FORMS OF TALK

University of Pennsylvania Publications in
Conduct and Communication

Erving Goffman and Dell Hymes, General Editors

ERVING GOFFMAN

FORMS OF TALK

UNIVERSITY OF PENNSYLVANIA PRESS
PHILADELPHIA
1981

Library of Congress Cataloging in Publication Data

Goffman, Erving.
   Forms of talk.

   (University of Pennsylvania publications in conduct
and communication)
   Includes bibliographies and index.
   1. Oral communication. I. Title. II. Series:
Pennsylvania. University. University of Pennsylvania
publications in conduct and communication.
P95.G58   001.54'2   80–52806
ISBN 0–8122–7790–2
ISBN 0–8122–1112–x (pbk.)

CONTENTS

INTRODUCTION

I

The five papers in this volume were written between 1974 and 1980, and are arranged in order of their completion. All deal with talk, and mainly the speaker's side of it. The first three were published as journal articles; they have been slightly revised. The last two are printed here for the first time. The three published papers are analytic and programmatic, leading to the very general statement in the third, the paper called "Footing." The two new papers could stand as substantive application of notions developed in the analytic ones. All the papers (least so the first) are written around the same frame-analytic themes, so the whole has something more than topical coherence. The whole also contains a very considerable amount of repetition. I state this last without much apology. The ideas purport to be general (in the sense of always applicable), and worth testing out. This is the warrant for repeated approaches from different angles and the eventual retracing of practically everything. Yet, of course, none of the concepts elaborated may have a future. So I ask that these papers be taken for what they merely are: exercises, trials, tryouts, a means of displaying possibilities, not establishing fact. This asking may be a lot, for the papers are proclamatory in style, as much distended by formulary optimism as most other endeavors in this field.

II

Everyone knows that when individuals in the presence of others respond to events, their glances, looks, and postural shifts carry all kinds of implication and meaning. When in these settings

1

words are spoken, then tone of voice, manner of uptake, restarts, and the variously positioned pauses similarly qualify. As does manner of listening. Every adult is wonderfully accomplished in producing all of these effects, and wonderfully perceptive in catching their significance when performed by accessible others. Everywhere and constantly this gestural resource is employed, yet rarely itself is systematically examined. In retelling events—an activity which occupies much of our speaking time—we are forced to sketch in these shadings a little, rendering a few movements and tones into words to do so. In addition to this folk transcription, we can employ discourse theatrics, vivifying the replay with caricaturized reenactments. In both cases, we can rely on our audience to take the part for the whole and cooperatively catch our meaning. Thus, in talk about how individuals acted or will act, we can get by with a small repertoire of alludings and simulations. Fiction writers and stage performers extend these everyday capacities, carrying the ability to reinvoke beyond that possessed by the rest of us. But even here only sketching is found.

So it remains to microanalysts of interaction to lumber in where the self-respecting decline to tread. A question of pinning with our ten thumbs what ought to be secured with a needle.

I I I

With my own thumbs, in this volume I want to hold up three matters for consideration. First, the process of "ritualization"—if I may slightly recast the ethological version of that term. The movements, looks, and vocal sounds we make as an unintended by-product of speaking and listening never seem to remain innocent. Within the lifetime of each of us these acts in varying degrees acquire a specialized communicative role in the stream of our behavior, looked to and provided for in connection with the displaying of our alignment to current events. We look simply to see, see others looking, see we are seen looking, and soon become knowing and skilled in regard to the evidential uses made of the appearance of looking. We clear our throat, we pause to think, we turn attention to a next doing, and soon we specialize these acts, performing them with no felt contrivance right where others in our gestural community would also, and like them, we do so apart from the original instrumental reason for the act. Indeed, gestural conventions once established in a community can be acquired directly, the initial noncommunicative character of the practice (when there is such) serving merely as a guide in our acquiring gestural competency, ensuring that our learning how to be unthinkingly expressive won't be entirely rote. The purpose and functions of these displays cannot of course be caught by the term "expression," but only by closely examining the consequence each several gesture commonly has in samples of actual occurrences—with due consideration to the sorts of things that might be conveyed in the context had no such gesture been offered.

Second, "participation framework." When a word is spoken, all those who happen to be in perceptual range of the event will have some sort of participation status relative to it. The codification of these various positions and the normative specification of appropriate conduct within each provide an essential background for interaction analysis—whether (I presume) in our own society or any other.

Third, there is the obvious but insufficiently appreciated fact that words we speak are often not our own, at least our current "own." Who it is who can speak is restricted to the parties present (and often more restricted than that), and which one is now doing so is almost always perfectly clear. But although who speaks is situationally circumscribed, in whose name words are spoken is certainly not. Uttered words have utterers; utterances, however, have subjects (implied or explicit), and although these may designate the utterer, there is nothing in the syntax of utterances to require this coincidence. We can as handily quote another (directly or indirectly) as we can say something in our own name. (This embedding capacity is part of something more general: our linguistic ability to speak of events at any remove in time and space from the situated present.)

I V

So three themes: ritualization, participation framework, and embedding. It is their interplay that will be at issue. Every utterance and its hearing have gestural accompaniments, these under some control of the actors. Every utterance and its hearing bear the marks of the framework of participation in which the uttering and hearing occur. All these markings we can openly mimic, mime, and reenact, allowing us dramatic liberties. Thus, when we speak we can set into the current framework of participation what is structurally marked as integral to another, enacting a dozen voices to do so. (For example, in describing a conversation, we, as speaker, can enact what had been our unstated response as *listener.*)

In what follows, then, I make no large literary claim that social life is but a stage, only a small technical one: that deeply incorporated into the nature of talk are the fundamental requirements of theatricality.

1

REPLIES AND RESPONSES

This paper examines conversational dialogue.[1] It is divided into four parts. The first presents arguments for dialogic analysis, the second lists some failings, the third applies this critical view to the notion of a "reply"; the final part is an overview.

PART ONE

I

Whenever persons talk there are very likely to be questions and answers. These utterances are realized at different points in "sequence time." Notwithstanding the content of their questions, questioners are oriented to what lies just ahead, and depend on what is to come; answerers are oriented to what has just been said, and look backward, not forward. Observe that although a question anticipates an answer, is designed to receive it, seems dependent on doing so, an answer seems even more dependent, making less sense alone than does the utterance that called it forth. Whatever answers do, they must do this with something already begun.

1. Grateful acknowledgment is made to *Language in Society,* where this paper first appeared (5[1976]:257–313). Originally presented at NWAVE III, Georgetown University, 25 October 1974. A preprint was published by the Centro Internazionale di Semiotica e di Linguistica, Università di Urbino. I am grateful to Theresa Labov, William Labov, Susan Philips, and Lee Ann Draud for critical suggestions, many of which have been incorporated without further acknowledgment. I alone, therefore, am not responsible for all of the paper's shortcomings.

In questions and answers we have one example, perhaps the canonical one, of what Harvey Sacks has called a "first pair part" and a "second pair part," that is, a couplet, a minimal dialogic unit, a round two utterances long, each utterance of the same "type," each spoken by a different person, one utterance temporally following directly on the other; in sum, an example of an "adjacency pair." The first pair part establishes a "conditional relevance" upon anything that occurs in the slot that follows; whatever comes to be said there will be inspected to see how it might serve as an answer, and if nothing is said, then the resulting silence will be taken as notable—a rejoinder in its own right, a silence to be heard (Sacks 1973).

On the face of it, these little pairings, these dialogic units, these two-part exchanges, recommend a linguistic mode of analysis of a formalistic sort. Admittedly, the meaning of an utterance, whether question or answer, can ultimately depend in part on the specific semantic value of the words it contains and thus (in the opinion of some linguists) escape complete formalization. Nonetheless, a formalism is involved. The constraining influence of the question-answer format is somewhat independent of *what* is being talked about, and whether, for example, the matter is of great moment to those involved in the exchange or of no moment at all. Moreover, each participating utterance is constrained by the rules of sentence grammar, even though, as will be shown, inferences regarding underlying forms may be required to appreciate this.

II

What sort of analyses can be accomplished by appealing to the dialogic format?

First, there is the possibility of recovering elided elements of answers by referring to their first pair parts, this turning out to be evidence of a strength of sentence grammar, not (as might first appear) a weakness. To the question "How old are you?" the answer "I am eleven years old" is not necessary; "I am eleven" will do, and even, often, "Eleven." Given "Eleven" as an answer, a proper sentence can be recovered from it, provided only that one knows the question. Indeed, I believe that elements of the intonation contour of the underlying grammatical sentence are preserved, supplying confirmation to the interpretation and assurance that an appeal to the grammatically tacit is something more than the linguist's legerdemain. If, then—as Gunter has shown—the right pair parts are aptly chosen, answers with very strange surface structures can be shown to be understandable, and what seemed anything but a sentence can be coerced into grammatical form and be the better off for it. What is "said" is obscure; what is "meant" is obvious and clear:

> A: "Who can see whom?"
> B: "The man the boy." [Gunter 1974:17]

The same argument can be made about dangling or interrupted sentences, false starts, ungrammatical usage, and other apparent deviations from grammatical propriety.

Note that answers can take not only a truncated verbal form but also a wholly nonverbal form, in this case a gesture serving solely as a substitute—an "emblem," to use Paul Ekman's terminology (1969:63–68)—for lexical materials. To the question "What time is it?" the holding up of five fingers may do as well as words, even better in a noisy room. A semantically meaningful question is still being satisfied by means of a semantically meaningful answer.

Second, we can describe embedding and "side-sequence" (Jefferson 1972) features, whereby a question is not followed directly by an answer to it, but by another question meant to be seen as holding off proper completion for an exigent moment:

> A_1: "Can I borrow your hose?"
> B_2: "Do you need it this very moment?"
> A_2: "No."
> B_1: "Yes."

or even:

> A_1 [To trainman in station] : "Have you got the time?"
> B_2 : "Standard or Daylight Saving?"
> A_3 : "What are you running on?"
> B_3 : "Standard."
> A_2 : "Standard then."
> B_1 : "It's five o'clock."

Which, in turn, leads to a central issue so far not mentioned: the question of how adjacency pairs are linked together to form chains. For "chaining" presumably provides us with a means of moving analysis forward from single two-part exchanges to stretches of talk. Thus, one might want to distinguish the two-person interrogative chain:

> A_1
> B_1
> A_2
> B_2
> etc.

whereby whoever provides a current question provides the next one, too (this turning out to have been a presupposition of the current utterance all along [Schegloff 1968:1080–81]), from the two-person sociable chain, whereby whoever provides a second pair part then goes on to provide the first pair part of the next pair:

> A_1
> B_1/B_2
> $\quad A_2/A_3$
> etc.

Combining the notion of ellipsis with the notion of chaining, we have, as Marilyn Merritt (1976) has suggested, the possibility of eliding at a higher level. Thus the typical:

> i(a)A: "Have you got coffee to go?"
> B: "Milk and sugar?"
> A: "Just milk."

can be expanded to display an underlying structure:

> i(b)A_1: "Have you got coffee to go?"
> $[\overline{B_1}]$ B_2: "Yes/Milk and sugar?"
> $\quad\quad A_2$: "Just milk."

an elision presumably based on the fact that an immediate query by the queried can be taken as tacit evidence of the answer that would make such a query relevant, namely, affirmation. Nor does expansion serve only to draw a couplet pattern from a three-piece unit. Thus:

8

ii(a) A: "Are you coming?"
    B: "I gotta work."

can be viewed as a contraction of:

ii(b) A_1: "Are you coming?"
    ⌐ B_1: "No." ¬
      A_2: "Why aren't you?"
    B_2: "I gotta work."

illustrating one interpretation (and the example) of the practice suggested by Stubbs,[2] namely, that an answer can be replaced by a reason for that answer. I might add that in what is to follow it will be useful to have a term to match and contrast with adjacency pair, a term to refer not to a question-answer couplet but rather to the second pair part of one couplet and the first pair part of the very next one, whether these parts appear within the same turn, as in:

A_1 : "Are they going?"
B_1/B_2: "Yes./Are you?"
    A_2: "I suppose."

or across the back of two turns, as in:

A_1: "Are they going?"
B_1: "Yes."
A_2: "Are you?"
B_2: "I suppose."

I shall speak here of a "back pair."

III

Observe now that, broadly speaking, there are three kinds of listeners to talk: those who *over*hear, whether or not their unratified participation is inadvertent and whether or not it has been encouraged; those (in the case of more than two-person talk) who are ratified participants but are not specifically addressed by the speaker; and those ratified participants who *are* addressed, that is,

2. Stubbs (1973:18) recommends that a simple substitution rule can be at work not involving deletion.

oriented to by the speaker in a manner to suggest that his words are particularly for them, and that some answer is therefore anticipated from them, more so than from the other ratified participants. (I say "broadly speaking" because all sorts of minor variations are possible—for example, speaker's practice of drawing a particular participant into an exchange and then turning to the other participants as if to offer him and his words up for public delectation.)

It is a standard possibility in talk that an addressed recipient answers the speaker by saying that the sound did not carry or that although words could be heard, no sense could be made of them, and that, in consequence, a rerun is required, and if not that, then perhaps a rephrasing. There are many pat phrases and gestures for conveying this message, and they can be injected concerning any item in an ongoing utterance whensoever this fault occurs (Stubbs 1973:21).

All of this suggests that a basic normative assumption about talk is that, whatever else, it should be correctly interpretable in the special sense of conveying to the intended recipients what the sender more or less wanted to get across. The issue is not that the recipients should agree *with* what they have heard, but only agree with the speaker *as to what* they have heard; in Austinian terms, illocutionary force is at stake, not perlocutionary effect.

Some elaboration is required. Commonly a speaker cannot explicate with precision what he meant to get across, and on these occasions if hearers think they know precisely, they will likely be at least a little off. (If speaker and hearers were to file a report on what they assumed to be the full meaning of an extended utterance, these glosses would differ, at least in detail.) Indeed, one routinely presumes on a mutual understanding that doesn't quite exist. What one obtains is a working agreement, an agreement "for all practical purposes."[3] But that, I think, is quite enough.

3. The student, of course, can find another significance in this working agreement, namely, evidence of the work that must be engaged in locally on each occasion of apparently smooth mutual understanding and evidence of how thin the ice is that everyone skates on. More to the point, it seems that such cloudiness as might exist is usually located in higher order laminations. Thus, A and B may have the same understanding about what A said and meant, but one or both can fail to understand that this agreement exists. If A and B both appreciate that they both have the same understanding about what A said and

The edging into ambiguity that is often found is only significant, I think, when interpretive uncertainties and discrepancies exceed certain limits or are intentionally induced and sustained (or thought to be by hearers), or are exploited after the fact to deny a legitimate accusation concerning what the speaker indeed by and large had meant. A serious request for a rerun on grounds of faulty reception is to be understood, then, not as a request for complete understanding—God save anyone from that—but for understanding that is on a par with what is ordinarily accepted as sufficient: understanding subject to, but not appreciably impaired by, "normatively residual" ambiguity.

Observe that the issue here of "normatively residual" ambiguity does not have to do with the three kinds of speech efficiency with which some students have confused it. First, the matter is not that of deixis or, as it is coming to be called, indexicality. An indexical such as "me" or "that one" can be rather clear and unambiguous as far as participants in the circle of use are concerned, the ambiguity only occurring to readers of isolated bits of the text of the talk. Second, ellipsis is not involved, for here again participants can easily be quite clear as to what was meant even though those faced with a transcribed excerpt might not agree on an expansion of the utterance. Finally, the issue is not that of the difference between what is "literally" said and what is conveyed or meant. For although here, too, someone coming upon the line out of the context of events, relationships, and mutual knowingness in which it was originally voiced might misunderstand, the speaker and hearers nonetheless can be perfectly clear about what was intended—or at least no less clear than they are about an utterance meant to be taken at face value.[4] (Indeed, it is in contrast to these three forms of mere laconicity that we can locate *functional* ambiguities, difficulties such as genuine uncertainty, genuine misunderstanding, the simulation of these difficulties, the suspicion that real difficulty has occurred, the suspicion that difficulty has been pretended, and so forth.)

---

meant, one or both can still fail to realize that they both appreciate that they both have the same understanding.

4. A useful treatment of the situated clarity of apparently ambiguous statements is available in Crystal (1969:102–3). The whole article contains much useful material on the character of conversation.

Given the possibility and the expectation that effective transmission will occur during talk, we can ask what conditions or arrangements would facilitate this and find some obvious answers. It would be helpful, for example, to have norms constraining interruption or simultaneous talk and norms against withholding of answers. It would be helpful to have available, and oblige the use of, "back-channel"[5] cues (facial gestures and nonverbal vocalizations) from hearers so that *while* the speaker was speaking, he could know, among other things, that he was succeeding or failing to get across, being informed of this while attempting to get across. (The speaker might thereby learn that he was not persuading his hearers, but that is another matter.) Crucial here are bracket-confirmations, the smiles, chuckles, headshakes, and knowing grunts through which the hearer displays appreciation that the speaker has sustained irony, hint, sarcasm, playfulness, or quotation across a strip of talk and is now switching back to less mitigated responsibility and literalness. Useful, too, would be a hold signal through which an addressed recipient could signal that transmission to him should be held up for a moment, this hold signal in turn requiring an all-clear cue to indicate that the forestalled speaker might now resume transmission. It would also be useful to enjoin an addressed recipient to *follow* right after current speaker with words or gestures showing that the message has been heard and understood, or, if it hasn't, that it hasn't.

Given a speaker's need to know whether his message has been received, and if so, whether or not it has been passably understood, and given a recipient's need to show that he has received the message and correctly—given these very fundamental requirements of talk as a communication system—we have the essential rationale for the very existence of adjacency pairs, that is, for the organization of talk into two-part exchanges.[6] We have an understanding of why any next utterance after a question is examined for how it might be an answer.

More to the point, we have grounds for extending this two-

5. See Yngve (1970:567–78); and Duncan (1972:283–92).
6. See Goffman (1967:38); and Schegloff and Sacks (1973:297–98).

part format outward from pairs of utterances which it seems perfectly to fit—questions and answers—to other kinds of utterance pairs, this being an extension that Sacks had intended. For when a declaration or command or greeting or promise or request or apology or threat or summons is made, it still remains the case that the initiator will need to know that he has gotten across; and the addressed recipient will need to make it known that the message has been correctly received. Certainly when an explanation is given the giver needs to know that it has been understood, else how can he know when to stop explaining? (Bellack et al. 1966: 2). And so once again the first pair part co-opts the slot that follows, indeed makes a slot out of next moments, rendering anything occurring then subject to close inspection for evidence as to whether or not the conditions for communication have been satisfied.

Given that we are to extend our dialogic format—our adjacency pairs—to cover a whole range of pairs, not merely questions and answers, terms more general than "question" and "answer" ought to be introduced, general enough to cover all the cases. For after all, an assertion is not quite a question, and the rejoinder to it is not quite an answer. Instead, then, of speaking of questions and answers, I will speak of "statements" and "replies," intentionally using "statement" in a broader way than is sometimes found in language studies, but still retaining the notion that an initiating element is involved, to which a reply is to be oriented.

Once we have begun to think about the transmission requirements for utterances and the role of adjacency pairing in accomplishing this, we can go on to apply the same sort of thinking to sequences or chains of statement-reply pairs, raising the question concerning what arrangements would facilitate the extended flow of talk. We could attend the issue of how next speaker is selected (or self-selects) in more-than-two-person talk (Sacks, Schegloff, and Jefferson 1974:696–735), and (following the structuring the above have nicely uncovered) how utterances might be built up to provide sequences of points where transition to next speaker is facilitated and even promoted but not made mandatory, the speaker leaving open the possibility of himself continuing on as if he had not encouraged his own retirement from the speaker role. We could also examine how a speaker's restarts and pauses (filled and otherwise) might function both to allow for his momentary failure to obtain listener attention and to remind intended recipients of their inattention.[7] And after that, of course, we could pose the same question regarding the initiating and terminating of a conversation considered as a total unit of communication.[8] We would thus be dealing with talk as a communications engineer might, someone optimistic about the possibility of culture-free formulations. I shall speak here of system requirements and system constraints.

A sketch of some of these system requirements is possible:

1. A two-way capability for transceiving acoustically adequate and readily interpretable messages.
2. Back-channel feedback capabilities for informing on reception while it is occurring.
3. Contact signals: means of announcing the seeking of a channeled connection, means of ratifying that the sought-for channel is now open, means of closing off a theretofore open channel. Included here, identification-authentication signs.
4. Turnover signals: means to indicate ending of a message and the taking over of the sending role by next speaker. (In the case of talk with more than two persons, next-speaker selection signals, whether "speaker selects" or "self-select" types.)
5. Preemption signals: means of inducing a rerun, holding off channel requests, interrupting a talker in progress.

7. C. Goodwin (1977).
8. In this paper, following the practice in sociolinguistics, "conversation" will be used in a loose way as an equivalent of talk or spoken encounter. This neglects the special sense in which the term tends to be used in daily life, which use, perhaps, warrants a narrow, restricted definition. Thus, conversation, restrictively defined, might be identified as the talk occurring when a small number of participants come together and settle into what they perceive to be a few moments cut off from (or carried on to the side of) instrumental tasks; a period of idling felt to be an end in itself, during which everyone is accorded the right to talk as well as to listen and without reference to a fixed schedule; everyone is accorded the status of someone whose overall evaluation of the subject matter at hand—whose editorial comments, as it were—is to be encouraged and treated with respect; and no final agreement or synthesis is demanded, differences of opinion to be treated as unprejudicial to the continuing relationship of the participants.

6. Framing capabilities: cues distinguishing special readings to apply across strips of bracketed communication, recasting otherwise conventional sense, as in making ironic asides, quoting another, joking, and so forth; and hearer signals that the resulting transformation has been followed.
7. Norms obliging respondents to reply honestly with whatever they know that is relevant and no more.[9]
8. Nonparticipant constraints regarding eavesdropping, competing noise, and the blocking of pathways for eye-to-eye signals.

We can, then, draw our basic framework for face-to-face talk from what would appear to be the sheer physical requirements and constraints of any communication system, and progress from there to a sort of microfunctional analysis of various interaction signals and practices. Observe that wide scope is found here for formalization; the various events in this process can be managed through quite truncated symbols, and not only can these symbols be given discrete, condensed physical forms, but also the role of live persons in the communication system can be very considerably reduced. Observe, too, that although each of the various signals can be expressed through a continuum of forms—say as "commands," "requests," "intimations"—none of this is to the point; these traditional discriminations can be neglected provided only that it is assumed that the participants have jointly agreed to operate (in effect) solely as communication nodes, as transceivers, and to make themselves fully available for that purpose.

I V

No doubt there are occasions when one can hear:

A: "What's the time?"
B: "It's five o'clock."

as the entire substance of a brief social encounter—or as a self-contained element therein—and have thereby a naturally bounded unit, one whose boundedness can be nicely accounted

9. In the manner of H. P. Grice's "conversational maxims," deriving from the "cooperative principle" (Grice 1975).

for by appealing to system requirements and the notion of an adjacency pair. But much more frequently something not quite so naked occurs. What one hears is something like this:

(i)   A: "Do you have the time?"
(ii) B: "Sure. It's five o'clock."
(iii) A: "Thanks."
(iv) B: [Gesture] " 'T's okay."

in which (i) albeit serving as a request, also functions to neutralize the potentially offensive consequence of encroaching on another with a demand, and so may be called a "remedy"; in which (ii) demonstrates that the potential offender's effort to nullify offense is acceptable, and so may be called "relief"; in which (iii) is a display of gratitude for the service rendered and for its provider not taking the claim on himself amiss, and may be called "appreciation"; and in which (iv) demonstrates that enough gratitude has been displayed, and thus the displayer is to be counted a properly feeling person, this final act describable as "minimization" (Goffman 1971:139–43). What we have here is also a little dialogic unit, naturally bounded in the sense that it (and its less complete variants) may fill out the whole of an encounter or, occurring within an encounter, allow for a longish pause upon its completion and an easy shift to another conversational matter. But this time actions are directed not merely to system constraints; this time an additional set apply, namely, constraints regarding how each individual ought to handle himself with respect to each of the others, so that he not discredit his own tacit claim to good character or the tacit claim of the others that they are persons of social worth whose various forms of territoriality are to be respected. Demands for action are qualified and presented as mere requests which can be declined. These declinables are in turn granted with a show of good spirit, or, if they are to be turned down, a mollifying reason is given. Thus the asker is hopefully let off the hook no matter what the outcome of his request.

Nor are these ritual contingencies restricted to commands and requests. In making an assertion about facts, the maker must count on not being considered hopelessly wrongheaded; if a greeting, that contact is wanted; if an excuse, that it will be acceptable; if an avowal of feeling and attitude, that these will be credited; if a summons, that it will be deferred to; if a serious offer, that it won't be considered presumptuous or mean; if an overgenerous one, that it will be declined; if an inquiry, that it won't be thought intrusive; if a self-deprecating comment, that it will be denied. The pause that comes after a tactfully sustained exchange is possible, then, in part because the participants have arrived at a place that each finds viable, each having acquitted himself with an acceptable amount of self-constraint and respect for the others present.

I have called such units "ritual interchanges."[10] Ordinarily each incorporates at least one two-part exchange but may contain additional turns and/or additional exchanges. Observe that although system constraints might be conceived of as pancultural, ritual concerns are patently dependent on cultural definition and can be expected to vary quite markedly from society to society. Nonetheless, the ritual frame provides a question that can be asked of anything occurring during talk and a way of accounting for what does occur. For example, back-channel expression not

---

10. Goffman (1967:19–22). The notion of ritual interchange allows one to treat two-part rounds, that is, adjacency pairs, as one variety and to see that ritual as well as system considerations have explanatory power here; that ritual considerations help produce many naturally bounded interchanges that have, for example, three or four parts, not merely two; and that delayed or nonadjacent sequencing is possible.

The term "ritual" is not particularly satisfactory because of connotations of otherworldliness and automaticity. Gluckman's recommendation, "ceremonious" (in his "Les rites de passage" [1962:20–23]), has merit except that the available nouns (ceremony and ceremonial) carry a sense of multiperson official celebration. "Politeness" has some merit, but rather too closely refers to matters necessarily of no substantive import, and furthermore cannot be used to refer to pointed offensiveness, "impoliteness" being too mild a term. The term "expressive" is close because the behavior involved is always treated as a means through which the actor portrays his relation to objects of value in their own right, but "expressive" also carries an implication of "natural" sign or symptom.

A compendium of ritual interchanges analyzed in terms of the "second assessments" which follow first pair parts, such as evaluative judgments, self-deprecations, and compliments, has recently been presented in Pomerantz (1975).

only lets the speaker know whether or not he is getting across while he is trying to, but also can let him know whether or not what he is conveying is socially acceptable, that is, compatible with his hearers' view of him and of themselves.

Note that insofar as participants in an encounter morally commit themselves to keeping conversational channels open and in good working order, whatever binds by virtue of system constraints will bind also by virtue of ritual ones. The satisfaction of ritual constraints safeguards not only feelings but communication, too.

For example, assuming a normatively anticipated length to an encounter, and the offensiveness of being lodged in one without anything to say, we can anticipate the problem of "safe supplies," that is, the need for a stock of inoffensive, ready-to-hand utterances which can be employed to fill gaps. And we can see an added function—the prevention of offensive expressions—for the organizational devices which reduce the likelihood of gaps and overlaps.

In addition to making sure someone (and only one) is always at bat, there will be the issue of sustaining whatever is felt to be appropriate by way of continuity of topic and tone from previous speaker's statement to current speaker's, this out of respect both for previous speaker (especially when he had provided a statement, as opposed to a reply) and, vaguely, for what it was that had been engrossing the participants.[11]

As suggested, communication access is itself caught up in ritual concerns: to decline a signal to open channels is something like declining an extended hand, and to make a move to open a channel is to presume that one will not be intruding. Thus, opening is ordinarily requested, not demanded, and often an initiator

---

11. We thus find that participants have recourse to a series of "weak bridges"—transparent shifts in topic hedged with a comment which shows that the maker is alive to the duties of a proper interactant: "reminds me of the time," "not to change the subject," "oh, by the way," "now that you mention it," "speaking of," "incidentally," "apropos of," etc. These locutions provide little real subject-matter continuity between currently ending and proposed topic, merely deference to the need for it. (Less precarious bridges are found when one individual "matches" another's story with one from his own repertoire.)

will preface his talk with an apology for the interruption and a promise of how little long the talk will be, the assumption being that the recipient has the right to limit how long he is to be active in this capacity. (On the whole, persons reply to more overtures than they would like to, just as they attempt fewer openings than they might want.) Once a state of talk has been established, participants are obliged to temper their exploitation of these special circumstances, neither making too many demands for the floor nor too few, neither extolling their own virtues nor too directly questioning those of the others, and, of course, all the while maintaining an apparent rein on hostility and a show of attention to current speaker. So, too, withdrawal by a particular participant aptly expresses various forms of disapproval and distance and therefore must itself be managed tactfully.

Instead, then, of merely an arbitrary period during which the exchange of messages occurs, we have a social encounter, a coming together that ritually regularizes the risks and opportunities face-to-face talk provides, enforcing the standards of modesty regarding self and considerateness for others generally enjoined in the community, but now incidentally doing so in connection with the special vehicles of expression that arise in talk. Thus, if, as Schegloff and Sacks suggest (1973: 300 ff.), a conversation has an opening topic which can be identified as its chief one, then he or she who would raise a "delicate" point might want to "talk past" the issue at the beginning and wait until it can be introduced at a later place in the conversation more likely to allow for lightly pressed utterances (say, as an answer to a question someone else raises), all of which management requires some understanding of issues such as delicacy. Participants, it turns out, are obliged to look not so much for ways of expressing themselves, as for ways of making sure that the vast expressive resources of face-to-face interaction are not inadvertently employed to convey something unintended and untoward. Motivated to preserve everyone's face, they then end up acting so as to preserve orderly communication.

The notion of ritual constraints helps us to mediate between the particularities of social situations and our tendency to think in terms of general rules for the management of conversational interplay. We are given a means of overcoming the argument that any generalization in this area must fall because every social situation is different from every other. In brief, we have a means of attending to what it is about different social situations that makes them relevantly different for the management of talk.

For example, although a request for coffee allows the counterman to elect to elide an answer and move directly into a question of his own, "Milk and sugar?", this option turns out, of course, to be available only in limited strategic environments. When an individual asks a salesperson whether or not a large object is in stock—such as a Chevy Nova with stick shift or a house with a corner lot—the server may well assume that he has a prospective customer, not necessarily an actual one, and that to omit the "Yes" and to go right into the next level of specification, i.e., "What color?" or "How many rooms?", might be seen, for example, to be snide. For a purchase at this scale ordinarily requires time and deliberation. The server can assume that whatever remarks he first receives, his job is to establish a selling relationship, along with the sociability-tinged, mutually committed occasion needed to support an extended period of salesmanship. The salesman will thus take the customer's opening remarks as a call for an appreciable undertaking, not merely a bid for a piece of information. At the other extreme, the question, "Do you have the time?" is designed never to be answered in such a way that another utterance, "Can you tell me it?" will be necessary—so much so that the setting up of this second request becomes available as an open joke or a pointed insult.

May I add that a feature of face-to-face interaction is not only that it provides a scene for playing out of ritually relevant expressions, but also that it is the location of a special class of quite conventionalized utterances, lexicalizations whose controlling purpose is to give praise, blame, thanks, support, affection, or show gratitude, disapproval, dislike, sympathy, or greet, say farewell, and so forth. Part of the force of these speech acts comes from the feelings they directly index; little of the force derives from the semantic content of the words. We can refer here to interpersonal verbal rituals. These rituals often serve a bracketing function, celebratively marking a perceived change in the physical and social accessibility of two individuals to each other (Goffman 1971: 62–94), as well as beginnings and endings—of a day's activity, a social occasion, a speech, an encounter, an interchange. So in addition to the fact that any act performed during talk will carry ritual significance, some seem to be specialized for this purpose—ritualized in the ethological sense—and these play a special role in the episoding of conversation.

We might, then, for purposes of analysis, try to construct a simple ritual model, one that could serve as a background for all those considerations of the person which are referred to as "ego," "personal feelings," *amour-propre,* and so forth. The general design, presumably, is to sustain and protect through expressive means what can be supportively conveyed about persons and their relationships.

1. An act is taken to carry implications regarding the character of the actor and his evaluation of his listeners, as well as reflecting on the relationship between him and them.

2. Potentially offensive acts can be remedied by the actor through accounts and apologies, but this remedial work must appear to be accepted as sufficient by the potentially offended party before the work can properly be terminated.

3. Offended parties are generally obliged to induce a remedy if none is otherwise forthcoming or in some other way show that an unacceptable state of affairs has been created, else, in addition to what has been conveyed about them, they can be seen as submissive regarding others' lapses in maintaining the ritual code.

And just as system constraints will always condition how talk is managed, so, too, will ritual ones. Observe that unlike grammatical constraints, system and ritual ones open up the possibility of corrective action as part of these very constraints. Grammars do not have rules for managing what happens when rules are broken (a point made by Stubbs [1973:19]). Observe, too, that the notion of ritual constraints complicates the idea of adjacency pairs but apparently only that; the flow of conversation can still be seen as parcelled out into these relatively self-contained units, the relevance of first slot for second slot appreciated—but now all this for added reasons.

PART TWO

System constraints reinforced by ritual constraints provide us with an effective means of interpreting some of the details of conversational organization. This is no longer news. The point of having reviewed the arguments is to question the adequacy of the analysis that results. For although a focus on system and ritual constraints has considerable value, it also has substantial limitations. It turns out that the statement-reply format generating dialoguelike structures covers some possibilities better than others. Consider, then, some problems introduced by this perspective.

I

First, the embarrassing question of units.

The environing or contextual unit of considerable linguistic concern is the sentence—". . . an independent linguistic form, not included by virtue of any grammatical construction in any larger linguistic form"[12]—in which the contained or dependent units are morphemes, words, and more extended elements such as phrases and clauses. In natural talk, sentences do not always have the surface grammatical form grammarians attribute to the well-formed members of the class, but presumably these defectives can be expanded by regular editing rules to display their inner normalcy.

The term "sentence" is currently used to refer to something that is spoken, but the early analysis of sentences seemed much caught up in examination of the written form. The term "utterance" has therefore come into use to underscore reference to a spoken unit. In this paper I shall use the term "utterance" residually to refer to spoken words as such, without concern about the naturally bounded units of talk contained within them or containing them.

Now clearly, a sentence must be distinguished from its interactional cousin, namely, everything that an individual says

12. Bloomfield (1946:170). His definition seems to have been a little optimistic. Grammatical elements of well-formed sentences can be dependent on neighboring sentences. See Gunter (1974:9–10).

during his exercise of a turn at talk, "a stretch of talk, by one person, before and after which there is silence on the part of the person."[13] I shall speak here of talk during a turn, ordinarily reserving the term "turn" or "turn at talk" to refer to an opportunity to hold the floor, not what is said while holding it.[14]

Obviously the talk of a turn will sometimes coincide with a sentence (or what can be expanded into one), but on many occasions a speaker will provide his hearers with more than a one sentence-equivalent stretch. Note, too, that although a turn's talk may contain more than one sentence-equivalent, it must contain at least one.

Now the problem with the concepts of sentence and talk during a turn is that they are responsive to linguistic, not interactional, analysis. If we assume that talk is somehow dialogic and goes on piecing itself out into interchange spurts, then we must obtain our unit with this in mind. As suggested, a sentence is not the analytically relevant entity, because a respondent could employ several in what is taken to be a single interactionally relevant event. Even something so glaringly answer-oriented and so dear to the grammarian's heart as a well-formed question regarding fact can be rhetorical in character, designed to flesh out the speaker's remarks, adding a little more weight and color or a terminal dollop, but not meant to be specifically answered in its own right. (In fact, so much is a rhetorical question not to be specifically answered that it becomes available as something the apt answering of which is automatically a joke or quip.)

But just as clearly, the talk during an entire turn can't be used either—at least not as the most elementary term—for, as suggested, one of the main patterns for chaining rounds is the one in which whoever answers a question goes on from there to provide the next question in the series, thereby consolidating during one turn at talk two relevantly different doings. And indeed, a question may be shared by two persons—one individ-

13. By which Zellig Harris (1951:14) defines utterance. Bloomfield (1946) apparently also used "utterance" to refer to talk done during one turn.

14. Susan Philips (1974:160) has suggested use of the term "a speaking" in this latter connection, and I have in places followed her practice, as well as Sacks' locution, "a turn's talk."

ual stepping in and finishing off what another has begun—all for the edification of a third party, the addressed recipient (Sacks 1967), who does not thereby lose a beat in the sequencing of his own reply. Thus, the talk during two different turns can yet function as one interactional unit. In fact, an addressed recipient can step in and help a slow speaker find the word or phrase he seems to be looking for, then follow this with a reply, thereby combining in one turn at talk some of two *different* parties' contribution to the dialogue. In general, then, although the boundary of a sequence-relevant unit and the boundary of a speaking commonly coincide, this must be seen as analytically incidental. We are still required to decide which concern will be primary: the organization of turns *per se* or the sequencing of interaction.[15] And we must sustain this discrimination even though the two terms, turn and interaction sequence, seem nigh synonymous.

In order to attack this problem, I propose to use a notion whose definition I cannot and want not to fix very closely—the notion of a "move."[16] I refer to any full stretch of talk or of its substitutes which has a distinctive unitary bearing on some set or other of the circumstances in which participants find themselves (some "game" or other in the peculiar sense employed by Wittgenstein), such as a communication system, ritual constraints, economic negotiating, character contests, "teaching cycles" (Bellack et al. 1966:119–20), or whatever. It follows that an utterance which is a move in one game may also be a move in another, or be but a part of such other, or contain two or more such others. And a move may sometimes coincide with a sentence and sometimes with a turn's talk but need do neither. Correspondingly, I redefine the notion of a "statement" to refer to a move characterized by an orientation to some sort of answering to follow, and the notion of "reply" to refer to a move characterized by its being seen as an answering of some kind to a preceding matter that has been raised. Statement and reply, then, refer to moves, not to sentences or to speakings.

15. A point also made, and made well, by Sinclair et al. (1970–72:72).
16. See Goffman (1961:35), and (1972:138 ff.). Sinclair et al. (1972), following Bellack et al. (1966), uses the term "move" in a somewhat similar way.

The notion of move gives some immediate help with matters such as types of silence. For example, there will be two kinds of silence after a conversational move has been completed: the silence that occurs between the back-pair moves a single speaker can provide during one turn at talk, and the one that occurs between his holding of the floor and the next person's holding.[17]

I I

Although it is clear that ritual constraints reinforce system ones, deepening a pattern that has already been cut, qualifications must be noted. A response will on occasion leave matters in a ritually unsatisfactory state, and a turn by the initial speaker will be required, encouraged, or at least allowed, resulting in a *three*-part interchange; or chains of adjacency pairs will occur (albeit typically with one, two, or three such couplets), the chain itself having a unitary, bounded character.

Moreover, standard conflicts can occur between the two sets of conditions. Ritual constraints on the initiation of talk, for example, are likely to function one way for the superordinate and another for the subordinate, so that what is orderliness from the superior's position may be excommunication from the inferior's.

Cultural variation is important here as well. Thus it is reported of Indians on the Warm Springs reservation in Oregon that because of obligations of modesty, young women may have answers they can't offer to questions (V. Hymes 1974: 7–8), and questioning itself may be followed with a decorum a communications engineer might well deplore:

> Unlike our norm of interaction, that at Warm Springs does not require that a question by one person be followed immediately by an answer or a promise of an answer from the addressee. It *may* be followed by an answer but may also be followed by silence or by

17. Silences *during* the completion of a move differently figure, recommending concern for cognitive, as much as ritual, matters. Thus there appears to be a difference between a "juncture pause" occurring after an encoding unit such as a "phonemic clause," and one occurring during such a unit. The first is likely to be easily disattendable, the second is more likely to be seen as a break in fluency. Here see Boomer (1965:148–58); and Dittmann (1972:135–51).

an utterance that bears no relationship to the question. Then the answer to the question may follow as long as five or ten minutes later. [ibid., p.9]

Also when utterances are not heard or understood, the failing hearer can feel obliged to affect signs of comprehension, thus forestalling correction and, in consequence, forestalling communication. For to ask for a rerun can be to admit that one has not been considerate enough to listen or that one is insufficiently knowledgeable to understand the speaker's utterance or that the speaker himself may not know how to express himself clearly— in all cases implying something that the uncomprehending person may be disinclined to convey.

III

Once we have considered the differential impact of system and ritual constraints upon talk we can go on to consider a more complicated topic, namely, the inversionary effects of both these sets of constraints.

When, during a conversation, communication or social propriety suddenly breaks down, pointed effort will likely follow to set matters right. At such moments what ordinarily function as mere constraints upon action become the ends of action itself. Now we must see that this shift from means to ends has additional grounds.

Although rerun signals are to be initially understood in obvious functional terms, in fact in actual talk they are much employed in a devious way, a standard resource for saying one thing—which propositional content can be withdrawn to if needs be—while meaning another. The same can be said of apparent "unhearings" and misunderstandings, for these also provide the apparently beset recipient a means of intentionally breaking the flow of the other's communication under the cover of untendentious difficulty.

What is true here of system constraints is, I think, even more true of ritual ones. Not only will conventional expressions of concern and regard be employed transparently as a thin cover for allusions to one's own strengths and others' failings, but just what might otherwise be protected by tact can delineate the target of abuse. As if on the assumption that other's every move is to be taken as something requiring remedial correction (lest one be seen as lax in the exaction of justice to oneself), assertions can be followed by direct denials, questions by questioning the questioner, accusations by counter-accusations, disparagement by insults in kind, threats by taunting their realization, and other inversions of mutual consideration. Here adjacency pairing and the normative sequence of remedy, relief, appreciation, and minimization continue to provide a scaffold of expectations, but now employed as a means for rejecting blame, according it without license, and generally giving offense. Neatly bounded interchanges are produced, well formed to prevent at least one of the participants from establishing a tenable position.[18]

I V

Having accounted for the prevalence of the two-person dialogic format by reference to the effective way in which it can satisfy system and ritual constraints, we can go on to examine organization that doesn't fit the format.

1. There are, for example, standard three-person plays:

1st speaker: "Where is this place?"
2nd speaker: "I don't know. You know, don't you?"
3rd speaker: "It's just north of Depoe Bay." [Philips 1974:160]

in which the third speaker's reply will bear a relation to first speaker's question, but a complicated one. Also to be noted are

18. Close recordings and analysis of chronic set-tos are available in M. Goodwin (1978). See also M. Goodwin (1975). An attempt at structural analysis of some standard adult gambits is made in Goffman (1971:171–83). Polite forms of these inversionary tactics constitute the repartee in plays and other literary texts, these neat packagings of aggression being taken as the essence of conversation, when in fact they are probably anything but that. Note, it is children more than adults who are subject to open blaming and given to making open jibes, so it is children who are the mature practitioners here. In any case, the great catalogue of inversionary interchanges was published some time ago in two volumes in connection with children by Lewis Carroll, thereby providing the Englishry with linguistic models to follow in the pursuit of bickering as an art form.

standard arrangements, as, for example, in classrooms, in which a speaker obliges a number of persons to cite their answers to a problem or opinions on an issue. In such cases, second respondent will wait for first respondent to finish, but second respondent's reply will not be an *answer* to first respondent, merely something to follow in sequence, resulting at most in a comparative array. This is but an institutionalized form of what is commonly found in conversation. As Clancy suggests, a speaker can answer to a topic or theme, as opposed to a statement:

> A large number of interruptions, however, do not appear to be so specifically precipitated by the preceding message. Instead, the interrupting speaker says something brought to mind by the whole general topic of conversation. In this case, speaker ignores the immediately preceding sentences to which he has proudly not paid attention since his idea occurred to him, and he interrupts to present his idea despite the non-sequitur element of his sentence. [1972:84]

Further, there is the obstinate fact that during informal conversation, especially the multiperson kind, an individual *can* make a statement such that the only apparent consequence is that the next speaker will allow him to finish before changing the topic, a case of patent disregard for *what* a person says. And, of course, when this happens, a third participant can decide to reply not to the last statement, the adjacent one, but to the one before, thus bypassing last speaker (Philips 1974:166). And if the first speaker himself reenters immediately after receiving a nonreply, he will be well situated to continue his original statement as if he had not terminated it, thus recognizing that a nonreply has occurred (Clancy 1972:84).

2. It is also an embarrassing fact that the ongoing back-channel cues which listeners provide a speaker may, as it were, "surface" at episodic junctures in the speaking, providing, thus, a clear signal that understanding and sympathy have followed this far. *Gee, gosh, wow, hmm, tsk, no!* are examples of such keep-going signals. Now these boosterlike encouragements could be counted as a turn at talk, yet obviously the individual who provides them does not "get the floor" to do so, does not become the ratified speaker. Thus, what is perceived as a single speaking, a

single go at getting something said, a single period of having the floor, can carry across several of these looked-for and appreciated interruptions.

Furthermore, it appears that the possibility of speaking *without having the floor or trying to get it* can itself be pointedly used, relied upon, in conveying asides, parenthetical remarks, and even quips, all of whose point depends upon their not being given any apparent sequence space in the flow of events. (Asides cause their maker embarrassment if ratified as something to be given the floor and accorded an answer, indeed such a reception becomes a way of stamping out the act, not showing it respect.)

All of which leads to a very deep complaint about the statement-reply formula. Although many moves seem either to call for a replying move or to constitute such a move, we must now admit that not all do, and for the profoundest reasons. For it seems that in much spoken interaction participants are given elbow room to provide at no sequence cost an evaluative expression of what they take to be occurring. They are given a free ride. (The surfacing of back-channel communication is but one example.) Thereby they can make their position felt, make their alignment to what is occurring known, without committing others to address themselves openly to these communications. (The common practice, already mentioned, whereby a teacher uses an answer to his question as an occasion for evaluating the merit of the reply suggests how institutionalized this can become.) Although such "reacting" moves—to use Bellack's term (1966: 18–19)—may be occasioned by, and meant to be seen as occasioned by, a prior move, they have a special status in that the prior speaker need not take it from their occurrence that his statement has been replied to. Nor need anyone who follows the reacting move take it that a reply to it is due. (Which is not to say that evaluative responses are not often pressed into service as replies.)

PART THREE

I want now to raise the issue of replies and responses but require a preface to do so.

I

It is a central property of "well-formed" sentences that they can stand by themselves. One can be pulled out at random and stuck on the board or printed page and yet retain its interpretability, the words and their order providing all the context that is necessary. Or so it seems.[19]

It can be recommended that the power of isolated, well-formed sentences to carry meaning for students of language and to serve so well for so many of the purposes of grammarians is a paradoxical thing. In effect, it is not that the grammarian's perspective can make sense out of even single, isolated sentences, but that these sentences are the *only* things his perspective can make sense out of. Moreover, without the general understanding that this effort is an acceptable, even worthy, thing to do, the doing could not be done. The functioning of these sentences is as grammarians' illustrations, notwithstanding that due to the residual effects of unpleasant exercises in grade school, large sections of the public can construe sentences in the same frame. The mental set required to make sense out of these little orphans is that of someone with linguistic interests, someone who is posing a linguistic issue and is using a sample sentence to further his argument. In this special context of linguistic elaboration, an explication and discussion of the sample sentence will have meaning, and this special context is to be found anywhere in the world where there are grammarians. But

19. Of course, sentences can have structural ambiguity. "Flying airplanes can be dangerous" has two quite different possible meanings. But like a reversing picture, these two possibilities are themselves clearly established solely by the sentence itself, which thus retains the power all on its own to do the work required of it as an illustration of what linguistic analysis can disambiguate. The same can be said for deictic terms. Their analysis treats *classes* of terms whose members carry meanings that are situation-locked in a special way, but the analysis itself apparently is not hindered in any way by virtue of having to draw on these terms as illustrations, and instead of being constrained by indexicals is made possible by them. "The man just hit my ball over there" leaves us radically ignorant of whose ball was hit, when, and where it went, unless we can look out upon the world from the physical and temporal standpoint of the speaker; but just as obviously this sentence all by itself can be used as an apparently context-free illustration of this indexical feature of "just," "my," and "there."

present one of these nuggets cold to a man on the street or to the answerer of a telephone, or as the content of a letter, and on the average its well-formedness will cease to be all that significant. Scenarios *could* be constructed in which such an orphaned sentence would be meaningful—as a password between two spies, as a neurologist's test of an individual's brain functioning, as a joke made by and about grammarians, and so forth. But ingenuity would be required. So all along, the sentences used by linguists take at least some of their meaning from the institutionalization of this kind of illustrative process. As Gunter suggests:

> A deeper suspicion suggests that all isolated sentences, including those that linguists often use as examples in argumentation, have no real existence outside some permissive context, and that study of sentences out of context is the study of oddities at which we have trained ourselves not to boggle. [1974:17]

What can be said about the use of sample sentences can also be said about sample dialogue. A two-part interchange—an adjacency pair—can be put on the board or printed in a book, recommended to our attention without much reference to its original context, and yet will be understandable. Exchanges provide self-contained, packaged meaning. The following illustrates:

A: "What's the time?"
B: "It's five o'clock."

I suggest that as grammarians display self-sufficient sample sentences, apparently unembarrassed by the presuppositions of doing so, so interactionists display self-sufficient interchanges. Nor are interactionists alone in the enjoyment of this license. Those who give talks or addresses or even participate in conversations can plug in riddles, jokes, bon mots, and cracks more or less at their own option at the appropriate points on the assumption that these interpolations will be meaningful in their own right, apart from the context into which they have been placed, which context, of course, is supposed to render them apt or fitting. Thus the same little plum can be inserted at the beginning or end of quite different speakers' quite different talks with easy aptness. Stage plays provide similar opportunities in allowing for the performance of "memorable" exchanges, that is, sprightly bits of dialogue that bear repeating and can be repeated apart from the play in which they occurred.

Yet we must see that the dialogic approach inherits many of the limitations of the grammarian's, the sins of which, after all, it was meant to correct. I refer to the sins of noncontextuality, to the assumption that bits of conversation can be analyzed in their own right in some independence of what was occurring at the time and place.

First, an obvious but important point about single sentences. The reproduction of a conversation in the printed text of a play or in a novel or in a news account of an actual event satisfies the condition of any body of print, namely, that *everything* readers might not already know and that is required for understanding be alluded to, if not detailed, *in print.* Thus, a physical event may be relevant without which the talk that follows does not make sense, but inasmuch as the medium is print, a description, a *written* version of the event, will be provided in the text, in effect interspersing talk and stage directions—materials from two different frames. Cues for guiding interpretation which are imbedded in the physical and interpersonal setting are therefore not denied, at least on the face of it. And yet, of course, these unspoken elements are necessarily handled so as to sustain a single realm of relevant material, namely, words in print. To draw on these materials as sources in the analysis of talk is thus to use material that has already been systematically rendered into one kind of thing—words in print. It is only natural, therefore, to find support from sources in print for the belief that the material of conversations consists fundamentally of uttered words.

I think the same strictures can be suggested regarding "conversational implicature," that is, indirectly conveyed understanding. As with grammatical ambiguities and indexicals, it appears that a cited sentence can be used in and by itself as a pedagogic example of what can be meant but not said, conveyed but not directly—the difference, in short, between locutionary content and illocutionary force. Yet, of course, here the sentence in itself is quite clearly not enough. A bit of the context (or possible contexts) must be sketched in, and is, by the analyst, using more sentences to do so. It is these verbally provided stage directions which allow the writer correctly to assume that the reader will be able to see the point. And ordinarily these sketchings are not themselves made a subject of classification and analysis.[20]

When we turn from the analysis of sentences to the analysis of interchanges, matters become somewhat more complicated. For there are intrinsic reasons why any adjacency pair is likely to be considerably more meaningful taken alone than either of its pair parts taken alone. Some elaboration is required.

As suggested, the transcript or audio tape of an isolated statement plucked from a past natural conversation can leave us in the dark, due to deixis, ellipsis, and indirection, although auditors in the original circle of use suffered no sense of ambiguity. But there is a further matter. As Gunter (1974: 94ff.) has recently recommended, what is available to the student (as also to the actual participants) is not the possibility of predicting forward from a statement to a reply—as we might a cause to its effects—but rather quite a different prospect, that of locating in what is said now the sense of what it is a response to. For the individual who had accepted replying to the original statement will have been obliged to display that he has discovered the meaningfulness and relevance of the statement and that a relevant reaction is now provided. Thus, for example, although his perception of the phrasal stress, facial gestures, and body orientation of the speaker may have been necessary in order for him to have made the shift from what was said to what was meant, the *consequence*

---

20. An encouraging exception is provided by those attempting to formulate rules for the "valid" performance of various speech acts (such as commands, requests, offers) and therefore generalizations concerning circumstances in which alternate meanings are imputed. See Grice (1975); Searle (1975); Gordon and Lakoff (1971:63–84); Labov and Fanshel (1977, chap. 3); and Ervin-Tripp (1976:25–66). One problem with this line of work so far is that it tends to end up considering a sort of check list individuals might apply in the rare circumstances when they are genuinely uncertain as to intended meaning—circumstances, in short, when usual determinants have failed. How individuals arrive at an effective interpretation on all those occasions when the stream of experience makes this easy and instantaneous is not much explored, this exploration being rather difficult to undertake from a sitting position. Most promising of all, perhaps, is the argument by Gordon and Lakoff (1971:77) that what is conveyed as opposed to what is said may be marked grammatically through the distribution of particular words in the sentence. Whether such a distribution determines the reading to be given or merely confirms it might still be an open question, however.

of this guidance for interpretation can well be made evident in the *verbal* elements of the reply, and so in effect becomes available to we who review a verbal transcript later. In the same way the respondent's special background knowledge of the events at hand can become available to us through his words. Indeed, the more obscure the speaker's statement for his original auditors, the more pains his respondent is likely to have taken to display its sense through his own reply, and the more need we who come later will have for this help. Second pair parts turn out, then, to be incidentally designed to provide us with some of what we miss in first pair parts in our effort to understand them, and respondents in one circle can turn out to be ideally placed and knowing explicators for later circles. Admittedly, of course, laconicity can be answered with laconicity; but although matters therefore are not necessarily improved for us, they can hardly be worsened, any words being better than none.

But note that although the one who had accepted replying had had to come to a usable interpretation of the statement *before* providing evidence that he had caught the speaker's meaning, we who later examine an isolated excerpt will find the key to hand even as we find the door. By quietly reading (or listening) on, we may find just the help we need. Quite systematically, then, we students obtain a biased view of uttered sentences. Unlike the self-sufficient sample sentences referred to by traditional grammarians, excerpts from natural conversations are very often unintelligible; but when they *are* intelligible, this is likely to be due to the help we quietly get from someone who has already read the situation for us.

However, even in spite of the fact that there are deep reasons why adjacency pairs are more excerptible than first pair parts, we will still find that sample interchanges are biased examples of what inhabits actual talk.

With this warning about the dangers of noncontextuality, let us proceed to the theme, replies and responses.

Take as a start rerun signals, whether made with words or gestural equivalents. He who sends such a signal can be demonstrating that he is, in fact, oriented to the talk, but that he has not grasped the semantic meanings the speaker attempted to convey. He thus addresses himself to the *process* of communication, not to *what* was communicated—for, after all, he professes not to have understood that. Differently put, the recipient here abstracts from the sender's statement merely its qualifications as something to be heard and understood. It is to the situation of failed communication, not to what is being communicated, that the recipient reacts. To call these signals "replies" seems a little inappropriate, for in the closest sense, they do not constitute a reply to what was said; the term "response" seems better.

Take, then, as a basic notion the idea of *response,* meaning here acts, linguistic and otherwise, having the following properties:

1. They are seen as originating from an individual and as inspired by a prior speaker.
2. They tell us something about the individual's position or alignment in what is occurring.
3. They delimit and articulate just what the "is occurring" is, establishing what it is the response refers to.
4. They are meant to be given attention by others now, that is, to be assessed, appreciated, understood at the current moment.

And assume that *one* type of response is what might be called a *reply,* namely, a response in which the alignment implied and the object to which reference is made are both conveyed through words or their substitutes; furthermore, this matter addressed by the response is itself something that a prior speaker had referred to through words. Replies, I might note, are found in the artful dialogue of the theater and in novels, part of the transmutation of conversation into a sprightly game in which the position of each player is reestablished or changed through each of his speakings, each of which is given central place as the referent of following replies. Ordinary talk ordinarily has less ping-pong.

I I

Consider now the properties of responses in general, not merely replies in particular.

1. Recall that in the couplets so far considered, the second pair part incidentally can be seen as a reply to something of its own generic kind, namely, a brief spurt of words whose semantic

(or propositional) meaning is to be addressed, a restriction to same generic type to be seen when one move in a game of chess calls forth another move or one strike at a ping-pong ball calls forth another. A case simply of tit for tat. (Indeed, not only will a reply here answer a statement, but also it will be drawn from the same discourse-type, as in question-answer, summons-acknowledgment, etc.)

A minor qualification was admitted, namely, that words alone are not involved. We have, for example, a special way of knotting up the face to convey the fact that we do not understand what it is a speaker seems to be trying to convey, and that a rerun is in order. And gestures obviously can also be freighted with ritual significance. In both cases, we deal with signals that can also be conveyed by words, indeed are very often conveyed by both words and gestures, presenting, incidentally, no particular need to question the relevance of system and ritual constraints in the analysis of talk. Here I only want to suggest that although it is plain that such gestures figure in conversation, it is much easier to reproduce words than gestures (whether vocal, facial, or bodily), and so sample interchanges tend to rely on the verbal portion of a verbal-gestural stream or tacitly substitute a verbal version of a move that was entirely gestural, with consequent risk of glossing over relevant moves in the sequence. And what is true of gesture is true also of scenic contributions. In consequence, words themselves, including the most perfunctory of them, can conceal the interactional facts. Thus the transcription:

> A: "Have you got the time?"
> B: "Yes, it's 5:15."

suggests that the "Yes" is rather redundant, being replaceable by a good-tempered mention of the time alone. But in fact a scene is possible in which B, walking past A, who is in a parked car, wants it known that he, B, will honor the request, yet finds that the time taken to get at his watch removes him a couple of steps from the car and opens up the possibility of his being seen as declining to acknowledge the contact. The "Yes" then becomes an immediately available means of showing that an encounter has been ratified and will be kept open until its work is done.

Note, too, that ritual concerns are not intrinsically a matter of talk *or* talklike gestures. Talk is ritually relevant largely insofar as it qualifies as but another arena for good and bad conduct.[21] To interrupt someone is much like tripping over him; both acts can be perceived as instances of insufficient concern for the other, mere members of the class of events governed by ritual considerations. To ask an improperly personal question can be equivalent to making an uninvited visit; both constitute invasions of territoriality.

Of course, talk figures in an added way, because challenges given to someone seen as not having behaved properly can neatly be done with words. Moreover, if something is to be offered that is physically absent from the situation or not palpable, and this offering is to be accepted, then offering and acceptance may *have* to be done with words or emblems.

So, too, if past conduct—verbal or behavioral—is to be cited for the purposes of demanding corrective action or bestowing praise, then again words will be necessary. (And in both the latter cases, the little interpersonal rituals likely to accompany the transaction will be verbal in a sense.) Nonetheless, ritual is concerned with the expressive implication of acts, with the sense in which acts can be read as portraying the position the actor takes up regarding matters of social import—himself, others present, collectivities—and what sentences say constitutes but one class of these expressions.

It follows that events which are not themselves verbal in character, but which, for example, raise questions of propriety, may have to be verbally addressed, and will thereby be thrust into the center of conversational concern. In sum, once the exchange of words has brought individuals into a jointly sustained and ratified focus of attention, once, that is, a fire has been built, any visible thing (just as any spoken referent) can be burnt in it.

Here a terminological clarification is required. Utterances are inevitably accompanied by kinesic and paralinguistic gestures

---

21. Grice (1975) argues for a distinction between conventional maxims and conversational ones, the latter presumably special to talk. However, although the maxims that seem special to an effective communication system allow us to account for certain presuppositions, implications, and laconicities in speech—a reason for formulating the maxims in the first place—other maxims of conduct allow for this accounting, too.

which enter intimately into the organization of verbal expression. Following Kendon, one may refer here to the gesticulatory stream and also include therein all nonverbal gestures that have acquired an emblematic function, replacing words and replaceable by them. However, conversation involves more than verbal and gesticulatory communication. Physical doings unconnected with the speech stream are also involved—acts which for want of a better name might here be called nonlinguistic.

So conversation can burn anything. Moreover, as suggested, the conventionalized interpersonal rituals through which we put out these fires or add to the blaze are not themselves sentences in any simple sense, having speech-act characteristics quite different from, say, assertions about purported facts.

Observe, too, that something more than thrusts from the physical world into the spoken one are possible. For quite routinely the very structure of a social contact can involve physical, as opposed to verbal (or gestural) moves. Here such words as do get spoken are fitted into a sequence that follows a nontalk design. A good example is perfunctory service contacts. A customer who comes before a checkout clerk and places goods on the counter has made what can be glossed as a first checkout move, for this positioning itself elicits a second phase of action, the server's obligation to weigh, ring up, and bag. The third move could be said to be jointly accomplished, the giving of money and the getting of change. Presumably the final move is one the shopper makes in carrying the bag away. Simultaneously with this last move, the server will (when busy) begin the second move of the next service contact. Now it turns out that this sequence of moves may or may not be bracketed by a greeting-farewell ritual, may or may not be embroidered with simultaneously sustained small talk, may or may not be punctuated at various points with thank you—you're welcome exchanges. Obviously, talk can figure in such a service contact and quite typically does. Moreover, should any hitch develop in the routine sequence, words will smoothly appear as correctives as though a ratified state of talk had all along existed—giving us some reason to speak of a service encounter, not merely a service contact. But just as obviously, talk and its characteristic structure hardly provides a characterization of the service sequence in progress, this servicing being a game of a different kind. In the serious sense, what is going on is a service transaction, one sustained through an occasion of cooperatively executed, face-to-face, nonlinguistic action. Words can be fitted to this sequence; but the sequencing is not conversational.

With the strictures in mind that relevant moves in a conversation need be neither verbal nor gesticulatory, let us examine more closely the workings of some perfunctory interchanges.

A query concerning the time can be signalled by a phrase or by a gesture, such as pointing to the other's watch or one's own bare wrist. (Under many circumstances both verbal and nonverbal methods will be used to assure effectiveness.) The response to this query can be a verbal reply ("It's five o'clock") or a verbal substitute (five fingers held up). Both modes of response satisfy system and ritual constraints, letting the asker know that his message has been correctly received and seen as proper—as would, incidentally, the excuse, "I'm sorry, I don't have a watch." But in addition, the recipient of the query can react by showing his watch to the questioner—a tack common in multilingual settings. Here, too, the standard system and ritual constraints are satisfied, the implication clearly being that the person offering access to the time has correctly received the message and, in complying with its demands in good spirit, believes the request to have been proper. But, again, this answering action is not a reply in the strict sense: words are being addressed but what they are addressed by is not words or their gestural substitute but a physical doing, a nonlinguistic deed which complies with a request. So, too, when in reaction to being asked for the salt, the asked person passes it.[22] Here words may accompany the respon-

---

22. And, of course, standard sequences could involve a nonlinguistic doing, *then* a verbal response. Indeed, under the term "completives," Jerome Bruner has recently argued that the sequence consisting of a nonlinguistic act by an infant and an affirming comment by a parent is a very basic way in which the child is induced to articulate the stream of behavior into repeatable, identifiable, terminally bracketed segments. (See Bruner [1974: 75]). In later years the parent will monitor the child's behavior, ready to respond with a verbal or gestural sanction each time a lapse in acceptable conduct occurs. Ontogenetically, then, it could be argued that one basic model for talk (in addition to a greeting version of statement and reply) is deed and evaluative comment. And what we take to be a tidy adjacency pair is often a three-part interchange, the first part being a bit of improper or exemplary conduct.

sive action, but need not. (Of course, when such a request must be denied for some reason or temporarily put off, then words are likely to be necessary in order to provide an account, and when the request is for an action in the future—and/or in another place —words in the form of a promise are often the best that can be provided.) Indeed, a case might be made that when a speaker responds to a rerun signal by recycling his statement, *that* act is a doing, too, a deed—in this case, the making of a picture, a hieroglyph—and not in the strictest sense a reply (Quine 1962: 26).

A moment's thought will make it obvious that there are lots of circumstances in which someone giving verbal orders or suggestions expects something nonlinguistic as a response ("On your mark, get set, go"). Thus, one group of sociolinguists studying classroom interaction has even had cause to make a basic distinction between "elicitations" and "directives," the first anticipating a verbal response, the second a nonlinguistic one (Sinclair and Coulthard 1975:28). As already suggested, in starting a foot race or a classroom exercise (or a service transaction), the triggering words constitute a move in an action pattern that is not necessarily enclosed within a state of talk at all, but is rather something with a different character—a game of a different kind —whether involving a single focus of attention or a set of actions each supporting its own, albeit similar, focus of attention. The point to be made here, however, is that while some scenes of face-to-face interaction are set up specifically for nonlinguistic responses, no face-to-face talk, however intimate, informal, dyadic, "purely conversational," or whatever, precludes nonlinguistic responses or the inducing of such responses. Incidentally, it might be argued that children learn to respond with actions before they learn to respond with words.[23]

2. Another feature of responses in general, as opposed to replies in particular, must be addressed: their "reach." A contrast between answering a query regarding the time by words and by demonstration has just been argued. But the matter needs further consideration. If we take the case of verbal answers (or their emblematic substitutes), even here we find that

23. See Shatz (1974).

matters may not be merely verbal. Again look at answering a question about the time. What the respondent does is to look at his watch and then answer. His response, properly speaking, involves a strip of behavior which includes both these phases. Were he *not* to precede the verbal part of his answer with a glance at his watch, he could not answer in the same way. Should it happen that the queried person unbeknownst to the asker has just looked at his watch for an independent reason and now knows the time, making a second look (at that moment) unnecessary, it is quite likely that either he will make this unnecessary look or, if not, will express by gesture or words that there is something special in his response, namely, that he appreciates that he might appear to be answering irresponsibly—without checking, as it were—but that this is not actually so. (For similar reasons, if the time happens to be a round number, the respondent may feel it prudent to answer in a way calculated to forestall the interpretation that he is answering only roughly; thus, "It's *exactly* five o'clock.")

All of this is even more clear in other perfunctory interchanges. For example, when someone trips over another, offers an apology, and has that apology graciously accepted, the acceptance is not simply a reply to the apology; it is also a response to an apologized-for delict. (Again observe that the initial delict, although clearly a nonlinguistic act, is as fully a part of the interchange as are the words that follow the trouble in attempting to deal with it.) And the same would apply if the delict were not a physical event, such as a tripping over, but a statement that is badly managed, or untactful, or whatever.

> C: [Telephone rings]
> A: "Hello."
> C: "Is this the Y?"
> A: "You have the wrong number."
> C: "Is this KI five, double four, double o?"
> A: "Double four, double *six.*"
> → C: "Oh, I am sorry."
> A: "Good-bye." [Hangs up]

Here (in this verbatim record of an actual phone call) the caller's statement, "Oh, I am sorry," patently refers to his having caused someone to come to the phone without warrant; the answerer's

41

immediately previous statement is merely the clincher and is not, all in itself, the object of the caller's remedial action. The object here stretches back to include the whole call.

Another example. In conversation it is obviously possible for a third person to contribute a comment—say, of exasperation—concerning the way in which two other participants have been handling an extended exchange between themselves; and an individual may even choose to comment about what has been happening in a conversation up to the current moment between himself and another party, the immediately prior statement now being read as merely the final one in a sequence, the sequence as a whole being the subject. Thus, the juncture of turn-taking, the management of interruption, and the like, may indeed support a formalistic analysis, showing the bearing with respect to timing of current statement on immediately completed one; but the semantic content of the response can still pertain to something that extends back in time.

The backward reach of responses is illustrated again in the interaction associated with storytelling. A very common feature of informal interaction is an individual's replaying of a bit of his past experience in narrative form (Goffman 1974:503–6). Such replays are commonly only a few sentences long, but sometimes considerably longer, more like, for example, a paragraph than a sentence. And very often listeners are not meant to *reply* to what they have heard, for what form could a reply take? What they are meant to do is to give signs of appreciation, and these may be very brief indeed. In any case, the appreciation shown—like the applause at the end of a play—is not for the last sentence uttered but rather for the whole story and its telling. Thus we can account for something already described, a "rhetorical question" that takes the question-asking form but is not delivered with the intent of eliciting a specific answer; for often this sort of questioning is meant to be heard as but one element in a longer statement, the longer one being the move to which the speaker intends his recipients to address their responses. (So, too, when one individual uses up a turn by directly or indirectly quoting a statement purportedly made by an absent person, the listener cannot, strictly speaking, respond with a reply, but, at least ordinarily, only with an expression of his "reaction" or attitude to such a statement, for the original speaker would have to be produced if a reply in the full sense is to be offered.) Another illustration is the "buried query": wanting to obtain a bit of information but not wanting this to be known, an individual can set up a question series such that the answer he seeks is to one member of the class of questions, here seen as merely part of a series, not symptomatic in itself. The very possibility of employing this dodge assumes that a question series that elicits a string of answers will be perceived, first off, as addressed to the sequence as a whole.[24] Finally, observe that it is possible for a recipient to respond to a speaker by repeating his words, derisively mimicking his style of delivery, this response performing the subtle—but nonetheless common—shift in focus from *what* a speaker says to his saying it in this way, this being (it is now implied) the *sort* of thing he as a speaker would say in the circumstances.

Just as we see that a response may refer to more than a whole statement, so, of course, we must see that it can refer to something less—say, the way the last word is pronounced.

To say that the subject of a response can extend back over something more or less than the prior turn's talk is another way of saying that although a *reply* is addressed to meaningful elements of whole statements, *responses* can break frame and reflexively address aspects of a statement which would ordinarily be "out of frame," ordinarily part of transmission, not content—for example, the statement's duration, tactfulness, style, origin, accent, vocabulary, and so forth.[25] And as long as the respondent can make listeners understand what he is responding to and ensure that this expression is ritually tolerable, then that might be all that is required. Thus the practice during idle talk of abstracting from a just-finished sentence something that can be

24. Another expression of this possibility is found in the tendency, noted by Shuy (1974:21) for a respondent to provide increasingly truncated same-answers to progressive items in a series of questions, the series coming thus to function somewhat as a single whole.

25. "It's time for you to answer now," the Queen said, looking at her watch: "open your mouth a *little* wider when you speak, and always say 'your Majesty.'"

"I only wanted to see what the garden was like, your Majesty—"

"That's right," said the Queen, patting her on the head, which Alice didn't like at all. . . .

punned with or jokingly understood in "literal" form or made explicit in the face of anticipated elision; thus, too, the joking or disciplining practice of ratifying another's asides and rhetorical questions as something to be officially addressed.

This skittish use of more or less than a speaker's whole statement may, of course, be something that the speaker induces. Thus, as Roger Shuy has recently suggested, when a doctor asks two questions at the same time, it is likely that the patient will have the rather enforced option of deciding which to answer:

> D: "Well, how do you feel? Did you have a fever?"
> P: "No."
> D: "And in your family, was there any heart problem? Did you wake up short of breath?"
> P: "No."[26]

Further, statements can be made with the clear understanding that it is not their ordinary meaning that is to be addressed but something else—an ironic or sarcastic interpretation, a joking unseriousness, the accent in which they are delivered, and a host of other "keyings," the transformative power of which seems to have largely escaped linguistic effort at appreciation, let alone conceptualization, until relatively recently.[27] In brief, statements very often have a demand function, establishing what aspect or element of them is to be responded to.

But of course, speaker's implied interpretation demands can often be left unsatisfied as long as some sort of meaningful response is possible. A response that casts backward in time beyond the prior statement, or abstracts an aspect of a statement, or focuses on a particular piece of a statement—all this without encouragement or even anticipation on the part of the initial speaker—can nonetheless leave him with the sense that he has satisfied system constraints, that the response he evoked has done so, too, and, further, that the ritual considerations have been satisfied—or at least not unacceptably violated. When, therefore, I earlier suggested that cited interchanges might be meaningful because whoever originally supplied the second pair part has

26. See footnote 24.

27. A useful current statement may be found in Gumperz (forthcoming). See also Crystal (1969:104).

done our job of uncovering the initial speaker's meaning, I was uncritical. A respondent cannot make evident that he has understood *the* meaning of a statement, because in a sense there isn't one. All he can do is respond to what he can display as *a* meaning that will carry—although, of course, he may effectively sustain the impression (and himself believe) that his *a* is the *the.*

It should be apparent that an encounter itself can be a subject for response. Thus, when a "preclosing" has been given, the recipient can respond by introducing a fresh statement in a manner suggesting that his remark is knowingly being introduced out of order (Schegloff and Sacks 1973:319–20). The preclosing is the immediate stimulus of the last-minute contribution, but, behind this, concern is being directed to the closing that is being postponed.

3. Another characteristic of responses. An individual can, and not infrequently does, respond to himself. Sometimes this will take the form of an actual verbal reply to the semantic content of his own utterances:

> "Do you think they would do that for you?" [Pause, ostensibly for recipient's possible reply, and then with rising stress] "They certainly would not!"[28]

More commonly a "reflexive frame break" is involved, the individual responding "out of frame" to some aspect of his own just-past utterance:

> "Also there's a guy at Princeton you should talk to. Richard . . . (Christ, I'm bad with names. I can see his face now and I can't remember his last name. I'll think of it soon and tell you.)."[29]

28. It should be added that performers of all kinds—including, interestingly, auctioneers—can find it impractical for various reasons to engage in actual repartee with members of the audience, and so as a substitute end up feeding themselves their own statements to reply to or making a statement in the name of a member of the audience, to which they can then respond. Engendered, thus, on situational grounds, is expropriation of the dialogic other.

29. Out-of-frame comments open up the possibility of being incorrectly framed by recipients, in this case heard as part of the unparenthesized material. Here speakers will be particularly dependent on obtaining back-channel expressions from hearers confirming that the reframing has been effectively conveyed. And here radio speakers will have a very special problem, being cut off from this source of confirmation. They can try to deal with this issue by laughing at their own out-of-frame comments, assuming in effect the role of the listener,

All this, perhaps, is only to be expected, for "self-responding" seems to satisfy a basic condition of meaningful communication; a move in the form of a statement occurs and the next move demonstrates that the prior one has been heard and seen to be interpretable and relevant. Note, we have added reason for distinguishing the notion of "move" from that of a speaking, since here, once again, the same turn contains more than one move. Moreover, it is evident that the notions of speaker and respondent can get us into trouble unless we keep in mind that they refer not to individuals as such, but to enacted capacities. Just as a listener can self-select himself as next speaker, so, too, apparently, can speaker.

The self-responses described here may strike one as uncommon, but there is a form of self-response that is found everywhere, namely, self-correction. Requesting suffrance for muffing a word or apologizing for inadvertently stepping on relevant toes very often occurs "immediately" after the delict, the speaker providing a remedy before his hearers have had a chance to feel that they themselves, perhaps, should take some kind of priming action. Moreover, once a gaffe of some kind has been made, it can have a referential afterlife of considerable duration; an hour or a day later, when topic and context give some assurance that those present will be able to understand what incident is being referred to, the speaker in passing can gratuitously inject an ironic allusion, showing that chagrin has been sustained, which demonstration reaches back a goodly distance for its referent.

4. All of which should prepare us for the fact that what

---

but this tack will have the effect of interrupting the flow of utterances and of underlining a joke, the merit of which is often dependent on its striking the hearer as a well-timed throwaway line, an interjection that the interjector can make offhandedly and without missing a stroke. In consequence there has emerged the "displaced bracket." The speaker makes no pause after his aside has terminated, gets established in the next line of his main text, and then, part way through this, and while continuing on with this text, allows his voice to bulge out a little with a laugh, a laugh his hearers ideally would have contributed right after the frame-breaking remark, were they in the studio with him. What is thus accomplished, in effect, is a parenthesized parenthesis. The announcer's little laugh allows him to stand back from the person who saw fit to dissociate himself by means of a wry aside from the text he was required to read. Alas, this distancing from distance sometimes takes the speaker back to the position the script originally afforded him.

appears to be an anomalous statement-reply form may not be anomalous at all simply because replying of any kind is not much involved. Thus the basic pair known as a greeting exchange. It turns out that the two parts of such a round can occur simultaneously or, if sequenced in time, the same lexical item may be employed:

> A: "Hello."
> B: "Hello."

The reason for this apparent license is that the second greeting is not a *reply* to the first; *both* are reactive responses to the sudden availability of the participants to each other, and the point of performing these little rituals is not to solicit a reply or reply to a solicitation but to enact an emotion that attests to the pleasure produced by the contact. And no disorganization results from the apparent overlapping or repetition; indeed, if circumstances can be seen to prevent one of the participants from easily performing his part, then the exchange can be effected through a single person's single offering. Nor, then, need the following greeting-in-passing be as strange as it looks:

> A: "How are you?"
> B: "Hi."

for in the underlying ritual structure a question is not being asked nor an answer provided.

5. And so we can turn to the final point. If a respondent does indeed have considerable latitude in selecting the elements of prior speaker's speaking he will refer to, then surely we should see that the respondent may choose something nonlinguistic to respond to. Respondent can coerce a variety of objects and events in the current scene into a statement to which he can now respond, especially, it seems, when the something derives from someone who could be a speaker.

> A: [Enters wearing new hat]
> B: [Shaking head] "No, I don't like it."

If such a remark is seen to leave matters in a ritually unresolved state, then the retroactively created first speaker can properly close out the interchange more to his satisfaction:

A: [Enters wearing new hat]
B: "No, I don't like it."
A: "Now I know it's right."

giving us a standard three-move interchange, albeit one that started out with something that need not have been treated as a statement at all and must be somewhat coerced into retrospectively becoming one. In general, then, to repeat, it is not *the* statement of a speaker which his respondent addresses, nor even *a* statement, but rather anything the speaker and the other participants will accept as a statement he has made.

Bringing together these various arguments about the admixture of spoken moves and nonlinguistic ones, we can begin to see how misleading the notion of adjacency pair and ritual interchange may be as basic units of conversation. *Verbal* exchanges may be the natural unit of plays, novels, audiotapes, and other forms of literary life wherein words can be transcribed much more effectively than actions can be described. Natural conversation, however, is not subject to this recording bias—in a word, not subject to systematic transformation into words. What is basic to natural talk might not be a conversational unit at all, but an interactional one, something on the order of: mentionable event, mention, comment on mention—giving us a three-part unit, the first part of which is quite likely not to involve speech at all.

III

I have argued that the notion of statement-reply is not as useful as that of statement-response in the analysis of talk. Now we must see that the notion of a statement itself is to be questioned.

True, a statement is something worth differentiating from a response. As suggested, statements precede responses in sequence time. Statements orient listeners to the upcoming; responses, to what has come up. Conversationalists seem more at liberty to choose a statement than to choose a response. And most important, a speaker can be free to make statements about matters that theretofore have not been presented in the talk, whereas he who makes a response must more attend to something that has just been presented, although, of course, he may construe this material in an unanticipated way. Statements elicit; responses are elicited.

Nonetheless, there are problems. Persons who provide responses, no less than those who provide statements, attend to back channel effects for a continuous guide to the reception of their contribution. And in both cases, one must wait for the actor to decide what to address himself to before one can know what is going to be said. And just as an immediately prior statement may be needed if one is to make sense out of the response which follows, so the response which follows will often be necessary if —as an unaddressed recipient—one is to make sense out of a statement now before oneself.

Moreover, beyond the constraint of intelligibility there are others. There is the question of topicality: Often the subject matter must be adhered to, or a proper bridge provided to another. There is the question of "reach" and the etiquette concerning it: Just as an addressed recipient can—whether encouraged to or not—respond to something smaller or larger than the speaker's statement, or to only an aspect of it, or even to nonlinguistic elements in the situation, so, too, a statement can be addressed to something more than the immediately expected response. Thus, the opening statement, "Have you got a minute?" can anticipate, and receive, such a reply as, "Of course," but this is certainly not all that the request implied. For the intent is to open up a channel of communication which stays open beyond the hoped-for reply that ratifies the opening. Indeed, a statement that bears on the management of some phase transition of the business at hand may anticipate no specific response, at least of an overt kind. Thus, Sinclair's recent suggestion about classroom tasks: the bracket markers employed to voice the fact that a task episode has terminated or is about to begin (e.g., "Well, okay, now then") may be employed not to elicit a response but to help with the cadence and pulsing of activity.[30] (Here, along with asides and "reacting moves," we have another example of utter-

---

30. Sinclair and Coulthard (1975:22). These writers use the term "frame" here. A general treatment of bracket markers may be found in Goffman (1974: 251–69).

ances that fall outside the statement-response format.) In sum, given the conversational demands of intelligibility, topicality, episode management, and the like, statements serving as brackets themselves provide an appropriate coping, seen as such, and in a sense thereby constitute responses to these demands.

To complicate matters even more, we find that responses themselves can be acceptably read as calling for a response to them, as when a question is answered with a question, and this second asking is accepted as an answering to the first. (It is even the case that should two individuals meet under circumstances in which both know that one of them is waiting for the other's answer to a particular question, the other may *open* the conversation with the awaited response.)

It follows that the term "statement" itself might be a little ill-suited, and we might want to look for a word encompassing all the things that could be responded to by a person presenting something in the guise of a response. Call this the "reference" of the response. Our basic conversational unit then becomes reference-response, where the reference may, but need not, center in the semantic meaning of the talk just supplied by previous speaker. And now the issue of how chaining occurs in conversation becomes that of how reference-response units are (if at all) linked.

You will note that this formulation rather oddly recommends a backward look to the structuring of talk. Each response provides its auditors with an appreciation not only of what the respondent is saying, but also of what it is he is saying this about; and for this latter intelligence, surely auditors must wait until the respondent has disclosed what his reference is, since they will have no other way of discovering for sure what it will be. It is true, of course, that some verbal pronouncements can be seen to condition responses closely, especially, for example, when social arrangements have underwritten this, as in interrogation sessions; but this mode of constraint is precisely what provides these occasions with their special and individual character. And it is true, of course, that when we examine or present a *record* of a conversation—real, literary, or got up—and read or listen backwards and forwards in it, the indeterminacy I am speaking of will be lost to our senses. For as suggested, in many cases we need only read on (or listen on) a little and it will be clear that the reference proves to be only what we readers expected, thus encouraging the illusion that its selection was determined all along. But, of course, the issue had not really been settled until the moment the purported respondent provided his purported response. Only then could the actual auditors (let alone we readers) actually have known who the person then beginning to speak was to be and what he has hit upon to respond to out of what had already gone on. Even when listeners can properly feel that there is a very high probability that the forthcoming response will address itself in a certain way to a certain aspect of what has been stated, they must wait for the outcome before they can be sure.[31] A similar argument is to be made concerning place of transition from one speaker to another. If a speaker may provide additional transition points after his first one is not taken up, so it follows that he will not know which of his offers is to be accepted until it has been, and we, upon reading a transcript, will only know which possible

---

31. Schegloff and Sacks (1973:299), provide an extreme statement:

> Finding an utterance to be an answer, to be accomplishing answering, cannot be achieved by reference to phonological, syntactic, semantic, or logical features of the utterance itself, but only by consulting its sequential placement, e.g., its placement after a question.

One problem with this view is that in throwing back upon the asker's question the burden of determining what will qualify as an answer, it implies that what is a question will itself have to be determined in a like manner, by reference to the sequence it establishes—so where can one start? Another issue is that this formulation leaves no way open for disproof, for how could one show that what followed a particular question was in no way an answer to it? Granted, an utterance which appears to provide no answer to a prior question can fail pointedly, so that part of its meaning is, and is meant to be, understood in reference to its not being a proper answer—an implication that the adjacency pair format itself helps us to explicate. But surely assessments about how pointed is the rejection of the claims of a question can vary greatly, depending on whether it is the questioner or nonanswerer to whom one appeals, and in fact there seems to be no absolute reason why an individual can't deliver a next remark with no concern at all for its failure to address itself to the prior question. Finally, to say that an answer of a sort can certainly be provided to a prior question without employing the conventional markers of an answer (and that the slot itself must be attended, not what apparently gets put into it) need not deny that answers will *typically* be marked phonologically, syntactically, semantically, etc., and that these markers will be looked to as a means of deciding that what has been said is an answer.

transition point was taken up, not why an earlier actual one or later possible one was not used. Nor is that the end of it. For after it has been disclosed who will be speaking, and at what precise point he will take up his speaking, and what reference his speaking will address itself to, there is still the open question of *what* he will say—and no interchange is so perfunctory as to allow a first pair part to totally constrain a second pair part in that connection.

In sum, we can find lots of strips of verbal interaction which clearly manifest a dialogic form, clearly establishing a difference between statements and replies (and consequently jumping along, an interchange at a time), but this differentiation is sometimes hardly to be found, and in any case is variable. Instead of replies, we have less tidy responses. Such responses can bear so little on the immediate statement that they are indistinguishable from statements; and statements can be so closely guided by understandings of what constitutes an appropriate topic as to be reduced to something much like a response.

It follows, then, that our basic model for talk perhaps ought not to be dialogic couplets and their chaining, but rather a sequence of response moves with each in the series carving out its own reference, and each incorporating a variable balance of function in regard to statement-reply properties. In the right setting, a person next in line to speak can elect to deny the dialogic frame, accept it, or carve out such a format when none is apparent. This formulation would finally allow us to give proper credit to the flexibility of talk—a property distinguishing talk, for example, from the interaction of moves occurring in formal games—and to see why so much interrupting, nonanswering, restarting, and overlapping occurs in it.

We could also see that when four or more persons participate, even this degree of flexibility is extended, for here statements and replies can function as part of the running effort of speakers either to prevent their recipients from getting drawn into another state of talk or to extend the cast of their talk, or contrariwise, to induce a division. (Thus, a speaker who has obtained the attention of one participant may shift his concern to the next person in line, neglecting someone who can be assumed to be committed in favor of someone not yet recruited.) Similarly, an addressed recipient can turn from the addressor to initiate what he hopes will be a separate state of talk with another party, minimizing any tendency to reply in order to invoke the boundary required by the conversation he himself is fostering. Nor does the issue of splitting end it. Two out of three or more coparticipants can enter a jocular, mocked-up interchange in which each loyally plays out his appropriate part, ostensibly providing appropriate statements and ostensibly responding with appropriate replies, while all the while the other participants look on, prepared to enter with a laugh that will let the jokesters off the hook, assuring them that their set piece was appreciated—and with this tactful appreciation provide a response to a statement which is itself an unserious dialogue embedded in a less lightly toned encounter.[32] Here instead of a story being narrated, it is—in a manner of speaking—enacted, but no less to be treated as an embedded whole.) More commonly, the difference between what is said and what is meant, and the various different things that can be meant by what is said, allow a speaker to knowingly convey through the same words one meaning to one auditor and a different meaning (or additional meanings) to another. For if statements or responses can draw their interpretability from the knowingly joint experience of speaker and hearer, then a speaker with more than one hearer is likely to be able to find a way of sustaining collusive communication with one of them through the winks and under-the-breath remarks that words themselves can be tricked into providing. (This three-party horizontal play can be matched in two-person talk through the use of innuendo, the common practice of phrasing an utterance so that two readings of it will be relevant, both of which are meant to be received as meanings intended but one deniably so.)

So, too, we would be prepared to appreciate that the social setting of talk not only can provide something we call "context" but also can penetrate into and determine the very structure of the interaction. For example, it has been argued recently that in classroom talk between teacher and students it can be understood

---

32. Another glimpse of this sort of complexity can be found in Jefferson's illustration of the "horizontal," as opposed to the "vertical," interplay of moves in a multiperson conversation. See Jefferson (1972:306).

that the teacher's purpose is to uncover what each and every pupil has learned about a given matter and to correct and amplify from this base. The consequence of this educational, not conversational, imperative is that classroom interaction can come to be parcelled out into three-move interchanges:

Teacher: Query
Pupil: Answer
Teacher: Evaluative comment on answer

the word "turn" here taken to mean sequencing of pupil obligations to participate in this testing process; furthermore, it is understood that the teacher's concern is to check up on and extend what pupils know, not add to her knowledge from their knowledge, and that it would not be proper for a pupil to try to reverse these roles.[33]

IV

Given an interactional perspective that recommends "move" as a minimal unit, that is concerned with ritual constraints as well as system ones, and that shifts attention from answers to replies and then from replies to responses in general, we can return to perfunctory interchanges and make a closer pass at analyzing them.

1. Take, for example, a standard rerun signal. A simple embedding can apparently result, this involving a "side sequence" whereby one two-part exchange is held open so that another can occur within it:

A_1: "It costs five."
⌐ B_2: "How much did you say?"
∟ A_2: "Five dollars."
B_1: "I'll take it."

33. Sinclair et al. (1972:88, 104). Shuy (1974:12), also provides examples of three-move play. Riddles might be thought to have a three-move structure: (1) question, (2) thought and give-up, (3) answer. Again, the purpose of the asked person's move is not to inform the asker about the answer but to show whether he is smart enough to uncover what the asker already knows. But here the interaction falls flat if indeed the correct answer is uncovered (unlike the asking done by teachers) or if, upon being told the answer, the asked person does not do an appreciable "take," this latter constituting a fourth move.

This is (apparently) an "unhearing." In the case of a misunderstanding, something less tidy can result, something less neatly parceled into two-part exchanges:

(i) D: "Have you ever had a history of cardiac arrest in your family?"
(ii) P: "We never had no trouble with the police."
(iii) D: "No. Did you have any heart trouble in your family?"
(iv) P: "Oh, that. Not that I know of."[34]

The structural difference between an unhearing and a misunderstanding is to be found in terms of how the difficulty gets corrected. With unhearings, the recipient signals there is trouble; with misunderstandings, the speaker. Consequently, unhearings can be nicely managed with turns containing only one move, but misunderstandings lead to a two-move third turn, its first part signalling that trouble has occurred, and its second providing a rerun. Therefore (iii) could be seen as an elision and contraction of something like this:

iii(a) D: "No, that's not what I said."
P: "What did you say?"
D: "Did you have any heart trouble in your family?"

and its collapse into one turn perhaps based on the maxim that in serious matters, anyone who misunderstands another will rather be corrected than protected. Note that (iv) is more complicated than (iii). For although elision does not seem involved in what the speaking accomplishes, it still seems that three different kinds of work are ventured, indeed, three different moves, two involving system constraints and one involving ritual ones. A gloss might go like this:

1. "Oh." [Now I see what you really said and I tell you that I do.]
2. "That." [Although I didn't get you the first time around, what you said comes from a corpus of questions not unfamiliar to me that I can readily deal with.]
3. "Not that I know of." [An answer to the now correctly heard question.]

34. The first two lines are drawn from Shuy (1974:22), and are real; the second two I have added myself, and aren't.

Here, resolving the interchange into two-move couplets doesn't help very much. For although (i) and (ii) can be seen as a two-part exchange of sorts, (iii) is a rejection of (ii) and a restatement of (i), and (iv) is a redoing of (ii) along with a defense against (iii). Observe that an admitted failure to hear (an unhearing) need expose the unhearing recipient to nothing more deprecatory than the imputation of inattentiveness. A misunderstanding, however, causes the misunderstanding recipient to expose what he thinks the speaker might have said and thereby a view both of what he thought might be expected from the speaker and what the recipient himself might expect to receive by way of a question—all this to the possible embarrassment of the definition of self and other that actually comes to prevail.

2. In examining (iv) we found that different moves within the same turn at talk were sustained by *different* words, a convenient fact also true of the chaining examples given at the beginning of the paper. But there is no reason why this must be so. The *same* words can embody different moves in different games. This dismal fact allows us to return to the five dollar unhearing example and examine some of its complications.

There is a way of saying "How much did you say?" so as to imply a "literal" reading, that is, a reading (whether actually literal or not) that stresses what is taken to be the standard meaning of the sentence—its propositional content—and suppresses all other possibilities. But work and care will be required to secure this locutionary effect, as much, perhaps, as would be required to speak the line with any of its other freightings.

About these other freightings. Obviously, in context, "How much did you say?" can mean "That's an awfully high price"—at least in a manner of speaking.[35] And when it does,

---

35. Two kinds of qualifications are always necessary. First, the translation from what is said to what is meant is necessarily an approximation. One should really say, ". . . can mean something like 'That's an awfully high price.'" But I take this to be an instance of "normatively residual" ambiguity. More important, an utterance designed to be made a convenience of, that is, intended to be accepted solely for what it indirectly conveys, never has *only* this significance —apart from the inherent ambiguity of this significance. For, as suggested, a directly made statement inevitably leaves its maker in a different strategic position from the one in which an indirectly equivalent statement would leave him. For example, if a recipient takes violent exception to what a speaker meant

the fact that a move of this kind has been made, a move which questions the honesty and integrity of the informant, will show up in the rerun that comes at the next turn, for then that line ("Five dollars") is likely to be spoken in an apologetic way, its speaker commiserating with the unhearer for the way prices are now; or in a slightly taunting tone, meeting the implied accusation head on and not giving way before it; or, most complicated of all, in what amounts to a serious mimicking of a straightforward standard rerun, providing thereby the functional equivalent of a silence produced and heard as something to take note of. Observe, the practicality of the customer using a sarcastic or ironic phrasing of a rerun signal not only depends on there being a rerun signal to overlay in this way, but also upon there being a conventionalized interchange into which the server's response to this sally can be neatly fitted—whether "directly," by openly addressing the implied meaning of the customer's query, or "indirectly," by inducing through intonation and stress a special reading of what is otherwise a standard response to a standard request for a rerun. Note that the same general interchange format will allow the customer to begin the display of disgruntlement in another way, namely, by means of an utterance such as "You gotta be kidding," which in its turn can lead on to "I know what you mean," or (straight-faced), "No, that's what it really costs," and we are back once again to the same position: a customer who reserves the right to complete a transaction even as he injects note of the fact that he feels the pricing is out of line. May I add that an important possibility in the analysis of talk is to uncover the consequence of a particular move for the anticipated sequence; for that is a way to study the move's functioning (Goffman 1971:171–83). One should examine, then, the way in which a move can precipitously bring an interchange to an end before its initial design would have prefigured or extend the interchange after its termination had been expected or induce an interchange without using up the first slot to do so or cause a "break in step," as when he who gives up the floor in a manner to ensure getting it back after the

---

to convey indirectly, the speaker can always take the line that he meant the literal meaning all along.

next turn finds that the person who obtained the floor has managed matters so as to undercut the built-in return, or when someone being presented at court asks the royal personage questions instead of merely answering them, thereby committing *lèse-majesté* linguistically, for although monarchs may deign to penetrate a commoner's preserve conversationally, the understanding is that the exposure is not to be reciprocated.

3. Consider now that just as interchanges can incorporate nonlinguistic actions along with verbal utterances concerning these actions, so interchanges can incorporate references to past doings as occasions for now doing praise or blame, thereby placing responses to wider circumstances before or after verbal reference to these circumstances and thus bringing them into the interchange:

> B comes home from work, apparently not having brought what he promised to bring, and shows no sign that he is mindful of his failure.
> A_1: "You forgot!" [An utterance whose propositional form is that of an assertion of fact, but here can be understood as blame-giving]
> B_1: "Yes. I *am* sorry."
> A_2: "You're always doing it."
> B_2: "I know."

However, because the accuser cannot be sure of the accused's situation, a tactful hedge may be employed, and sometimes with good reason:

> A_1: "Did you forget?"
> B_1: "No."
> A_2: "Where is it?"
> B_2: "It's in the car."
> A_3: "Well?"
> B_3: "I'm on my way out to get it."

an interchange that can be nicely managed in a more elliptical form:

> A_1 :"Did you forget?"
> $B_1/B_2/B_3$: "No, it's in the car; I'm just on my way to get it."

Observe that the accuser can extend this sort of strategic hedging by asking a question, the affirmative answer to which constitutes an acceptable excuse for the action at fault, thereby giving the apparent offender an easy opportunity either to demonstrate that indeed this (or a similarly effective accounting) can be given or to initiate an admission of guilt (along with an apology) without actually having been asked for either. Thus:

> A: "The store was closed by the time you got out?"
> B: "Darn it. I'm afraid it was."
> etc: . . .
> A: "The store was closed by the time you got out?"
> B: "It was open but they won't have any 'til next week."
> etc: . . .

are possibilities (as initial rounds) the asker leaves open while actually priming the following self-rebuke, thereby allowing the blameworthy person first slot in an apology interchange:

> A: "The store was closed by the time you got out?"
> B: [Striking head] "God. I'm sorry. I'm hopeless."
> etc: . . .

4. Finally, observe how passing interchanges can bear on nonlinguistic actions and balance the claims of different games off against each other, presenting us with utterances that are routine yet functionally complex:

> At an airport a man approaches a stranger, a woman, who is seated at one end of a three-seat row. He places his small bag on the far seat of the three and prepares to walk away to a distant ticket counter.

The basic alternatives open to the man seem to be:

> a. Leave his bag, civilly disattend the sitter (thus neither obliging her to do anything nor presuming on her in any other manner), and go on his way, leaving his bag at risk.
> b. Openly approach the sitter in the manner of someone politely initiating talk with an unacquainted cross-sexed other, saying, for example, "Excuse me, Ma'am, I'll only be gone a minute. If you're going to be here, would you mind keeping an eye on my bag?" (to which the response would likely be a granting of the request or the provision of an explained decline).

With these possibilities as part of the actual situation confronting the two, the following interchange can easily transpire:

He: [Laconically, almost *sotto voce,* as if already lodged in conversation with the recipient]: "Don't let them steal it."
She: [Immediately utters an appreciative conspiratorial chuckle as speaker continues on his way.]

Here a man is taking license to treat a woman with whom he is unacquainted as though they were in a state of "open talk," i.e., the right but not the obligation to initiate brief states of talk at will. But the price for taking this liberty—and what neutralizes it as a liberty and therefore permits it—is that the speaker not only thereby forgoes the outright possibility of obtaining a formal commitment concerning the guarding of his bag, but also physically removes himself from the possibility of further threatening the sitter with an extension of the contact. The recipient responds with a laugh patently directed to the sally—the little joke that is to bring the two momentarily together in acknowledgment of the theft level at the airport—and not to the man's underlying need to have his bag guarded. But the sitter's response does not deny outright that she will indeed be responsive to the man's unstated hope, that prospect being scrupulously left open. The little laugh that follows the unserious command is, then, not merely a sign of appreciation for a joke made, but also evidence of a strategic position which neither denies nor accepts the buried request. (Thus, she is free to leave before the man returns and is free to help out without formally having to accept talk from a stranger.) And this hedged response to the man's deeply hedged request is what he was all along ready to settle for, namely, a hope, not a promise. Thus, an interchange that is entirely verbal and apparently unserious can yet draw upon and implicate wider nonlinguistic matters, such as guardianship, the rules for initiating spoken contact between strangers, and the like. Different orders of interaction, different interaction games, are simultaneously in progress, each involving a different amalgam of linguistic and nonlinguistic doings, and yet the same stretch of words must serve. Note that here the words that realize a move in one game can do so because they can be presented as realizing a move in another.[36]

36. Puns and other "double meanings" are not mere double meanings, for without the occurrence of the straight meaning in the context in which it occurs

V

1. Ordinary language philosophers have recently brought help in the study of the structure of interchanges, for these units of interaction appear to contain and to meld what students of Austin would refer to as quite different speech acts. Drawing on John Searle's analysis (1976:1–23), consider that the following argument is possible.

In theory at least, a speaker should be able to present a statement that solely reports pure fact (an "assertion") and receive a reply that simply attests to system constraints having been satisfied:

> (i) A: "I think I'll do the wrapping."
> B: "Oh."

Very often, in contrast, a speaker presents a "directive," that is, words whose point (or illocutionary force) is to urge the hearer to do something, the urging varying in degree from gentle requests to harsh commands.

One basic kind of directive is aimed at inducing the hearer to impart verbal information on a particular matter, giving us again the question-answer pair.[37]

> ii(a) A: "Is that the parcel I'm supposed to start with?"
> B: "Yes."

Observe that instead of speaking simply of system and ritual constraints, we might want to see B's "Yes" as a move in three different games; the requested information is provided but *also* (by implication) assurance is given that the question was correctly heard, *and* that it was not intrusive, stupid, overeager, out of order, and the like. Consequently the following recovery of two preliminary exchanges is thinkable:

(and thus in the context which allows it to occur) the sophisticated meaning could not be introduced. There is thus a hierarchical ordering of the two meanings, that is, of the unmarked and marked forms; one must be introducible before the other can be introduced.

37. A directive in the sense that "I request that you tell me" is implied. See Gordon and Lakoff (1971:66); Searle (1976:11).

A₁: "Can you hear and understand me?"
B₁: "Yes."
A₂: "Is it all right to ask you a question about the wrapping?"
B₂: "Yes."
A₃: "Is that the parcel I'm supposed to start with?"
B₃: "Yes."

The possibility that the asker needs assurance either that he has gotten across or that his question is proper seems quite remote here, and consequently the argument for elision seems extremely labored. But, of course, there are lots of circumstances in which these two considerations (especially the ritual one) are acutely problematic, being expressed either explicitly in preliminary exchanges or tacitly through intonation and stress.

Move on now to a second basic kind of directive, to the request or command for a nonlinguistic doing:

iii(a) A: "Would you put your finger on the knot?"
B: [Puts finger on knot]

Here again the response (a doing) performs triple work: it does what was requested and simultaneously affirms that the request was correctly heard and deemed to be in order. But now we can see more readily that directives involve (among other things) a timing condition, and this can imply a tacit back pair, or at least the expansion is thinkable in which this underlying possibility is exhibited:

iii(b) A: "Would you put your finger on the knot when I say now?"
B: "Yes."
A: "Now."
B: [Puts finger on knot]

which almost surfaces in the following:

iii(c) A: "Would you put your finger on the knot nnnnnnnnow!"
B: [Puts finger on knot]

The examples given here of requests for information and requests for nonlinguistic doings are simpler than ordinarily found in nature, for there quite commonly what is *meant* as a request for information or action is *said* as a request for yes/no information either about having information or being able to perform an action. ("Do you know the time?"; "Can you reach the salt?") So in many examples of both kinds of directives a further expansion is thinkable in order to recover another elided back pair:

A_1: "Do you know the time?" A_1: "Can you reach the salt?"

    B_1: "Yes." B_1: "Yes."
    A_2: "What is it?" A_2: "Would you?"
    B_2: "Five o'clock." B_2B_3: "Yes." [Gets it, gives it]
                                 A_3: "Thanks."

Furthermore, although what is "literally" said in these cases can be so thoroughly a dead issue as to provide the basis for joking "literal" replies, there will, as suggested, be other occasions when both understandings are relevant, allowing for the possibilities of one utterance figuring as a move in four games: a request for evidence that one is being correctly heard; a request for information about possessing information or ability; a request for divulgence of the information or performance of the capacity; a stand taken concerning the social propriety of making these requests.

Now just as directives aim at inducing words or actions from the addressed recipient, so we can anticipate a class of speech acts through which speaker commits himself to a course of action—"commissives," in Searle's phrasing—comprising promises, pledges, threats, offerings, and the like (1976:17–18).

Commissives are similar to directives in that interchanges involving either can intimately interweave words and actions. Further, both commissives and directives raise the issue of the character of the ritual tags typically associated with them, namely, some variant of please and thank you. Thus:

Directive A_1: "Would you put your finger on the knot?"
     B_1: [Does so]

     A_2: "Thanks."
     B_2: "'t's okay."

Commissive A_1: "Would you like me to put my finger on the knot?"
     B_1: "Yes."
     A_2: [Puts finger on knot]

     B_2: "Thanks."

Although these politeness forms consist of lexicalized verbal utterances, the feeling with which they are spoken is always an important element; as already suggested, the point of employing these forms is not so much to state something as to exhibit feeling. In turn, we might want to distinguish this sort of verbal doing from a second sort, the sort identifiable as involving classic performatives, whereby uttering a formulaic statement in the proper circumstances accomplishes the doing of something, the formula and the circumstances being required, not the feelings of the speaker.[38]

2. A classification of speech acts—such as the one recommended by Searle—provides us with an opportunity to see that how an interchange unfolds will depend somewhat on the type of speech act involved, especially upon the type that initiates the interchange. Thus, a simple declarative statement of fact (if indeed there is such a thing in natural talk) creates a quite different second pair part from a request for information, and such a request has different sequencing implications from a request for a nonlinguistic doing. A "commissive" has still other sequential consequences. And an interpersonal ritual such as a greeting proves to be linked with a matching expression, but now much more loosely than is true of other adjacency pairs.

But if a typology of speech acts is to guide us, we must see that something equally fundamental is presumed.

In English, speech acts tend to be identified with particular syntactic structures (such as imperative and interrogative forms) and particular lexical items (such as "please" and "pardon"), the position being that here the locutionary form "directly" conveys a speech act. It is said that the speech form can "literally" express or realize the corresponding speech act.[39] It is then rea-

38. Note that all classical performatives are moves in at least two games, one that of informing hearers about, say, the name to be given, the bid to be made, the judgment to be rendered, and the other that of achieving this naming, bidding, judging (see Searle [1975]). Words are not alone in having this capacity. Every move in a board game similarly figures, both informing what move the player is to take and committing him to having taken this move. See Goffman (1961:35).

39. "Literal" here is a wonderfully confusing notion, something that should constitute a topic of linguistic study, not a conceptual tool to use in making studies. Sometimes the dictionary meaning of one or more of the

soned that a particular speech form may be routinely employed in accomplishing a speech act different from the one that would be performed were the speech form to be understood literally, that is, taken directly. So a given speech form can come to have a standard significance as a speech act different from its literal significance as a speech act.[40] Only one more step is needed to appreciate that in a particular context, a speech form having a standard significance as a speech act can be employed in a still further way to convey something not ordinarily conveyed by it —whatever, of course, it happens to say. (Indeed, on occasion the special meaning conveyed by a speech form may consist of its "literal" meaning, as when James Bond leaves his recently shot dancing partner at a stranger's table, saying that she is dead on her feet.)

Given all of this, an attempt must be made to uncover the principles which account for whatever contrast is found on a particular occasion between what is said (locutionary effect), what is *usually* meant by this (standard illocutionary force), and what in fact is meant on that particular occasion of use. Further, consideration must be given to the fact that in some cases, standard meaning is closely dependent on literal meaning, in other cases not; in some cases, particular force is closely dependent on the standard one (either as a contrast or as something that can retroactively be claimed as what was intended), in other cases there seems hardly any relation at all between them.[41]

One problem with this perspective is that a set of prear-

---

words of the utterance is meant, although how *that* meaning is arrived at is left an open question. And the underlying, commonsense notion is preserved that a word *in isolation* will have a general, basic, or most down-to-earth meaning, that this basic meaning is sustained in how the word is commonly used in phrases and clauses, but that in many cases words are used "metaphorically" to convey something that they don't really mean.

40. In fact, as recently suggested (Shatz 1974), indirect significance may be learned *before* literal meaning is appreciated.

41. A good example of this latter, one that did not show respect for linguistic doctrines of the time, can be found in the once-popular John-Marsha record, wherein a male voice repeating only the female name and a female voice repeating only the male name managed to convey through timing, stress and other paralinguistic cues a complete seduction. Dostoyevsky's version is reviewed in Vološinov (1973:103–5); and Vygotsky (1962:142–44).

ranged harmonies tends to be assumed. Speech forms are taken to be of the same number and kind as are standard speech acts; and the latter are taken to provide a matching for the variety of meanings that occur in particular contexts. The same list of possibilities is assumed to be found in each of the three classes of cases, the only issue being which instances of this list are to appear together, as when, for example, a question is said but an order is meant or an order is said but an offer is meant or an offer is what is usually meant but in this case a request is intended.[42] (A similar argument can be made about the issue of "strength"; the "strength" of an utterance is ordinarily attached to, and indicated by, a set speech form, but in context a particular usage can convey much less or much more force.)[43] The point, of course, is that although standard speech acts may form a relatively small, well-demarcated set, this applies largely to what is said; what is meant seems to draw on additional sets of meanings, too. For example, the interruptive utterance, "What?", presents the proposition that something has not been heard and the illocutionary intent of inducing a rerun. But in very many cases of actual use, these possibilities are the cover for some sort of boggling at what is occurring, and these various bogglings don't aptly fit into the standard speech act boxes.

Further, there is a degenerative relation between what is said and what is conveyed, for the special use to which a standard speech act is put on occasion can after a time become itself a standard overlayed meaning, which can then, in turn, allow for a second-order use to be employed for still other purposes. For example, "I shall hate you if you do not come to my party" has

42. Here, as Ervin-Tripp (1976) suggests, misunderstandings are to be located; so also seriously pretended misunderstandings, openly unserious misunderstandings, concern by speaker about misunderstanding, etc.

43. Linguists seem to have a special commitment to the analysis of directives. They start with a series that is marked syntactically and phonetically, beginning with imperative forms and then on to the various "mitigations" until something like a vague wish is being said. And there does seem to be a general social understanding that such a series exists; witness the fact that the series is drawn upon as a resource when formulating joking moves. But what sort of series, if any (and if only one), any particular social circle of users actually employs and what relation this may have, if any, to the grammarian's stereotypes is an open question, no doubt to be differently answered by every group one might study. Here see the useful analysis in Ervin-Tripp (1976).

to do with issuing strong invitations, not with warning of strong dislike consequent on failure to perform a particular act. But what is here conveyed as opposed to what is said may well itself be employed in a mock voice as mimicry of refinement. And some of these mockeries have themselves become rather standardized, opening up the prospect of a still further twist between what is said and what is meant. Moreover, two different standardized meanings may be established. For example, rerun signals very commonly constitute a sanctioning move against a speaker, pointedly giving him a chance to recast the way he has said something or to proceed now to account for why he did what he has just reported having done; however, the same signals are also used in their more "literal" sense to accomplish improved communication.

3. Commonly, critiques of orthodox linguistic analysis argue that although meaning depends on context, context itself is left as a residual category, something undifferentiated and global that is to be called in whenever, and only whenever, an account is needed for any noticeable deviation between what is said and what is meant. This tack fails to allow that when no such discrepancy is found, the context is still crucial—but in this case the context is one that is usually found when the utterance occurs. (Indeed, to find an utterance with only one possible reading is to find an utterance that can occur in only one possible context.) More important, traditionally no analysis was provided of what it is in contexts that makes them determinative of the significance of utterances, or any statement concerning the classes of contexts that would thus emerge—all of which if explicated, would allow us to say something other than merely that the context matters.

Here Austin has helped. He raises the question of how a speech act can fail to come off and suggests an analysis: there are infelicities (including misfirings and abuses), restrictions on responsibility, misunderstandings, and etiolations, namely, the reframings illustrated when an act turns out to be embedded in a report, a poem, a movie, and so on (Austin 1965:12–24). In asking how a speech act can fail, Austin points to conditions that must be fulfilled if the act is to succeed, this in turn suggesting how contexts might be classified according to the way they affect the illocutionary force of statements made in them. And indeed, the prospect is implied that a whole framework might be uncovered which establishes the variety of ways in which an act can be reread and a determinative account of the relations among these several bases for reinterpretation.

Say that there is in any given culture a limited set of basic reinterpretation schemas (each, of course, realized in an infinite number of ways), such that the whole set is potentially applicable to the "same" event. Assume, too, that these fundamental frameworks themselves form a framework—a framework of frameworks. Starting, then, from a single event in our own culture, in this case, an utterance, we ought to be able to show that a multitude of meanings are possible, that these fall into distinct classes limited in number, and that the classes are different from each other in ways that might appear as fundamental, somehow providing not merely an endless catalogue but an entree to the structure of experience. It will then seem obvious that the schema of schemas applicable to (and even derived from) the possible meanings of our chosen event will similarly apply to any other event. Of course, the shape of such a metaschema need only be limned in to provide the reader with a focus for easy complaint; but complaints can lead to what we are looking for.

Start, then, with a conventionalized, perfunctory social litany, one that begins with A's "Do you have the time?" and restricting ourselves to B's verbal response, consider the following unfoldings:

A. Consensual
  1. The "standard" response, comprising variants of a more or less functionally equivalent kind:
  "Five o'clock."
  "Yes I do. It's five o'clock."
  "Sorry, my watch isn't working."
  "There it is" [pointing to big wall clock].
  2. A standard schema of interpretation fundamentally different from the one pertaining to clocks proves to be the one that both participants are applying:
  "No, but I still have the *Newsweek.*"
  "Sure. Anyway, what you want won't take but a minute."
  "No, I left it with the basil."
  3. A mutually and openly sustained full transformation of the original (a "keying") proves to prevail:

Director to actress: "No, Natasha. Turn your head or you'll never reach beyond the footlights."

Librarian: "No, that wasn't the title, but it was something like that."[44]

Language teacher: "That's just fine, Johann. A few more times and you'll have the 't' right."

4. Indirect meaning given direct reply:

"Stop worrying. They'll be here."

"All right, all right, so I did lose your present."

Prospective john: "How much for the whole night?"

B. Procedural problems holding off illocutionary concerns

1. System constraints not satisfied:

"What did you say?"

"Bitte, ich kann nur Deutsch sprechen."

"What dime?"

2. Ritual constraints not satisfied:

"I'm sorry, we are not allowed to give out the time. Please phone TI 6-6666."

"Nurse, can't you see I'm trying to tie off this bleeder?"

"Shh, that mike carries."

C. Addressing ritual presuppositions so that the illocutionary point of the initial statement is denied at least temporarily, and a side sequence is established in which the erstwhile respondent becomes the initiator:

---

44. Borrowed from Fillmore (1973:100), who not only provides some illustrations (in connection with his article's title), but also goes on to offer an injunction:

> We must allow ourselves, first of all, to disregard the infinite range of possible situations in which the sentence was *mentioned* or merely *pronounced,* rather than *used.* It may be that somebody was asked, for example, to pronounce four English monosyllables, putting heavy stress and rising intonation on the last one, and he accidentally came up with our sentence; or a speaker of a foreign language might have been imitating an English sentence he once overheard; or a librarian might have been reading aloud the title of a short story. Since the properties of this infinitely large range of possibilities are in no way constrained by the structure or meaning of this particular sentence, this whole set of possibilities can safely be set aside as an uninteresting problem.

Here I think Fillmore is overdespairing, confusing members and classes. There is an unmanageable number of different ways a sentence can figure, but perhaps not so many *classes* of ways it can figure, and the delineation of these classes can be an interesting problem. That different students will be free to come up with different classes does not undermine the value of examining various attempts to see which seems currently the most useful.

"Why the formality, love?"
"Could I ask where you learned your English?"
"Don't you remember me?"

D. Warranted or unwarranted treatment of asker's move as trick-
   ery—in this particular case the assumption being that once a
   claim is established for initiating talk, it will come to be exploited:
   "No." [Not meeting the asker's eyes and hurrying away from
   him on the assumption that the question might be an instance
   of the now standard ploy to ready a robbery]
   "Say, are you trying to pick me up?"
   "Never mind the time, Peterkins, you know you're supposed
   to be in bed."

E. Jointly sustained fabrication relative to passers-by; e.g.:
   [Spy recognition signal] "Yes. Do you happen to have a
   match?"

F. Unilateral use of features of interaction for the open purpose of
   play or derision:
   1. Failure to perform anticipated ellipsis:
      "Yes, I do. . . ."
   2. Use of unanticipated schema of interpretation:
      "Yes, do you have the inclination?"
      [In mock Scots accent] "And may I ask what you want it
      for?"
   3. Anything covered in A through E but reframed for playful
      use, e.g.:
      [Huge, tough-looking black in black neighborhood, on being
      asked the time by a slight middle-class, white youth, looks
      into youth's eyes while reaching for watch] "You ain' fixin'
      to rob me, is you?"

It is some such framework of frameworks that we must seek
out; it is some such metaschema that will allow us to accumulate
systematic understanding about contexts, not merely warnings
that in another context, meaning could be different.

PART FOUR

What, then, is talk viewed interactionally? It is an example of
that arrangement by which individuals come together and sustain matters having a ratified, joint, current, and running claim
upon attention, a claim which lodges them together in some

sort of intersubjective, mental world.[45] Games provide another example, for here the consciously intended move made by one participant must be attended to by the other participants and has much the same meaning for all of them. A sudden "striking" event can constitute another source for this joint arrangement; for at such moments, and typically only for a moment, a common focus of attention is provided that is clearly not the doing of the witnesses, which witnessing is mutually witnessed, the event then having the power to collapse persons theretofore not in a state of talk into a momentary social encounter. But no resource is more effective as a basis for joint involvement than speakings. Words are the great device for fetching speaker and hearer into the same focus of attention and into the same interpretation schema that applies to what is thus attended. But that words are the best means to this end does not mean that words are the only one or that the resulting social organization is intrinsically verbal in character. Indeed, it is when a set of individuals have joined together to maintain a state of talk that nonlinguistic events can most easily function as moves in a conversation. Yet, of course, conversation constitutes an encounter of a special kind. It is not positional moves of tokens on a board that figure as the prime concern; it is utterances, very often ones designed to elicit other utterances or designed to be verbal responses to these elicitations.

Now when an individual is engaged in talk, some of his utterances and nonlinguistic behavior will be taken to have a special temporal relevance, being directed to others present as something he wants assessed, appreciated, understood, *now*. I have spoken here of a move. Now it seems that sometimes the

45. An argument recently pressed by Rommetveit (1974:23):

Once the other person accepts the invitation to engage in the dialogue, his life situation is temporarily transformed. The two participants leave behind them whatever were their preoccupations at the moment when silence was transformed into speech. From that moment on, they became inhabitants of a partly shared social world, established and continuously modified by their acts of communication. By transcribing what they say into atemporal contents of utterances, moreover, we clearly disregard those dynamic and subjective aspects of their discourse which Merleau Ponty seems to have in mind when referring to "synchronizing change of . . . own existence" and "transformation of . . . being."

speaker and his hearers will understand this move to be primarily a comment on what has just been said, in that degree allowing us to speak of a response; at other times the move will be primarily seen as something to which a response is called for, in which degree it can be called a statement.

And the possibility of each leaves radically open another possibility, namely, that some mixture of the two will occur and in such a way as to discourage the value of the differentiation in the first place. Left open also will be the status of the reference and also the question as to whether or not the move involves action or talk or both. What we are left with, then, is the conversational move carving out a reference, such that the reference and the move may, but need not, be verbal. And what conversation becomes then is a sustained strip or tract of referencings, each referencing tending to bear, but often deviously, some retrospectively perceivable connection to the immediately prior one.

In recommending the notion of talk as a sequence of reference-response moves on the part of participants, such that each choice of reference must be awaited before participants can know what that choice will be (and each next speaker must be awaited before it can be known who he is), I do not mean to argue against formalistic analysis. However tortured the connection can become between last person's talk and current speaker's utterance, that connection must be explored under the auspices of determinism, as though all the degrees of freedom available to whosoever is about to talk can somehow be mapped out, conceptualized, and ordered, somehow neatly grasped and held, somehow made to submit to the patterning-out effected by analysis. If contexts can be grouped into categories according to the way in which they render the standard force of an utterance inapplicable and principles thus developed for determining when this meaning will be set aside, then such must be attempted. Similarly, sequencing must be anticipated and described. We must see, for example, that current speaker's shift from the ordinarily meant meaning of last speaker's statement to an ordinarily excluded one, with humorous intent, can lead to a groan intoned jointly and simultaneously by all other participants and then return to seriousness; or the maneuver can lead to the temporary establishment of a punning rule, thus encouraging an answering pun from next speaker. Standard sequences are thus involved, but these are not sequences of statement and reply but rather sequences at a higher level, ones regarding choice with respect to reach and to the construing of what is reached for. (A compliment seems totally different from an insult, but a likeness is involved if each has been elicited by its kind.) It is thus that uniformities might be uncovered in regard to reference selection, including how standard utterances will be construed as a reference basis for response. In this way we could recognize that talk is full of twists and turns and yet go on to examine routinized sequences of these shiftings. Conversational moves could then be seen to induce or allow affirming moves or countermoves, but this gamelike back-and-forth process might better be called interplay than dialogue.

And with that, the dance in talk might finally be available to us. Without diffidence, we could attend fully to what it means to be in play and we could gain appreciation of the considerable resources available to a speaker each time he holds the floor. For he can use what he is pleased to of the immediate scene as the reference and context of his response, provided only that intelligibility and decorum are maintained. His responses themselves he can present with hedges of various sorts, with routine reservations, so that he can withdraw from the standpoint, and hence the self, these remarks would ordinarily imply. Part-way through his turn he can break frame and introduce an aside, alluding to extraneous matters, or, reflexively, to the effort at communication now in progress—his own—in either case temporarily presenting himself to his listeners on a changed footing. And after he is ostensibly finished speaking, he can beat his listeners to the punch by gesturing a final bracketing comment on what he has just said and upon the person who would engage in such a saying, this comment, too, requiring a shift in stance, the taking up of a new relationship to, a new footing with, his audience. And in artfully managing this sequence of altered footings, he can but succeed, however else he fails, in extending the choices in depth available to the speakers who follow—choices as to what to address their own remarks to. Every conversation, it seems, can raise itself by its own bootstraps, can provide its participants with something to flail at, which process in its entirety can then be made the reference of an aside, this side remark then responsively provoking a joking refusal to disattend it. The box that conversation stuffs us into is Pandora's.

But worse still. By selecting occasions when participants have tacitly agreed to orient themselves to stereotypes about conversation, we can, of course, find that tight constraints obtain, that, for example, a statement by A will be followed by a demonstration from B that he found this statement meaningful and within bounds, and here supplies a response that displays the relevance of this statement and relevance for it. And we can collect elegantly structured interchanges, whether by drawing on occasions when incidental mutual impingement is handled by perfunctory politeness on both sides, or conversely, when two individuals are positioned to sustain having a verbal go at each other, or better still, by drawing on literary texts. But there are other arrangements to draw upon. Individuals who are on familiar, ritually easy terms can find themselves engaged close together (whether jointly or merely similarly) in a nonlinguistic doing that claims their main attention. While thusly stationed, one amongst them may occasionally speak his passing thoughts aloud, half to himself, something equivalent to scratching, yawning, or humming. These ventings call on and allow the license available to those sustaining an open state of talk. An adjacent hearer can elect to let the matter entirely pass, tacitly framing it as though it were the stomach rumblings of another's mind, and continue on undeflected from his task involvements; or, for example, he can hit upon the venting as an occasion to bring the remaining company into a focus of conversational attention for a jibe made at the expense of the person who introduced the initial distraction, which efforts these others may decline to support, and if declining, provide no display of excuse for doing so. In these circumstances the whole framework of conversational constraints —both system and ritual—can become something to honor, to invert, or to disregard, depending as the mood strikes. On these occasions it's not merely that the lid can't be closed; there is no box.

REFERENCES

Austin, J. L. 1965. *How to do things with words.* New York: Oxford University Press.

Bellack, Arno A.; Kliebard, H. M.; Hyman, R. T.; and Smith, F. L. 1966. *The language of the classroom.* New York: Columbia Teachers College Press.

Bloomfield, Leonard. 1946. *Language.* New York: Henry Holt & Co.

Boomer, Donald S. 1965. "Hesitation and grammatical encoding." *Language and Speech* 8:148–58.

Bruner, Jerome. 1974. "The ontogenesis of speech acts." In *Social rules and social behavior,* edited by Peter Collett. Oxford: Department of Experimental Psychology, Oxford University, multigraph.

Clancy, Patricia. 1972. "Analysis of a conversation." *Anthropological Linguistics* 14: 78–86.

Crystal, David. 1969. "The language of conversation." In *Investigating English style,* edited by David Crystal and Derek Davy, pp. 95–124. Bloomington: Indiana University Press.

Dittmann, Allen T. 1972. "The body movement–speech rhythm relationship as a cue to speech encoding." In *Studies in dyadic communication,* edited by A. W. Siegman and B. Pope, pp. 135–51. New York: Pergamon Press.

Duncan, Starkey, Jr. 1972. "Some signals and rules for taking speaking turns in conversations." *Journal of Personality and Social Psychology* 23:283–92.

Ekman, Paul, and Friesen, Wallace. 1969. "The repertoire of nonverbal behavior: Categories, origins, usage and coding." *Semiotica* 1:63–68.

Ervin-Tripp, Susan. 1976. "Is Sybil there? The structure of American directives." *Language in Society* 5:25–66.

Fillmore, Charles J. 1973. "May we come in?" *Semiotica* 9:97–116.

Gluckman, Max. 1962. "Les rites de passage." In *Essays on the ritual of social relations,* edited by Max Gluckman. Manchester: Manchester University Press.

Goffman, Erving. 1961. *Encounters.* Indianapolis: Bobbs-Merrill, Inc.

———. 1967. *Interaction ritual.* New York: Anchor Books.

———. 1971. *Relations in public.* New York: Harper and Row.

———. 1974. *Frame analysis.* New York: Harper and Row.

Goodwin, Charles. 1977. Ph.D. dissertation, University of Pennsylvania.

Goodwin, Marjorie. 1975. "Aspects of the social organization of children's arguments: Some procedures and resources for restructuring positions." Unpublished paper.

————. 1978. "Conversational practices in a peer group of urban black children." Ph.D. dissertation, University of Pennsylvania.

Gordon, David, and Lakoff, George. 1971. "Conversational postulates." In *Papers of the Chicago Linguistic Society,* pp. 63–84. Chicago: Department of Linguistics, University of Chicago.

Grice, H. Paul. 1975. "Logic and conversation." In *syntax and semantics: Speech acts,* vol. 3, edited by Peter Cole and Jerry L. Morgan, pp. 41–58. New York: Academic Press.

Gumperz, John J. Forthcoming. "Language, communication and public negotiation." In *Anthropology and the public interest: Fieldwork and theory,* edited by Peggy R. Sanday. New York: Academic Press.

Gunter, Richard. 1974. *Sentences in dialog.* Columbia, S.C.: Hornbeam Press.

Harris, Zellig. 1951. *Structural linguistics.* Chicago: University of Chicago Phoenix Books.

Hymes, Virginia. 1974. "The ethnography of linguistic intuitions at Warm Springs." Paper presented at NWAVE III, Georgetown University, October 25, 1974.

Jefferson, Gail. 1972. "Side sequences." In *Studies in social interaction,* edited by David Sudnow. New York: The Free Press.

Labov, William, and Fanshel, David. 1977. *Therapeutic discourse: Psychotherapy as conversation.* New York: Academic Press.

Merritt, Marilyn. 1976. "Resources for saying in service encounters." Ph.D. dissertation, Department of Linguistics, University of Pennsylvania.

Pomerantz, Anita May. 1975. "Second assessments: A study of some features of agreements/disagreements." Ph.D. dissertation, University of California, Irvine.

Philips, Susan U. 1974. "The invisible culture: Communication in classroom and community on the Warm Springs Reservation." Ph.D. dissertation, Department of Anthropology, University of Pennsylvania.

Quine, Willard van Orman. 1962. *Mathematical logic.* Rev. ed. New York: Harper and Row.

Rommetveit, Ragnar. 1974. *On message structure: A framework for the study of language and communication.* New York: John Wiley and Sons.

Sacks, Harvey. 1967. Unpublished lecture notes. University of California, Irvine.

————. 1973. Lecture notes. Summer Institute of Linguistics. Ann Arbor, Michigan.

Sacks, Harvey; Schegloff, Emanuel; and Jefferson, Gail. 1974. "A simplest systematics for the organization of turn-taking for conversation." *Language* 50: 696–735.

Schegloff, Emanuel. 1968. "Sequencing in conversational openings." *American Anthropologist* 70:1075–95.

Schegloff, Emanuel, and Sacks, Harvey. 1973. "Opening up closings." *Semiotica* 8:289–327.

Searle, John R. 1975. "Indirect speech acts." In *Syntax and semantics,* edited by Peter Cole and Jerry L. Morgan, pp. 59–82. New York: Academic Press.

76

————. 1976. "A classification of illocutionary acts." *Language in Society* 5:1–23.

Shatz, Marilyn. 1974. "The comprehension of indirect directives: Can two-year-olds shut the door?" Paper presented at the Summer Meeting, Linguistic Society of America, Amherst, Massachusetts.

Shuy, Roger. 1974. Problems of communication in the cross-cultural medical interview. *Working Papers in Sociolinguistics,* no. 19, December 1974.

Sinclair, J. McH., and Coulthard, R. M. 1975. *Towards an analysis of discourse: The English used by teachers and pupils.* London: Oxford University Press.

Sinclair, J. McH., et al. 1972. The English used by teachers and pupils. Unpublished Final Report to SSRC for the period September 1970 to August 1972.

Stubbs, Michael. 1973. Some structural complexities of talk in meetings. *Working Papers in Discourse Analysis,* no. 5. University of Birmingham: English Language Research.

Vološinov, V. N. 1973. *Marxism and the philosophy of language.* New York: Seminar Press.

Vygotsky, L. S. 1962. *Thought and language.* MIT Press and John Wiley and Sons.

Yngve, Victor H. 1970. On getting a word in edgewise. In *Papers from the Sixth Regional Meeting, Chicago Linguistic Society,* edited by M. A. Campbell et al., pp. 567–78. Chicago: Department of Linguistics, University of Chicago.

2

RESPONSE CRIES

Utterances are not housed in paragraphs but in turns at talk, occasions implying a temporary taking of the floor as well as an alternation of takers.[1] Turns themselves are naturally coupled into two-party interchanges. Interchanges are linked in runs marked off by some sort of topicality. One or more of these topical runs make up the body of a conversation. This inter-actionist view assumes that every utterance is either a statement establishing the next speaker's words as a reply, or a reply to what the prior speaker has just established, or a mixture of both. Utterances, then, do not stand by themselves, indeed, often make no sense when so heard, but are constructed and timed to support the close social collaboration of speech turn-taking. In nature, the spoken word is only to be found in verbal interplay, being inte-grally designed for such collective habitats. This paper considers some roguish utterances that appear to violate this interdepend-ence, entering the stream of behavior at peculiar and unnatural places, producing communicative effects but no dialogue. The

---

1. Grateful acknowledgment is made to *Language,* where this paper first appeared (54[1978]:787–815). Without specific acknowledgment I have incor-porated a very large number of suggestions, both general and specific, provided by John Carey, Lee Ann Draud, John Fought, Rochel Gelman, Allen Grimshaw, Gail Jefferson, William Labov, Gillian Sankoff, Joel Sherzer, W. John Smith, and an anonymous reviewer. I am grateful to this community of help; with it I have been able to progress from theft to pillage. Comments on broadcasters' talk are based on a study reported in this volume.

paper begins with a special class of spoken sentences, and ends with a special class of vocalizations, the first failing to qualify as communication, the second failing not to.

I

To be all alone, to be a "solitary" in the sense of being out of sight and sound of everyone, is not to be alone in another way, namely, as a "single," a party of one, a person not in a *with,* a person unaccompanied "socially" by others in some public undertaking (itself often crowded), such as sidewalk traffic, shopping in stores, and restaurant dining.[2]

Allowing the locution "in our society," and, incidentally, the use of *we* as a means of referring to the individual without specifying gender, it can be said that when we members of society are solitary, or at least assume we are, we can have occasion to make passing comments aloud. We kibitz our own undertakings, rehearse or relive a run-in with someone, speak to ourselves judgmentally about our own doings (offering words of encouragement or blame in an editorial voice that seems to be that of an overseer more than ourselves), and verbally mark junctures in our physical doings. Speaking audibly, we address ourselves, constituting ourselves the sole intended recipient of our own remarks. Or, speaking in our own name, we address a remark to someone who isn't present to receive it. This is self-communication, specifically, "self-talk." Although a conversationlike exchange of speaker-hearer roles may sometimes occur, this seems unusual. Either we address an absent other or address ourselves in the name of some standard-bearing voice. Self-talk of one type seems rarely replied to by self-talk of the other. I might add that the voice or name in which we address a remark to ourselves can be just what we might properly use in addressing a remark to someone else (especially someone familiar enough with our

2. This easy contrast conceals some complications. For a *with*—a party of more than one—can be solitary, too, as when a lone couple picnics on a deserted beach. Strictly speaking, then, a *single* is a party of one present among other parties, whereas a solitary individual is a party of one with no other parties present.

world to understand cryptic references), or what another might properly use in talking to us. It is not the perspective and standards that are peculiar or the words and phrases through which they are realized, but only that there are more roles than persons. To talk to oneself is to generate a full complement of two communication roles—speaker and hearer—without a full complement of role-performers, and which of the two roles—speaker or hearer —is the one without its own real performer is not the first issue.

Self-talk could, of course, be characterized as a form of egocentricity, developmentally appropriate in childhood years and only reappearing later "in certain men and women of a puerile disposition" (Piaget 1974:40). Common sense, after all, recommends that the purpose of speech is to convey thoughts to others, and a self-talker necessarily conveys them to someone who already knows them. To interrogate, inform, beseech, persuade, threaten, or command oneself is to push against oneself or at best to get to where one already is, in either case with small chance of achieving movement. To say something to someone who isn't there to hear it seems equally footless.

Or worse, self-talk might appear to be a kind of perversion, a form of linguistic self-abuse. Solitary individuals who can be happily immersed in talking to themselves need not in that degree seek out the company of their fellows; they need not go abroad to find conversational company, a convenience that works to the general detriment of social life. Such home consumption in regard to the other kind of intercourse qualifies either as incest or masturbation.

A more serious argument would be that self-talk is merely an out-loud version of reverie, the latter being the original form. Such a view, however, misses the sense in which daydreaming is different from silent, fuguelike, well-reasoned discussion with oneself, let alone the point (on which Piaget [1962:7] and Vygotsky [1962:19–20] seem to agree) that the out-loud version of reverie and of constructive thought may precede the silent versions developmentally. And misses, too, the idea that both the autistic and constructive forms of "inner speech" are considerably removed from facially animated talk in which the speaker overtly gives the appearance of being actively engrossed in a spirited exchange with invisible others, his eyes and lips alive with the proceedings.

In any case, in our society at least, self-talk is not dignified as constituting an official claim upon its sender-recipient—true, incidentally, also of fantasy, "wool gathering," and the like. There are no circumstances in which we can say, "I'm sorry, I can't come right now, I'm busy talking to myself." And anyway, hearers ordinarily would not *reply* to our self-talk any more than they would to the words spoken by an actor on the stage, although they might otherwise *react* to both. Were a hearer to say, "What?", that would stand as a rebuke to conduct, not a request for a rerun, much as is the case when a teacher uses that response to squelch chatter occurring at the back of the room; or, with a different intonation, that the self-talk had been misheard as the ordinary kind, a possibility which could induce a reply such as, "Sorry, I was only talking to myself."

Indeed, in our society a taboo is placed on self-talk. Thus, it is mainly through self-observation and hearsay that one can find out that a considerable amount goes on. Admittedly, the matter has a Lewis Carroll touch. For the offense seems to be created by the very person who catches the offender out, it being the witnessing of the deed which transforms it into an improper one. (Solitary self-talkers may occasionally find themselves terminating a spate of self-talk with a self-directed reproach, but in doing so would seem to be catching *themselves* out—sometimes employing self-talk to do so.) In point of fact, the misdoing is not so much tied up with doing it in public as *continuing* to do it in public. We are all, it seems, allowed to be caught stopping talking to ourselves on one occasion or another.

It is to be expected that questions of frames and their limits will arise. Strictly speaking, dictating a letter to a machine, rehearsing a play to a mirror, and praying aloud at our bedside are not examples of self-talk, but should others unexpectedly enter the scene of this sort of solitary labor, we might still feel a little uneasy and look for another type of work. Similarly, there are comedy routines in which the butt is made vulnerable by having to sustain a full-blown discussion with someone who is hidden from general view. And there are well-known comic gestures by which someone caught talking to himself attempts to transform the delict into a yawn or into the just-acceptable vocalizations of whistling, humming, or singing.[3] But behind these risible issues of frame is the serious fact that an adult who fails to attempt to conceal his self-talk, or at least to stop smartly on the appearance of another person, is in trouble. Under the term verbal hallucination we attribute failure in decorum here to "mental illness."[4]

Given the solitary's recourse to self-addressed remarks well into adult life, and that such talk is not merely a transitional feature of primary socialization (if, indeed, a natural phase of childhood development), one is encouraged to shift from a developmental to an interactional approach. Self-talk, when performed in its apparently permissible habitat—the self-talker all alone—is by way of being a mimicry of something that has its initial and natural provenance in speech between persons, this in turn implying a social encounter and the arrangement of participants through which encounters are sustained. (Such transplantation, note, is certainly not restricted to deviant activity; for example, a writer does it when he quotes in the body of his own single sentence an entire paragraph from a cited text, thereby pseudomorphically depositing in one form something that in nature belongs to another.)

With self-talk, then, one might want to say that a sort of impersonation is occurring; after all, we can best compliment or upbraid ourselves in the name of someone other than the self to whom the comments are directed. But what is intended in self-talk is not so much the mere citation or recording of what a

3. Nor should the opposite framing issue be neglected. A man talking to himself at a bar may cause the bartender to think him drunk, not peculiar, and if he wants to continue drinking may suffer more hardship from the first imputation than the second. (An instance is reported to me of a barroom self-talker being misframed as always having had too much and temporarily solving this threat to his drinking rights by retreating to the tavern's telephone booth to do his self-talking.)

4. I leave open the question of whether the individual who engages in verbal hallucination does so in order to create an impression of derangement, or for other reasons, and is merely indifferent to how he appears, or carries on in spite of some concern for the proprieties. And open, too, the question of whether in treating unabashed self-talk as a natural index of alienation, we have (in our society) any good grounds for our induction.

monitoring voice might say, or what we would say to another if given a chance, but the stage-acting of a version of the delivery, albeit only vaguely a version of its reception. What is set into the ongoing text is not merely words, but their animator also—indeed, the whole interactional arrangement in which such words might get spoken. To this end we briefly split ourselves in two, projecting the character who talks and the character to whom such words could be appropriately directed. Or we summon up the presence of others in order to say something to them. Self-talk, then, involves the lifting of a form of interaction from its natural place and its employment in a special way.

Self-talk described in this way recommends consideration of the soliloquy, long a feature of western drama, although not currently fashionable.[5] An actor comes stage center and harangues himself, sometimes at enormous length, divulging his inner thoughts on a pertinent matter with well-projected audibility. This behavior, of course, is not really an exception to the application of the rule against public self-talk. Your soliloquizer is really talking to self when no one is around; we members of the audience are supernatural, out-of-frame eavesdroppers. Were a character from the dramatized world to approach, our speaker would audibly (to us) self-direct a warning:

> But soft, I see that Jeffrey even now doth come. To the appearance of innocent business then.

and would stop soliloquizing. Were he to continue to self-talk, it would be because the script has instructed him to fail to notice the figure all the rest of us have seen approach.

Now, if talking to oneself in private involves a mocking-up of conversation and a recasting of its complementarity, then the production of this recasting on the stage in the bloated format of a soliloquy obviously involves a further insetting, and a transformation of what has already been transformed. The same could be

5. Never necessary in novels and comics where the author has the right to open up a character's head so the reader can peer into the ideas it contains, and technologically no longer necessary in the competing modes of commercial make-believe—movies and television plays. In these latter a voice-over effect allows us to enter into the inner thoughts of a character who is shown silently musing.

said, incidentally, about a printed advertisement which features realistically posed live models whose sentiments are cast into well-articulated inner speech in broken-line balloons above their heads, providing a text that the other figures in the pictured world can't perceive but we real people can, to be distinguished from the continuous-line balloon for containing words that one figure openly states to another.

Here, I believe, is a crucial feature of human communication. Behavior and appearance are ritualized—in something like the ethological sense—through such ethologically defined processes as exaggeration, stereotyping, standardization of intensity, loosening of contextual requirements, and so forth. In the case under question, however, these transformations occur to a form of interaction, a communication arrangement, a standard set of participant alignments. I believe that any analysis of self-talk (or for that matter, any other form of communication) that does not attend to this nonlinguistic sense of embedding and transformation is unlikely to be satisfactory.

I I

These parables about self-talk provide entrance to a mundane text. First, definitions: by a *social situation* I mean any physical area anywhere within which two or more persons find themselves in visual and aural range of one another. The term "gathering" can be used to refer to the bodies that are thus present. No restriction is implied about the relationship of those in the situation: they may all be involved in the same conversational encounter, in the sense of being ratified participants of the same state of talk; some may be in an encounter while others are not, or are, but in a different one; or no talk may be occurring. Some, all, or none of those present may be definable as together in terms of social participation, that is, in a "with."

Although almost every kind of mayhem can be committed in social situations, one class of breaches bears specifically on social situations as such, that is, on the social organization common to face-to-face gatherings of all kinds. In a word, although many delicts are *situated,* only some are *situational.* As for social situations as such, we owe any one in which we might find ourselves evidence that we are reasonably alive to what is already in it, and furthermore to what might arise, whether on schedule or unexpectedly. Should need for immediate action be required of us, we will be ready; if not mobilized, then able to mobilize. A sort of communication tonus is implied. If addressed by anyone in the situation we should not have far to go to respond, if not to reply. All in all, a certain respect and regard is to be shown to the situation-at-large. And these demonstrations confirm that we are able and willing to enter into the perspective of the others present, even if no more than is required to collaborate in the intricacies of talk and pedestrian traffic. In our society, then, it is generally taboo in public to be drunken, to belch or pass wind perceptibly, to daydream or doze, or to be disarrayed with respect to clothing and cosmetics—and all these for the same reason. These acts comprise our conventional repertoire, our prescribed stock of "symptoms," for demonstrating a lack of respectful alertness in and to the situation, their inhibition our way of "doing" presence, and thereby self-respect. And the demonstration can be made with sound; audible indicators are involved as well as visual ones.

It is plain, then, that self-talk, in a central sense, is situational in character, not merely situated. Its occurrence strikes directly at our sense of the orientation of the speaker to the situation as a whole. Self-talk is taken to involve the talker in a situationally inappropriate way. Differently put, our self-talk—like other "mental symptoms"—is a threat to intersubjectivity; it warns others that they might be wrong in assuming a jointly maintained base of ready mutual intelligibility among all persons present. Understandably, self-talk is less an offense in private than in public; after all, the sort of self-mobilization and readiness it is taken to disprove is not much required when one is all alone.

This general argument makes sense of a considerable number of minor details. In a waiting room or public means of transportation, where it is evident that little personal attention to pedestrian traffic is required, and therefore less than a usual amount of aliveness to the surround, reading is allowed in our society, along with such self-withdrawal to a printed world as this makes possible. (Observe that reading itself is institutionalized as something that can be set aside in a moment should a reason present itself, something that can be picked up and put down without ceremony, a definition that does not hold for all of our pleasures.) However, chuckling aloud to ourselves in response to what we are reading is suspect, for this can imply that we are too freely immersed in the scene we are reading about to retain dissociated concern for the scene in which our reading occurs. Interestingly, should we mouth the read words to ourselves and in the process make the mouthings audible, we will be taken to be unschooled, not unhinged—unless, of course, our general appearance implies a high educational status and therefore no "natural" reason for uncontained reading. (This is not to deny that some mumbled reading gives the impression of too much effort invested in the sheer task of reading to allow a seemly reserve for the situation-at-large.)

In public, we are allowed to become fairly deeply involved in talk with others we are with, providing this does not lead us to block traffic or intrude on the sound preserve of others; presumably our capacity to share talk with one other implies we are able to share it with those who see us talking. So, too, we can conduct a conversation aloud over an unboothed street phone while either turning our back to the flow of pedestrian traffic or watching it in an abstracted way, without the words being thought improper; for even though our coparticipant is not visually present, a natural one can be taken to exist, and an accounting is available as to where, cognitively speaking, we have gone, and, moreover, that this "where" is a familiar place to which the others could see themselves traveling, and one from which we could be duly recalled should events warrant.[6]

Observe also that we can with some impunity address words in public to a pet, presumably on the grounds that the animal can

6. I once saw an adolescent black girl collapse her male companion in laughter on a busy downtown street by moving away from him to a litter can in which she had spied a plastic toy phone. Holding the phone up to her mouth and ear while letting the cord remain in the can, and then, half-turning as if to view the passing parade in a dissociated manner (as one does when anchored to an open telephone kiosk), she projected a loud and lively conversation into the mouthpiece. Such an act puts on public order in a rather deep way, striking at its accommodative close readings, ones we all ordinarily support without much awareness.

appreciate the affective element of the talk, if nothing else. We extend the same sort of regard to infants. Although on both these occasions a full-fledged recipient is not present to reply to our words, it is clear that no imagined person or alien agency has captured our attention. Moreover, special forms of talk are involved: for example, the praising/admonishing sort of evaluative utterance that routinely leads to no verbal reply when employed in talk between competents, or mimicked babytalk projected as the talk the incompetent would employ were it able to speak ("say-foring"). Should a pet or infant be addressed in quite ordinary speech, then, of course, something would be heard as very odd indeed. Incidentally, to be seen walking down the street alone while *silently* gesticulating a conversation with an absent other is as much a breach as talking aloud to ourselves—for it is equally taken as evidence of alienation.

Finally, there are the words we emit (sometimes very loudly) to summon another into talk. Although such a speaking begins by being outside of talk with actual others, its intended recipient is likely quickly to confirm—by ritualized orientation, if not by a verbal reply—the existence of the required environment, doing so before our utterance is completed.[7] A summons that is openly snubbed or apparently undetected, however, can leave us feeling that we have been caught engaging in something like talking to ourselves, and moreover very noticeably.[8]

To say that self-talk is a situational impropriety is not to say

---

7. A pet or a small child can be repeatedly summoned with a loud cry when it is not in sight, with some disturbance to persons in range; but a "mental" condition is not ordinarily imputed. Typically it is understood that the words are merely a signal—a toy whistle would do—to come home, or to come into view to receive a message, not to come into protracted conversation from wherever the signal is heard.

8. Such an occurrence is but one instance of the deplorable class of occasions when we throw ourselves full face into an encounter where none can be developed, as when, for example, we respond to a summons that was meant for someone behind us, or warmly greet a total stranger mistakenly taken to be someone we know well, or (as already mentioned) mistakenly reply to someone's self-talk. The standard statement by which the individual whom we have improperly entangled sets us right, for example, "Sorry, I'm afraid you've . . . ," itself has a very uneasy existence. Such a remark is fully housed within a conversational exchange that was never properly established, and its purpose is to deny a relationship that is itself required for the remark to be made.

that it is a *conversational* delict—no more, that is, than any other sounded breach of decorum, such as an uncovered, audible yawn. Desisting from self-talk is not something we owe our fellow conversationalists as such; that is, it is not owed to them in their capacity as coparticipants in a specific encounter and thus to them only. Clearly it is owed to all those in sight and sound of us, precisely as we owe them avoidance of the other kinds of improper sounds. The individual who begins to talk to himself while in a conversational encounter will cause the other participants in the encounter to think him odd; but for the same reason and in the same way those not in the encounter but within range of it will think him odd, too. Clearly, here the conversational circle is not the relevant unit; the social situation is. Like catching a snail outside its shell, words are here caught outside of conversations, outside of ratified states of talk; one is saved from the linguistic horror of this fact only because the words themselves ought not to have been spoken. In fact, here talk is no more conversational than is a belch; it merely lasts longer and reflects adversely on a different part of personality.

So a rule: *No talking to oneself in public.* But, of course, the lay formulation of a rule never gets to the bone, it merely tells us where to start digging. In linguistic phrasing, *No talking to oneself in public* is a prescriptive rule of communication; the descriptive rule —the practice—is likely to be less neat and is certain to be less ready to hand, allowing, if not encouraging, variously grounded exceptions. The framework of normative understandings that *is* involved is not recorded, or cited, or available in summary form from informants. It must be pieced out by the student, in part by uncovering, collecting, collating, and interpreting all possible exceptions to the stated rule.

III

An unaccompanied man—a single—is walking down the street past others. His general dress and manner have given anyone who views him evidence of his sobriety, innocent intent, suitable aliveness to the situation, and general social competency. His left foot strikes an obtruding piece of pavement and he stumbles. He instantly catches himself, rights himself more or less efficiently, and continues on.

Up to this point his competence at walking had been taken for granted by those who witnessed him, confirming their assessment of him in this connection. His tripping casts these imputations suddenly into doubt. Therefore, before he continues he may well engage in some actions that have nothing to do with the laws of mechanics. The remedial work he performs is likely to be aimed at correcting the threat to his reputation, as well as his posture. He can pause for a moment to examine the walk, as if intellectually concerned (as competent persons with their wits about them would be) to discover what in the world could possibly have caused him to falter, the implication being that anyone else would certainly have stumbled, too. Or he can appear to address a wry little smile to himself to show that he himself takes the whole incident as a joke, something quite uncharacteristic, something that can hardly touch the security he feels in his own manifest competency and therefore warranting no serious account. Or he can "overplay" his lurch, comically extending the disequilibrium, thereby concealing the actual deviation from normal ambulatory orientation with clowning movements, implying a *persona* obviously not his serious one.

In brief, our subject externalizes a presumed inward state and acts so as to make discernible the special circumstances which presumably produced it. He tells a little story to the situation. He renders himself easy to assess by all those in the gathering, even as he guides what is to be their assessment. He presents an act specialized in a conventional way for providing information—a *display*—a communication in the ethological, not the linguistic, sense. The behavior here is very animal-like, except that what the human animal seems to be responding to is not so much an obvious biological threat as a threat to the reputation it would ordinarily try to maintain in matters of social competence. Nor is it hard to catch the individual in a very standard look—the hasty, surreptitious survey sometimes made right after committing a fleeting discreditable deed. The purpose is to see whether witnessing has occurred and remedial action is therefore necessary, this assessment itself done quickly enough so that a remedy, if necessary, can be provided with the same dispatch as occurs when there is no doubt from the start that it will be necessary.

However, instead of (or as a supplement to) engaging in a choreographed accounting that is visually available, our subject may utter a cry of wonderment, such as *What in the world!* Again he renders readily accessible to witnesses what he chooses to assign to his inward state, along with directing attention to what produced it, but this time the display is largely auditory. Moreover, if nonvocal gestures in conjunction with the visible and audible scene can't conveniently provide the required information, then self-talk will be the indicated alternative. Suddenly stopping in his tracks, the individual need only grimace and clutch at his heart when the issue is an open manhole at his feet; the same stopping consequent on his remembering that he was supposed to be somewhere else is more likely to be accounted for by words. (Presumably the more obscure the matter, the more extended the self-remarks will have to be and perhaps the less likely is the individual to offer them.)

I am arguing here that what in some sense is part of the subject matter of linguistics can require the examination of our relation to social situations at large, not merely our relation to conversations. For apparently verbalizations quite in the absence of conversations can play much the same role as a choreographed bit of nonvocal behavior. Both together are like other situational acts of propriety and impropriety in that they are accessible to the entire surround and in a sense designed for it. They are like clothing more than like speech. However, unlike clothing or cosmetics, these displays—be they vocal or in pantomime—are to be interpreted as bearing on a passing event, an event with a limited course in time. (What we wear can certainly be taken as an indication of our attitude to the social occasion at hand but hardly to specific events occurring during the occasion.) Necessarily, if unanticipated passing events are to be addressed, a marker must be employed that can be introduced just at the moment the event occurs, and withdrawn when concern for the event has been.

I V

It has been argued that there is a prohibition against public self-talk, and that breachings of this rule have a display character; yet also that there are social situations in which one could expect self-talk. Indeed, I think that the very force which leads us to refrain from self-talk in almost all situations might itself cause us to indulge in self-talk during certain exceptional ones. In this light, consider now in greater detail a few environments in which exposed self-talk is frequently found.

On our being "informed" of the death of a loved one (only by accident are we "told," this latter verb implying that the news might be conveyed in passing), a brief flooding out into tears is certainly not amiss in our society. As might be expected, it is just then that public self-talk is also sanctioned. Thus Sudnow (1967:141) describes the giving of bad news in hospitals:

> While no sympathy gestures are made, neither does the doctor withdraw from the scene altogether by leaving the room, as, for example, does the telegram delivery boy. The doctor is concerned that the scene be contained and that he have some control over its progress, that it not, for example, follow him out into the hall. In nearly all cases the first genuine interchange of remarks was initiated by the relative. During the period of crying, if there is any, relatives frequently "talk." Examples are: "I can't believe it," "It's just not fair," "Goddamn," "Not John . . . no. . . ." These remarks are not responded to as they are not addressed to anyone. Frequently, they are punctuated by crying. The physician remains silent.

The commonsense explanation here is that such informings strike at our self so violently that self-involvement immediately thereafter is reasonable, an excusable imposition of our own concerns upon everyone else in the gathering. Whatever the case, convention seems to establish a class of "all-too-human" crises that are to be treated as something anyone not directly involved ought yet to appreciate, giving us victims the passing right to be momentary centers of sympathetic attention and providing a legitimate place for "anything" we do during the occasion. Indeed, our utter self-containment during such moments might create uneasiness in others concerning our psychological habitat, causing them to wonder how responsive we might be to ordinary situated concerns directly involving them.

Not all environments which favor self-talk are conventionally understood to do so. For example, podium speakers who suddenly find themselves with a page or line missing from their texts or with faulty microphones will sometimes elect to switch from talking to the audience to talking to themselves, addressing a full sentence of bewilderment, chagrin, or anger for their own ears and (apparently) their own benefit, albeit half-audibly to the room. Even in broadcast talk, speakers who lose their places, misplace their scripts, or find themselves with incoherent texts or improperly functioning equipment, may radically break frame in this way, apparently suddenly turning their backs on their obligations to sustain the role of speaker-to-an-audience. It is highly unprofessional, of course, to engage in *sotto voce,* self-directed remarks under just those microphonic conditions which ensure their audibility; but broadcasters may be more concerned at this point to show that some part of them is shocked by the hitch and in some way not responsible for it than to maintain broadcasting decorum. Also, being the sole source of meaningful events for their listeners, they may feel that the full text of their subjective response is better than no text at all. Note, there are other social situations which provide a speaker with an audience that is captive and concerned, and which thereby encourage self-talk. Drivers of buses, taxis, and private cars can shout unflattering judgments of invasive motorists and pedestrians when these have passed out of range, and feel no compunction about thus talking aloud to themselves in the presence of their passengers. After all, there is a sense in which their contretemps in traffic visibly and identically impinge on everyone in the vehicle simultaneously.[9]

9. And, of course, there will be occasions of equivalent license for nonverbal signs, both vocal and gesticulatory. In trying on a shoe we can emit all manner of grimaces and obscure sounds, for these signs provide running evidence of fit, and such information is the official, chief concern at that moment of all parties to the transaction, including the shoe clerk. Similarly, a sportsman or athlete is free to perform an enormous flailing-about when he flubs; among other reasons for this license, he can be sure (if anyone can) that his circumstances are fully attended and appreciated by everyone who is watching the action. After all, such clarity of intent is what sports are all about.

That drivers may actually wait until the apparent target of their remarks cannot hear them points to another location for self-talk, which is also suggested by the lay term "muttering." Frustrated by someone's authority, we can mutter words of complaint under the breath as the target turns away out of apparent conversational earshot. (Here is a structural equivalent of what children do when they stick out their tongues or put their thumbs to their noses just as their admonisher turns away.) For these subvocalizations reside in the very interstice between a state of talk and mere copresence, more specifically, in the transition from the first to the second. And here function seems plain. In muttering we convey that although we are now going along with the line established by the speaker (and authority), our spirit has not been won over, and compliance is not to be counted on. The display is aimed either at third parties or at the authority itself, but in such a way that we can deny our intent and the authority can feign not hearing what we have said about him. Again a form of communication that hardly fits the linguistic model of speaker and addressed recipient; for here we provide a reply to the speaker that is displaced from him to third parties and/or to ourselves. Instead of being the recipient of our reply, the initial speaker becomes merely the object or target of our response. Observe, as with tongue-sticking, muttering is a time-limited communication, entering as a "last word," a post-terminal touch to a just-terminated encounter, and thus escapes for incidental reasons the injunction against persisting in public self-talk.

Consideration of self-talk in one kind of interstice recommends consideration of self-talk in others. For example, if we are stopped for a moment's friendly chat just before entering or leaving an establishment or turning down a street, we may provide a one-sentence description of the business we are about to turn to, this account serving as a rationale for our withdrawing and as evidence that there are other calls upon our time. Interestingly enough, this utterance is sometimes postponed until the moment when the encounter has just finished, in which case we may mumble the account half-aloud and somewhat to ourselves. Here again is self-talk that is located transitionally between a state of talk and mere copresence, and again self-communication that is self-terminating, although this time because the communicator, not the hearer, is moving away. Here it is inescapably clear that the self-talker is providing information verbally to others present, merely not using the standard arrangement—a ratified state of talk—for doing so.

Finally, it must be allowed that when circumstances conspire to thrust us into a course of action whose appearance might raise questions about our moral character or self-respect, we often elect to be seen as self-talkers in preference. If we stoop to pick up a coin on a busy street, we might well be inclined to identify its denomination to ourselves aloud, simultaneously expressing surprise, even though we ourselves are no longer in need of the information. For the street is to be framed as a place of passage not—as it might be to a child or a vagrant—a hunting ground for bits of refuse. If what we thought was a coin turns out to be a worthless slug, then we might feel urged to externalize through sound and pantomime that we can laugh at the fools we have made of ourselves.[10] Trying to open the door of a car we have mistaken for our own and discovering our mistake, we are careful to blurt out a self-directed remark that properly frames our act for those who witness it, advertising inadequate attentiveness to deny we are a thief.

With these suggestions of where self-talk is to be found, one can return and take a second look at the conventional argument that children engage in it because they aren't yet socialized into the modesties of self-containment, the proprieties of persondom. Vygotsky, responding to what he took to be Piaget's position, long ago provided a lead ([1934], 1962:16):

10. Picking money off the street is, of course, a complicated matter. Pennies and even nickels we might well forgo, the doubt cast on our conduct of more concern to us than the money. (We accept the same small sums in change when paying for something in a shop, but there a money transaction is the official business at hand.) Should another in our sight drop such a coin, we might well be inclined to retrieve and return it, for we are allowed a distractive orientation to the ground we walk on so long as this is patently in the interests of others. (If we don't retrieve our own small coins, then we run the risk of others doing so for us and the necessity, therefore, of showing gratitude.) If the sum is large enough to qualify as beyond the rule of finders keepers, we might quickly glance around to see if we have been seen, carefully refraining from saying or gesturing anything else. Covert also may be our act whenever we spy a coin of any denomination to see if any others are not to be found, too.

In order to determine what causes egocentric talk, what circumstances provoke it, we organized the children's activities in much the same way Piaget did, but we added a series of frustrations and difficulties. For instance, when a child was getting ready to draw, he would suddenly find that there was no paper, or no pencil of the color he needed. In other words, by obstructing his free activity we made him face problems.

We found that in these difficult situations the coefficient of egocentric speech almost doubled, in comparison with Piaget's normal figure for the same age and also in comparison with our figure for children not facing these problems. The child would try to grasp and to remedy the situation in talking to himself: "Where's the pencil? I need a blue pencil. Never mind, I'll draw with the red one and wet it with water; it will become dark and look like blue."[11]

The implication is that self-talk serves a self-guidance function, and will be most evident, presumably, when the child senses that task performance is problematic. Given that Vygotsky's early work required an adult observer to be within listening distance, one could go on to suggest an additional interpretation, namely that for children the contingencies are so great in undertaking any task, and the likelihood so strong that they will be entirely discounted as reasonably intentioned persons if they fail (or indeed that they will be seen as just idling or fooling around anyway), that some voicing of what they are about is something

11. Piaget, as his reply (1962:3–4) to a reading of Vygotsky's manuscript suggests, apparently meant "egocentricity" to refer to speech (or any other behavior) that did not take into consideration the perspective of the other in some way, and only incidentally (if at all) to speech not openly addressed to others, the latter being what Vygotsky described, and which I call "self-talk." (Piaget's concept of egocentricity has led to another confusion, a failure to discriminate two matters: taking the point of view of the other in order to discover what his attitude and action will be, and accepting for oneself, or identifying with, the perspective of the other. The classic con operation illustrates how fully the first form of sympathy may be required and produced without leading to the second.) It is probably the case that there is a whole array of different forms of talk that are not fully other-involving, that some of these decrease with age, some increase to a point, and still others are not especially age-related. For a review of some of the possibilities, the Piaget-Vygotsky debate, and the developmental literature on self-talk in general (under the perhaps better title, "Private Speech"), see Kohlberg et al. (1968).

they are always prepared to offer. An adult attempting to learn to skate might be equally self-talkative.[12]

Some loose generalizations might be drawn from these descriptions of places for self-talk. First, when we address a remark to ourselves in public, we are likely to be in sudden need of reestablishing ourselves in the eyes and ears of witnesses as honest, competent persons not to be trifled with, and an expression of chagrin, wonderment, anger, and so forth would seem to help in this—at least establishing what our expectations for ourselves are, even if in this case they can't be sustained. Second, one could argue that self-talk occurs right at the moment when the predicament of the speaker is evident to the whole gathering in a flash or can be made so, assuring that the utterance will come as an understandable reaction to an understood event; it will come from a mind that has not drifted from the situation, a mind readily tracked. The alien world reflected in hallucinatory talk is therefore specifically avoided, and so, too, therefore, some of the impropriety of talking outside the precincts of a ratified conversation. Nor is "understandable" here merely a matter of cognition. To appreciate quickly another's circumstances (it seems) is to be able to place ourselves in them empathetically. Correspondingly, the best assurance another can have that we will understand him is to offer himself to us in a version with which we can identify. Instead, then, of thinking of self-talk as something blurted out under pressure, it might better be thought of as a mode of response constantly readied for those circumstances in which it is excusable. Indeed, the time and place when our private

---

12. Recently Jenny Cook-Gumperz and William Corsaro have offered a more compelling account (1976:29): "We have found that children consistently provide verbal descriptions of their behavior at various points in spontaneous fantasy in that it cues other interactants to what is presently occurring as well as provides possibilities for plugging into and expanding upon the emerging social event." The authors imply that if a fantasy world is to be built up during *joint* play, then words alone are likely to be the resource that will have to be employed, and an open recourse to self-talk then becomes an effective way to flesh out what is supposed to be unfolding for all the participants in the fantasy.

A purely cognitive interpretation of certain action-oriented, self-directed words ("nonnominal expressions") has also been recently recommended by Alison Gopnik (1977:15–20).

reaction is what strangers present *need* to know about is the occasion when self-talk is more than excusable.[13]

v

Earlier it was suggested that when an unaccompanied man stumbles, he may present his case by means of self-talk instead of silent gesture. However, there is another route to the advertisement of self-respect. He can emit one or two words of exclamatory imprecation, such as *hell* or *shit*. Observe, these ejaculatory expressions are nothing like the pointed shout of warning one individual might utter to and for another, nor even like an openly directed broadcast to all-in-hearing, such as a street vendor's cry or a shriek for help. Talk in the ordinary sense is apparently not at issue. In no immediate way do such utterances belong to a conversational encounter, a ritually ratified state of talk embracing ratified participants, nor to a summoning to one. First speaker's utterance does not officially establish a slot which second speaker is under some obligation to fill, for there is no ratified speaker and recipient—not even imaginary ones—merely actor and witness. To be sure, an interjection is involved, but one that interrupts a course of physical action, not an utterance.

When, unaccompanied, we trip and curse ourselves (or the walk, or the whole wide world), we curse *to* ourselves; we appear to address ourselves. Therefore, a kind of self-remarking seems to be involved. Like the publicly tolerated self-talk already considered, imprecations seem to be styled to be overheard in a gathering. Indeed, the styling is specific in this regard. With no one present in the individual's surround, I believe the expression is quite likely to be omitted. If women and children are present, your male self-communicator is quite likely to censor his cries accordingly—a man who utters *fuck* when he stumbles in a

---

13. Understandably, stage soliloquies occur only when the character's personal feelings about his circumstances are exactly what we members of the audience require to be privy to if we are to be properly positioned in the drama unfolding.

foundry is quite likely to avoid that particular expletive should he trip in a day-nursery. If we can see that persons very close by can see what we have just done (or failed to do), then whispered expletives are possible; if witnesses are far away, then shouted sounds will be required. "Recipient design" is involved (to use Harvey Sacks's term) and so quickly applied as to suggest that continuous monitoring of the situation is being sustained, enabling just this adjustment to take place when the moment requiring it comes. Of course, in any case we will have taken the time to encode our vocalization in the conventional lexicon of our language (which is, incidentally, likely to be the local one), a feat that is instantaneously accomplished even sometimes by bilinguals who in addition must generally select their imprecations from the language of their witnesses.[14] (This is not to say that bilinguals won't use a harsh imprecation from one language in place of a less harsh one drawn from the language in use, foreignness apparently serving as a mitigation of strength.) Significantly, here is a form of behavior whose very meaning is that it is something blurted out, something that has escaped control, and so such behavior very often is and has; but this impulsive feature does not mark the limits to which the utterance is socially processed, rather the conventionalized styling to which it is obliged to adhere.

It is plain that singles use imprecations in a variety of circumstances. Racing unsuccessfully to enter a turnstile before it automatically closes, or a door before it is locked for the evening, may do it; coming up to what has just now become a brick wall, we may exhibit frustration and chagrin, often with a curse. (Others, having formulated a possible reading of the precipitous rush we have made, can find that our imprecations are a way of confirming their interpretation, putting a period to the behavioral sentence we have played out, bringing the little vignette to a close, and reverting us to someone easily disattendable.) Precariously carrying too many parcels, we may curse at the moment they fall. The horse we have bet on being nosed out at the finish line, we may damn our misfortune while tearing up our tickets;

14. It would be interesting to know whether or not bilingual children who self-talk select the code likely to be employed by the others in their presence.

our cause for disappointment, anger, and chagrin amply evident, or at least easily surmisable, we have license to wail to the world. Walking along a wintry street that carries a record-breaking snow now turned to slush, we are in a position to cry *God!* in open private response, but as it happens we do so just at the point of passing another, the cause of our remark and the state of our mind perfectly plain and understandable. It might be added that the particular imprecations I have so far used as illustrations seem in our society to be the special domain of males—females, traditionally at least, employing softer expressions. Nor, as is now well known, is this gender convention impervious to rapid politically inspired change.

Finally, I want to recommend that although imprecations and extended self-remarks can be found in much the same slot, do much the same work, and indeed often appear together, raising the question as to why they should be described separately, judgment should be reserved concerning their equivalence. Other questions must be considered first.

V I

The functioning of imprecations raises the question of an allied set of acts that can be performed by singles: *response cries,* namely, exclamatory interjections which are not full-fledged words. *Oops!* is an example. These nonlexicalized, discrete interjections, like certain unsegmented, tonal, prosodic features of speech, comport neatly with our doctrine of human nature. We see such "expression" as a natural overflowing, a flooding up of previously contained feeling, a bursting of normal restraints, a case of being caught off guard. That is what would be learned by asking the man in the street if he uses these forms and, if so, what he means by them.

I am assuming, of course, that this commonsense view of response cries should give way to the co-occurrence analysis that sociolinguists have brought to their problems. But although this naturalistic method is encouraged by sociolinguists, here the subject matter moves one away from their traditional concern. For a response cry doesn't seem to be a statement in the linguistic sense (even a heavily elided one), purportedly doing its work through the concatenated semantic reference of words. A remark is not being addressed to another, not even, it seems, to oneself. So, on the face of it at least, even self-communication is not involved, only a simpler sign process whereby emissions from a source inform us about the state of the source—a case of exuded expressions, not intentionally sent messages. One might better refer to a "vocalizer" or "sounder" than to a speaker. Which, of course, is not to deny the capacity of a well-formed, conventionally directed sentence to inform us about the state of the protagonist who serves as its subject, nor that the speaker and protagonist can be the "same"—for indeed through the use of first-person pronouns they routinely are. Only that this latter arrangement brings us information through a message, not an expression, a route fundamentally different from and less direct than the one apparently employed in response cries, even though admittedly such cries routinely come to be employed just in order to give a desired impression. Witnesses can seize the occasion of certain response cries to shake their heads in sympathy, cluck, and generally feel that the way has been made easy for them to initiate passing remarks attesting to fellow-feeling; but they aren't obliged to do so. A response cry may be uttered in the hope that this half-license it gives to hearers to strike up a conversation will be exercised; but, of course, this stratagem for getting talk going could not work were an innocent reading not the official one. As might be expected, the circumstances which allow us to utter a response cry are often just the ones that mitigate the impropriety of a different tack we could take, that of opening up an encounter by addressing a remark to an unacquainted other; but that fact, too, doesn't relieve one of the necessity to distinguish between this latter, fully social sort of comment and the kind that is apparently not even directed to the self.

A response cry is (if anything is) a ritualized act in something like the ethological sense of that term. Unable to shape the world the way we want to, we displace our manipulation of it to the verbal channel, displaying evidence of the alignment we take to events, the display taking the condensed, truncated form of a discretely articulated, nonlexicalized expression. Or, suddenly able to manage a tricky, threatening set of circumstances, we deflect into nonlexicalized sound a dramatization of our relief and self-congratulation in the achievement.

VII

Consider now some standard cries.

1. The *transition display*. Entering or leaving from what can be taken as a state of marked natural discomfort—wind, rain, heat, or cold—we seem to have the license (in our society) to external-ize an expression of our inner state. *Brr!* is a standard term for wind and cold upon leaving such an atmosphere. (Other choices are less easily reproduced in print.) *Ahh!* and *Phew!* are also heard, this time when leaving a hot place for a cool one. Function is not clear. Perhaps the sounding gives us a moment to orient ourselves to the new climatic circumstances and to fall into cadence with the others in the room, these requirements not ordinarily a taxing matter and not ordinarily needful, therefore, of a pause for their accomplishment. Perhaps the concentration, the "holding our-selves in" sometimes employed in inclement places (as a sort of support for the body), gets released with a flourish on our escap-ing from such environments. In any case, we can be presumed to be in a state of mind that any and all those already safe might well appreciate—for, after all, weather envelops everyone in the vicin-ity—and so self-expression concerning our feelings does not take us to a place that is mysterious to our hearers. Incidentally, it appears that, unlike strong imprecations, transition displays in our society are not particularly sex-typed.

2. The *spill cry*. This time the central examples, *Oops!* and *Whoops!*, are well-formed sounds, although not in every sense words, and again something as much (perhaps even more) the practice of females as males. Spill cries are a sound we emit to follow along with our having for a moment lost guiding control of some feature of the world around us, including ourselves. Thus a woman, rapidly walking to a museum exit, passes the door, catches her mistake, utters *Oops!*, and backtracks to the right place. A man, dropping a piece of meat through the grill to coals below, utters *Oops!* and then spears the meat to safety with his grill fork.

On the face of it, the sound advertises our loss of control, raising the question of why we should want to defame ourselves through this publicity. An obvious possibility is that the *Oops!* defines the event as a mere accident, shows we know it has happened, and hopefully insulates it from the rest of our behavior, recommending that failure of control was not generated by some obscure intent unfamiliar to humanity or some general defect in competence. Behind this possibility is another: that the expression is presumably used for *minor* failings of environmental control, and so in the face of a more serious failure, the *Oops!* has the effect of downplaying import and hence implication as evidence of our incompetence. (It follows that to show we take a mishap *very* seriously we might feel constrained to omit the cry.) Another reason for (and function of) spill crying is that, a specific vocalization being involved, we necessarily demonstrate that at least our vocal channel is functioning and, behind this, at least some presence of mind. A part of us proves to be organized and standing watch over the part of us that apparently isn't watchful. Finally, and significantly, the sound can provide a warning to others present that a piece of the world has gotten loose and that they might best be advised to take care. Indeed, close observation shows that the *oo* in *Oops!* may be nicely prolonged to cover the period of time during which that which got out of control is out of control.

Note, when we utter *Oops!* as we slip on the ice, we can be making a plea to the closest other for a steadying hand and simultaneously warning others as to what they themselves should watch out for, these circumstances surely opening up our surround for vocalizations. When in fact there is no danger to the self, we may respond to *another's* momentary loss of control with an *Oops!* also, providing him a warning that he is in trouble, a readied framework within which he can define the mishap, and a collectively established cadence for his anticipated response. That some sort of help for others is thus intended seems to be borne out by the fact that apparently men are more likely to *Oops!* for another when that other is a child or a female, and thus definable as someone for whom responsibility can be taken. Indeed, when a parent plucks up a toddler and rapidly shifts it from one point to another or "playfully" swings or tosses it in the air, the prime mover may utter an *Oopsadaisy!*, stretched out to cover the child's period of groundlessness, counteracting its feeling of being out of control, and at the same time instructing the child in the terminology and role of spill cries. In any case, it is apparent that *oopsing* is an adaptive practice with some survival value. And the fact that individuals prove (when the occasion does arise) to have been ready all along to *oops* for themselves or an appropriate other suggests that when nothing eventful is occurring, persons in one another's presence are still nonetheless tracking one another and acting so as to make themselves trackable.

3. The *threat startle*, notably *Eek!* and *Yipe!* Perhaps here is a response cry sex-typed (or at least so believed) for feminine use. Surprise and fear are stated—in lay terms, "expressed"—but surprise and fear that are very much under control, indeed nothing to be really concerned about. A very high open stairwell, or a walk that leads to a precipice, can routinely evoke *yipes* from us as we survey what might have been our doom, but from a position of support we have had ample time to secure. A notion of what a fear response would be is used as a pattern for mimicry. A sort of overplaying occurs that covers any actual concern by extending with obvious unseriousness the expressed form this concern would take. And we demonstrate that we are alive to the fearsome implications of the event, albeit not overthrown by them, that we have seen the trouble and by implication will assuredly control for it, and are, therefore, in need of no warning, all of this releasing others from closely tracking us. And the moment it takes to say the sound is a moment we can use actually to compose ourselves in the circumstances. In a very subtle way, then, a verbal "expression" of our state is a means of rising above it—and a release of concern now no longer necessary, coming after the emergency is really over.

Here an argument made earlier about multiple transformations can be taken up. Precipitous drops are the sorts of things that an individual can be very close to without the slightest danger of dropping over or intent to do so. In these circumstances it would seem that imagery of accident would come to the fore or at least be very readily available. It is this easily achieved mental set that the response cry in question would seem to participate in. Thus the uncompelling character of the actual circumstances can be nicely reflected in the light and almost relaxed character of the cry. One has, then, a warning*like* signal in dangerous*like* circumstances. And ritualization begins to give way to a copy of itself, a playful version of what is already a formalized version, a display that has been retransformed and reset, a second order ritualization.

4. *Revulsion sounds,* such as *Eeuw!,* are heard from a person who has by necessity or inadvertence come in contact with something that is contaminating. Females in our society, being defined as more vulnerable in this way than males, might seem to have a special claim on the expression. Often once we make the sound, we can be excused for a moment while decontamination is attempted. At other times, our voice performs what our physical behavior can't, as when our hands must keep busy cleaning a fish, leaving only the auditory and other unrequired channels to correct the picture—to show that indelicate, dirty work need not define the person who is besmeared by it. Observe, again there is an unserious note, a hint of hyperritualization. For often the contamination that calls forth an *Eeuw!* is not *really* believed to contaminate. Perhaps only germ contamination retains that literal power in our secular world. So again a protectivelike cry is uttered in response to a contaminatinglike contact.

VIII

So far response crying has been largely considered as something that could be available to someone who is present to others but not "with" any of them. If one picks accompanied individuals, not singles, the behavior is still to be found; indeed, response crying is, if anything, encouraged in the circumstances. So, also, response cries are commonly found among persons in an "open state of talk," persons having the right but not the obligation to address remarks to the other participants, this being a condition that commonly prevails among individuals jointly engaged in a common task (or even similarly engaged in like ones) when this work situates them in immediate reach of one another.

1. The *strain grunt.* Lifting or pushing something heavy, or

wielding a sledgehammer with all our might, we emit a grunt at the presumed peak and consummation of our fully extended exertion, the grunt so attesting. The sound seems to serve as a warning that at the moment nothing else can claim our concern, and, sometimes, as a reminder that others should stand clear. No doubt the cry also serves as a means by which joint efforts can be temporally coordinated, as is said to be true of work songs. Observe that these sounds are felt to be entirely unintentional, even though the glottis must be partially closed off to produce them and presumably could be fully opened or closed to avoid doing so. In any case, it could be argued that the expression of ultimate exertion these sounds provide may be essentially overstated. I might add that strain grunts are routinely guyed, employed in what is to be taken as an unserious way, often as a cover for a task that is reckoned as undemanding but may indeed require some exertion, another case of retransformation. Note, too, that strain grunts are also employed during solitary doings that can be construed as involving a peaking of effort. The rise and falling away of effort contoured in sound dramatizes our acts, filling out the setting with their execution. I suppose the common example is the vocal accompaniment we sometimes provide ourselves when passing a hard stool.

2. The *pain cry, Oww!* (or *Ouch!*).[15] Here the functioning of this exclamation is rather clear. Ensconced in a dentist's chair, we use a pain cry as a warning that the drill has begun to hurt. Or when a finger is firmly held by a nurse, we *ouch* when the needle probing for a sliver goes too deep. Plainly the cry in these cases can serve as a self-regulated indicator of what is happening, providing a reading for the instigator of the pain, who might not otherwise have access to the information needed. The meaning, then, may not be "I have been hurt," but

---

15. Solitarily experiencing a bout of intense pain, we sometimes follow its course with a half-moaned, half-grunted sound tracing, as though casting the experience in a sort of dialogic form were a way of getting through the moment and maintaining morale. We sometimes also employ such sound tracings when witnesses are perceivedly present, producing in these circumstances a real scene-stopper, implying that our current inner acutely painful state is the business everyone should be hanging on.

rather, "You are just now coming to hurt me." This meaning, incidentally, may also be true of the response that a dog or cat gives us when we have begun to step accidentally on its tail, although *that* cry often seems to come too late. In any case, these are good examples of how closely a vocalizer can collaborate with another person in the situation.

4. The *sexual moan.* This subvocal tracking of the course of sexually climactic experience is a display available to both sexes, but said to be increasingly fashionable for females—amongst whom, of course, the sound tracing can be strategically employed to delineate an ideal development in the marked absence of anything like the real thing.

5. *Floor cues.* A worker in a typing pool makes a mistake on a clean copy and emits an imprecation, this leading to, and apparently designed to lead to, a colleague's query as to what went wrong. A fully communicated statement of disgust and displeasure can then be introduced, but now ostensibly as a reply to a request for information. A husband reading the evening paper suddenly brays out a laugh or a *Good God!,* thereby causing his wife to orient her listening and even to ease the transition into talk by asking what is it. (A middle-class wife might be less successful in having her floor cues picked up.) Wanting to avoid being thought, for example, self-centered, intrusive, garrulous, or whatever, and in consequence feeling uneasy about making an open request for a hearing in the particular circumstances, we act so as to encourage our putative listeners to make the initial move, inviting us to let them in on what we are experiencing. Interestingly, although in our society married couples may come to breach many of the standard situational proprieties routinely when alone together—this marking the gradual extension of symmetrical ritual license between them—the rule against persisting in public self-talk may be retained, with the incidental consequence that the couple can continue to use response crying as a floor cue.

6. *Audible glee.* A lower-middle-class adolescent girl sitting with four friends at a table in a crowded crêperie is brought her order, a large crêpe covered with ice cream and nuts. As the dish is set before her, she is transfixed for a moment, and wonder and

pleasure escape with an *Oooooo!* In a casino an elderly woman playing the slots alongside two friends hits a twenty-dollar payoff, and above the sound of silver dropping in her tray peeps out a *Wheee!* Tarzan, besting a lion, roars out a Hollywood version of the human version of a lay version of a mammalian triumph call.

I X

It is important, I believe, to examine the functioning of response cries when the crier is a ratified participant of ongoing conversation, not merely someone copresent to others or in an open state of talk. Walking along saying something to a friend, we can, tripping, unceremoniously interrupt our words to utter *Oops!*, even as the hand of our friend comes out to support us; and as soon as this little flurry is passed, we revert back to our speaking. All that this reveals, of course, is that when we are present to others as a fellow conversationalist we are also present to them —as well as to all others in the situation—as fellow members of the gathering. The conversational role (short of what the telephone allows) can never be the only accessible one in which we are active.

Now let us move on to a closer issue. If these responses are to be seen as ritualized expressions, and some as standardized vocal comments on circumstances that are not, or no longer, beyond our emotional and physical control, then there is reason to expect that such cries will be used at still further remove, this time in response to a *verbally presented* review of something settled long ago at a place quite removed. A broker tells a client over the phone that his stock has dropped, and the client, well socialized in this sort of thing, says *Yipe!* or *Eek!* (The comedian Jack Benny made a specialty of this response cry.) A plumber tells us what our bill will be and we say *Ouch!* Indeed, response cries are often employed thrice removed from the crisis to which they are supposed to be a blurted response: a friend tells us about something startling and costly that happened to him and at the point of disclosure we utter a response cry on his behalf, as it were, out of sympathetic identification and as a sign that we are fully following his exposition. In fact, we may offer a response cry when he recounts something that happened to someone *else.* In these latter cases, we are certainly far removed from the exigent event that is being replayed, and just as far removed from its consequences, including any question of having to take immediate rescuing action. Interestingly, there are some cries which seem to occur more commonly in our response to another's fate (good or bad) as it is recounted to us than they do in our response to our own. *Oh wow!* is an example.

And we can play all of these response games because our choice of vocalization allows the recipient, or rather hearer, to treat the sound as something to which a specific spoken reply is not required. To the plumber we are precisely not saying: "Does the bill have to be that high?"—*that* statement being something that would require a reply, to the possible embarrassment of all.

Having started with response cries in the street, the topic has been moved into the shelter of conversations. But it should not be assumed from this that the behaviors in question—response cries—have somehow been transmuted into full-fledged creatures of discourse. That is not the way they function. These cries are conventionalized utterances which are specialized for an informative role, but in the linguistic and propositional sense they are not statements. Obviously, information is provided when we utter response cries in the presence of others, whether or not we are in a state of talk at the time. That is about the only reason we utter them in the first place and the reason why they are worth studying. But to understand how these sounds function in social situations, particularly during talk, one must first understand where the prototype of which they are designed to be a recognizable version is seated. What comes to be made of a particular individual's show of "natural emotional expression" on any occasion is a considerably awesome thing not dependent on the existence anywhere of natural emotional expressions. But whatever is made of such an act by its maker and its witnesses is different from what is made of openly designed and openly directed communication.

X

At the beginning of this paper it was argued that extended self-talk, if discovered, reflects badly on the talker. Then it was recommended that elements in the situation can considerably mitigate the impropriety of talking to ourselves publicly, and that in any case we are prepared to breach the injunction against public self-talk when, in effect, to sustain this particular propriety would go even harder on our reputation. Much the same position could be taken with respect to interjected imprecations. In both cases, one can point to some hitch in the well-managed flow of controlled events and the quick application of an ostensibly self-directed pronouncement to establish evidence—a veneer —of control, poise, and competency. And although response cries do not on the surface involve words uttered even to oneself, being *in prototype* merely a matter of nonsymbolic emotional expression, they apparently come to function as a means of striking a self-defensible posture in the face of extraordinary events—much as does exposed self-talk. However, there is one source of trouble in the management of the world which is routine, and that, interestingly enough, is in the management of talk itself. So again response cries occur, but this time ones that are constantly uttered.

First, there is the well-known filled pause (usually written *ah* or *uh* or *um*) employed by speakers when they have lost their places, can't find a word, are momentarily distracted, or otherwise find they are departing from fluently sustained speech. Response *cries* seems an awkward term for such unblurted subvocalizations, but nonetheless they do, I think, function like response cries, if only in that they facilitate tracking. In effect, speakers make it evident that although they do not now have the word or phrase they want, they are giving their attention to the matter and have not cut themselves adrift from the effort at hand. A word search, invisible and inaudible in itself, is thus voluntarily accompanied by a sound shadow—a sound, incidentally, that could easily be withheld merely by otherwise managing the larynx—all to the end of assuring that something worse than a temporary loss of words has not happened, and incidentally holding the speaker's claim on the floor.[16] (Interestingly, in radio broadcasting, where visual facial signs of a word search can't be effective, the filling of pauses by a search sound or a prolongation of a vowel has much to recommend it, for speakers are under obligation to confirm that nothing has gone wrong with the studio's equipment, as well as their own, the floor in this case being a station. And if only inexperienced broadcasters employ filled pauses frequently, it is because professionals can manage speech flow, especially aloud reading, without the hitches in encoding which, were they to occur, would equally give professionals reasons to ritualize evidence of what was occurring.)

In addition to the filled-pause phenomenon, consider the very standard form of self-correction which involves the breaking off of a word or phrase that is apparently not the one we wanted, and our hammering home of a corrected version with increased loudness and tempo, as if to catch the error before it hit the ground and shattered the desired meaning. Here the effect is to show that we are very much alive to the way our words should have come out; we are somewhat shocked and surprised at our failure to encode properly an appropriate formulation the first time round, the rapidity and force of the correct version presumably suggesting how much on our toes we really are. We display our concern and the mobilization of our effort at the expense of smooth speech production, electing to save a little of our reputation for presence of mind over and against that for fluency. Again, as with filled pauses, one has what is ostensibly a bit of pure expression, that is, a transmission providing direct evidence (not relayed through semantic reference) of the state of the transmitter, but now an expression that has been cut and polished into a standard shape to serve the reputational contingencies of its emitter.

16. A case can be made that in some English-speaking circles the familiar hesitation markers are systematically employed in slightly different ways, so that, for example, *uh* might be heard when the speaker had forgotten a proper name, *oh* when he knew a series of facts but was trying to decide which of them could be appropriately cited or best described for the hearers. The unfilled or silent pause participates in this specialization, giving one reason, alas, to think of it as a response cry, too. Here see the useful paper by James (1972).

XI

Earlier it was suggested that imprecations were somewhat like truncated, self-addressed statements but not wholly so. Later these lexicalized exclamations were shown to function not unlike response cries. Now it is time to try to settle on where they belong.

Say, for example, someone brings you the news that they have failed in a task you have seriously set them. Your response to the news can be: "I knew it! Did you have to?" In the styling I have in mind, this turn at talk contains two moves and a change of "footing": the first move (uttered half under the breath with the eyes turned upward) is a bit of self-talk, or something presented in that guise—the sort of open aside that adults are especially prone to employ in exasperated response to children, servants, foreigners, and other grades who easily qualify for moments of nonperson treatment. The second move ("Did you have to?") is conventionally directed communication. Observe that such a turn at talk will oblige its recipient to offer an apology or a counteraccount, locking the participants into an interchange. But although the recipient of the initial two-move turn will be understood to have overheard the self-addressed segment, he will have neither the right nor the obligation to reply to it specifically, at least in the sense that he does in regard to the conventionally communicated second portion.

Now shift from extended self-talk to the truncated form—imprecation: "Shit! Did you have to?" Given the same histrionics, one again has a two-move turn with a first move that must be oriented to as something that can't be answered in a conventional way. If the recipient does address a remark to this blurted-out portion, it will be to the psychic state presumably indexed by it—much as when we comfort someone who has burst into tears or when we upbraid them for loss of self-control. Or the respondent may have to venture a frame ploy, attempting to counter a move by forcing its maker to change the interpretative conventions that apply to it—as in the snappy comeback, *Not here,* injected immediately after the expletive. In all of this, and in the fact that standard lexicalizations are employed, *I knew it!* and *Shit!* are similar. However, although *I knew it!* follows grammatical constraints for well-formed sentences, *Shit!* need not, even if one appeals to the context in order to see how it might be expanded into a statement. *Shit!* need no more elide a sentence than need a laugh, groan, sob, snicker, or giggle—all vocalizations that frequently occur except in the utterances ordinarily presented for analysis by linguists. Nor, I think, does it help understanding very much to define *Shit!* as a well-formed sentence with *NP!* as its structure. Here, of course, imprecations are exactly like response cries. For it is the essence of response cries that they be presented as if mere expression were involved, and not recipient-directed, propositional-like statements, at least on the face of it.

Imprecations, then, might best be considered not as a form of self-talk at all, but rather as a type of response cry. Whereas unlexicalized cries have come to be somewhat conventionalized, imprecations have merely extended the tendency, further ritualizing ritualizations. Religious life already setting aside a class of words to be treated with reserve and ranked with respect to severity, response crying has borrowed them. Or so it would seem.

Insofar as self-talk is structurally different from the normal kind, imprecatory utterances (like other response cries) are too, only more so. And because of this sharp underlying difference between conventionally directed statements and imprecatory interjections, the two can be given radically different roles in the functioning of particular interaction systems, serving close together in complementary distribution without confusion.

Consider tennis. During the open state of talk sustained in such a game, a player who misses an "easy" shot can response cry an imprecation loudly enough for opponents and partner to hear. On the other hand, a player making a "good" shot is not likely to be surprised if an opponent offers a complimentary statement about him to him. (As these two forms of social control help frame his own play, so he will participate in the two forms that frame his opponents'.) But, of course, good taste forbids a player addressing opponents in praise of his own efforts, just as they must allow him elbowroom and not reply directly to his cries of self-disgust. A player may, however, use directed, full-fledged statements to convey self-castigation and (when directed to his partner) apology. Response cries and directed statements here comprise a closely working pair of practices, part of the ritual resources of a single interaction system. And their workings can be intermingled because of their structural difference, not in spite of it. Given this arrangement, it is understandable that a player will feel rather free to make a pass at ironically praising himself in statements made to opponents or partner, correctly sensing that his words could hardly be misframed as literal ones. (That he might employ this device just to induce others to communicate a mitigated view of his failure merely attests again to the various conveniences that can be made of forms of interaction.)

And just as response cries can form a complementary resource with conventionally directed statements, so they can with self-directed ones. For example, in casino craps, a shooter has a right to preface a roll, especially a "come out," with self-encouraging statements of a traditional kind directed to the fates, the dice, or some other ethereal recipient. This grandstanding (as dignified gamblers call this self-talk) sometimes serves to bring the other players into a cadence and peaking of attention. When, shortly, the shooter "craps out," he is allowed a well-fleshed imprecation coincidental with the dissolution of the table's coordinated involvement. So again there is complementarity and a division of labor, with self-talk located where collective hope is to be built up, and imprecatory response cry where it is to be abandoned.

DISCUSSION

1. Written versions of response cries seem to have a speech-contaminating effect, consolidating and codifying actual response cries, so that, in many cases, reality begins to mimic artifice, as in *Ugh!, Pant pant, Gulp, Tsk tsk,* this being a route to ritualization presumably unavailable to animal animals.[17] This easy change is

17. The carryback from the written to the spoken form is especially marked in the matter of punctuation marks, for here writing has something that speaking hasn't. Commonly used lexicalizations are: "underline," "footnote,"

only to be expected. For response cries themselves are by way of being second order ritualizations, already part of an unserious, or less than serious, domain.

Here cartoons and comics are to be taken seriously. These printed pictures must present entire scenarios through a small number of "panels" or frozen moments, sometimes only one. The cartoonist has great need, then, for expressions that will clearly document the presumed inner state of his figures and clearly display the point of the action. Thus, if individuals in real life need response cries to clarify the drama of their circumstances, cartoon figures need them even more. So we obtain written versions of something that could be thought originally to have no set written form. Moreover, cartoon figures portrayed as all alone must be portrayed acting in such a way as to make their circumstances and inner states available to the viewer (much as real persons do when in the presence of others), and included in this situational-like behavior are response cries. (So also in the case of movies showing persons ostensibly all alone.) In consequence, the practice of emitting response cries when all alone is tacitly assumed to be normal, presumably with at least some contaminating effect upon actual behavior when alone.

2. A point might be made about the utterances used in response cries. As suggested, they seem to be drawn from two sources: taboo but full-fledged words (involving blasphemy and —in English—Anglo-Saxon terms for bodily functions) and from the broad class of nonword vocalizations ("vocal segregates," to employ Trager's term [1958:1–12]), of which response cries are one, but only one, variety.

There is a nice division of linguistic labor here. Full-fledged words that are well formed *and* socially acceptable are allocated to communication in the openly directed sense, whereas taboo words and nonwords are specialized for the more ritualized kind of communication. In brief, the character of the word bears the mark of the use that is destined for it. And one has a case of complementary distribution on a grand scale.

"period," "question mark," "quotes," "parenthetically." Written abbreviations (such as British *p* for *pence*) also enter the spoken domain. Moreover, there is a carryback to the spoken form of the pictorial-orthographic form of the presumed approximated sound effects of an action: *Pow! Bam!* are examples.

Nonwords as a class are not productive in the linguistic sense, their role as interjections being one of the few that have evolved for them. (Which is not to say that a particular vocal segregate can't have a very lively career, quickly spreading from one segment of a language community to others; the response cry *Wow!* is a recent example.) Many taboo words, however, are considerably productive, especially in the tradition maintained in certain subcultures, where some of these words occur (if not function) in almost every syntactical position.[18] Furthermore, curse words are drawn from familiar scales of such words, and choice will sharply reflect (in the sense of display, negotiate, etc.) the terms of the relationship between speaker and hearer; nonwords don't function very effectively in this way.

Nonwords, note, can't quite be called part of a language. For example, there tends to be no canonical "correct" spelling. When and where convention clearly does begin to establish a particular form and spelling, the term can continue to be thought of as not a word by its users, as if any written version must continue to convey a rough-and-ready attempt at transcription. (I take it here that in our society a feature of what we think of as regular words is that we feel the written form is as "real" a version as the spoken.) Further, although we have efficient means of reporting another's use of an expletive (either literally or by established paraphrastic form), this is not the case with nonwords. So, too, the voiced and orthographic realizations of some of these constructions involve consonant clusters that are phonotactically irregular; furthermore, their utterance can allow the speaker to chase after the course of an action analogically with stretches, glides, turns, and heights of pitch foreign to his ordinary speech. Yet the sound that covers any particular nonword can stand by itself, is standardized within a given language community, and varies from one language community to another, in each case as

18. Admittedly, even in these productive cases, taboo words are not entirely vulnerable to syntactical analysis. Saying that *the fuck* in a sentence like *What the fuck are you doing?* is adjectival in function, or that *bloody* in *What are you bloody well doing?* is an adverb, misses something of the point. In such cases specific syntactic location seems to be made a convenience of, for somehow the intensifying word is meant to color uniformly the whole of the utterance some place or other in which it occurs. Here see Quang Phuc Dong (1971).

do full-fledged words.[19] And the nonwords of a particular language comply with and introduce certain of the same phonotactic constraints as do its regular words (Jefferson 1974:183–86). Interestingly, there is some evidence that what one language community handles with a nonword, other language communities do, too.

On the whole, then, nonword vocalizations might best be thought of as semiwords. Observe that the characterization provided here (and by linguists) of these half-caste expressions takes no note that some (such as *Uh?* and *Shh!*) are clearly part of directed speech, and often interchangeable with a well-formed word (here *What?* and *Hush!*), but others (such as the *uh* as filled pause) belong to a radically different species of action, namely, putatively pure expression, response crying. (Imprecations and some other well-formed interjections provide an even more extreme case, for exactly the same such word may sometimes serve as an ostensibly undirected cry, and at other times be integrated directly into a recipient-directed sentence under a single intonation contour.) Here, again, one can see a surface similarity covering a deep underlying difference, but not the kind ordinarily addressed by transformationalists.

Apart from qualifying as semiwords, response cries can be identified in another way, namely, as articulated free-standing examples of the large class of presumed "natural expressions," namely, signs meant to be taken to index directly the state of the transmitter. (Some of those signs, like voice qualifiers, can paralinguistically ride roughshod across natural syntactical units of speech.) I might add that although gender differences in the basic semantic features of speech do not seem very marked in our society, response cries and other paralinguistic features of communication are. Indeed, speech *as a whole* might not be a useful base to employ in considering gender differences, cancelling out sharp contrasts revealable in special components of discourse.

3. Earlier it was suggested that a response cry can draw on the cooperation of listeners, requiring that they hear and under-

19. Quine (1959:6) has an example: " 'Ouch' is not independent of social training. One need only to prick a foreigner to appreciate that it is an English word."

stand the cry but act as though it had not been uttered in their hearing. It is in this way that a form of behavior ostensibly not designed for directed linguistic communication can be injected into public life, in certain cases even into conversations and broadcasts. In brief, a form of response perceived as native to one set of circumstances is set into another. In the case of blasphemous cries, what is inserted is already something that has been borrowed from another realm—semantic communication—so the behavior can be said to have been returned to its natural place, but now so much transformed as to be little like a native.

This structural reflexivity is, I believe, a fundamental fact of our communicative life. What is ritualized here, in the last analysis, is not an expression but a self-other alignment—an interactional arrangement. Nor, as earlier suggested, is that the bottom of embedding. For example, when a speaker finds he has skated rather close to the edge of discretion or tact, he may give belated recognition to where his words have gone, marking a halt by uttering a plaintive *Oops!,* meant to evoke the image of someone who has need of this particular response cry, the whole enactment having an unserious, openly theatrical character. Similarly, in the face of another's reminder that we have failed in fulfilling some obligation, we can utter *Darn it!* in an openly mock manner as a taunting, even insolent, denial of the imprecation we might normally be expected to employ in the circumstances. In brief, what is placed into the directed discourse in such cases is not a response cry but a mocked-up individual uttering a mocked-up response cry. (All of this is especially evident when the cry itself is a spoken version of the written version of the cry, as when a listener responds to the telling of another's near disaster by ungulpingly uttering the word *Gulp.*) So, too, the filled pause *uh,* presumably a self-expression designed to allow hearers to track speaker's engagement in relevant (albeit silent) production work, can apparently be employed with malice aforethought to show that the word that does follow (and is ostensibly the one that was all along wanted), is to be heard as one about which the speaker wants it known that he himself might not be naturally inclined to employ it (Jefferson 1974:192–94). In this case a "correction format" has been made a convenience of, its work set into an environment for which it was not originally designed. Similarly, on discovering that he has said "April the 21st" instead of "May the 21st," an announcer may (as one type of remedial work) repeat the error immediately, this time with a quizzical, speaking-to-oneself tone of voice, as though this sort of error were enough of a rarity to cause him to break frame; but this response itself he may try to guy, satirizing self-talk (and self-talkers) even as he engages in it, the retransformation confirmed by the little laugh he gives thereafter to mark the end to error-making *and* playful correction.

The moral of the story is that what is sometimes put into a sentence may first have to be analyzed as something that could not occur naturally in such a setting, just as a solitary's self-comments may first have to be analyzed as something exclusively found in social intercourse. And the transformations these alien bits of saying undergo when set into their new milieu speak as much to the competence of ethologists as of grammarians.

A turn at talk that contains a directed statement *and* a segment of self-talk (or an imprecation or a nonlexicalized response cry) does not merely involve two different moves, but *moves of two different orders.* This is very clear, for example, when someone in or out of a conversation finds cause to blurt out *Shit!* and then, in apparent embarrassment, quickly adds *Excuse me,* sometimes specifically directing the apology to the person most likely to have been offended. Here, patently, the first move is an exposed response cry, the second, a directed message whose implied referent happens to be the first. The two moves nicely fit together—indeed, some speakers essay an imprecation knowing that they will have a directed apology to compensate for it; but this fit pertains to how the two moves function as an action-response pair, self-contained within a single turn at talk, and not to any ultimate commonality of form. So, too, when an announcer coughs rather loudly, says *Excuse me* with greater urgency of tone than he likes, and then follows with a well-designed giggle; except here he gives us a three-move sequence of sounded interference, directed statement, and response cry, the second move a comment on the first, the third move a comment on the second move's comment. Any effort to analyze such strips of talk linguistically by trying to uncover a single deep structure that accounts for the surface sequence of words is destined to obscure the very archaeological issues that the generative approach was designed to develop. A blender makes a mush of apples and oranges; a student shouldn't.

And a student shouldn't, even when there is no obvious segmentation to help with the sorting. For now it is to be admitted that through the *way* we say something that is part of our avowedly directed discourse, we can speak—ostensibly at least—for our own benefit at the same time, displaying our self-directed (and/or nondirected) response to what is occurring. We thereby simultaneously cast an officially intended recipient of our propositional-like avowals into an overhearer of our self-talk. The issue is not merely that of the difference between what is said and what is meant, the issue, that is, of implicature; the issue is that one stream of information is conveyed as avowedly intended verbal communication, whilst simultaneously the other is conveyed through a structural ruse—our allowing witnesses a glimpse into the dealings we are having with ourselves. It is in this way that one can account for the apparently anomalous character of imprecations of the *Fuck you!* form. It might appear as if one person were making a directed verbal avowal to another by means of an imperative statement with deleted subject; in fact the format is restricted to a relatively small list of expletives, such as *screw,* and none qualifies as an ordinary verb, being constrained in regard to embedded and conjoined forms in ways in which standard verbs in the elided imperative form are not (Quang Phuc Dong 1971).

Nor is this analysis of the unconversational aspects of certain conversational utterances meant to deny the traditional conception of transformation and embedding; rather the power of the latter is displayed. Waiting with her husband and a friend for the casino cashier to count down her bucket of silver, a happy player says, "And when I saw the third seven come up and stop, I just let out 'Eeeee!' " Here, through direct quotation, the speaker brings to a well-circumscribed, three-person talk what was, a few minutes ago, the broadly accessible eruption of a single. This shows clearly that what starts out as a response cry (or starts out, for that matter, as any sounded occurrence, human, animal, or inanimate) can be conversationally replayed—can be reset into ordinary directed discourse—through the infinite coverage of sound mimicry.

CONCLUSION

The public utterance of self-talk, imprecations, and response cries constitutes a special variety of impulsive, blurted actions, namely, vocalized ones. Our tacit theory of human nature recommends that these actions are "purely expressive," "primitive," "unsocialized," violating in some way or other the self-control and self-possession we are expected to maintain in the presence of others, providing witnesses with a momentary glimpse behind our mask.

However, the point about these blurtings is not that they are particularly "expressive." Obviously, in this sense of that word, ordinary talk is necessarily expressive, too. Naked feelings can agitate a paragraph of discourse almost as well as they can a solitary imprecation. Indeed, it is impossible to utter a sentence without coloring the utterance with some kind of perceivable affect, even (in special cases) if only with the emotionally distinctive aura of affectlessness. Nor is the point about segmented blurtings that they are particularly unsocialized, for obviously they come to us as our language does and not from our own invention. Their point lies elsewhere. One must look to the light these ventings provide, not to the heat they dispel.

In every society one can contrast occasions and moments for silence and occasions and moments for talk. In our own, one can go on to say that by and large (and especially among the unacquainted) silence is the norm and talk something for which warrant must be present. Silence, after all, is very often the deference we will owe in a social situation to any and all others present. In holding our tongue, we give evidence that such thought as we are giving to our own concerns is not presumed by us to be of any moment to the others present, and that the feelings these concerns invoke in ourselves are owed no sympathy. Without such enjoined modesty, there could be no public life, only a babble of childish adults pulling at one another's sleeves for attention. The

120

mother to whom we would be saying, "Look, no hands," could not look or reply for she would be saying, "Look, no hands," to someone else.

Talk, however, presumes that our thoughts and concerns will have some relevance or interest or weight for others, and in this can hardly but presume a little. Talk, of course, in binding others to us, can also do so for protracted periods of time. The compensation is that we can sharply restrict this demand to a small portion of those who are present, indeed, often to only one.

The fugitive communications I have been considering constitute a third possibility, minor no doubt, but of some significance if only because of what they tell us about silence and talk. Our blurtings make a claim of sorts upon the attention of everyone in the social situation, a claim that our inner concerns should be theirs, too, but unlike the claim made by talk, ours here is only for a limited period of attention. And, simply put, this invitation into our interiors tends to be made only when it will be easy for other persons present to see where the voyage takes them. What is precipitous about these expressions, then, is not the way they are emitted but rather the circumstances which render their occurrence acceptable. The invitation we are free to extend in these situations we would be insane to extend in others.

Just as most public arrangements oblige and induce us to be silent, and many other arrangements to talk, so a third set allows and obliges us momentarily to open up our thoughts and feelings and ourselves through sound to whosoever is present. Response cries, then, do not mark a flooding of emotion outward, but a flooding of relevance in.

There is linguistic point to the consideration of this genre of behavior. Response cries such as *Eek!* might be seen as peripheral to the linguist's domain, but imprecations and self-talk are more germane, passing beyond semiword vocal segregates to the traditional materials of linguistic analysis. And the point is that all three forms of this blurted vocalization—semiword response cries, imprecations, and self-talk—are creatures of social situations, not states of talk. A closed circle of ratified participants oriented to engaging exclusively with one another in avowedly directed communications is not the base; a gathering, with its variously oriented, often silent and unacquainted members, is.

Further, all three varieties of this ejaculatory expression are conventionalized as to form, occasion of occurrence, and social function. Finally, these utterances are too commonly met with in daily life, surely, to justify scholarly neglect.

Once it is recognized that there is a set of conventionalized expressions that must be referred to social situations, not conversations, once, that is, it is appreciated that there are communications specifically designed for use outside states of talk, then it is but a step to seeing that ritualized versions of these expressions may themselves be embedded in the conventionally directed talk to be found in standard conversational encounters. And appreciating this, then to go on to see that even though these interjections come to be employed in conversational environments, they cannot be adequately analyzed there without reference to their original functioning outside of states of talk.

It is recommended, then, that linguists have reason to broaden their net, reason to bring in uttering that is not talking, reason to deal with social situations, not merely with jointly sustained talk. Incidentally, linguists might then be better able to countenance inroads that others can be expected to make into their conventional domain. For it seems that talk itself is intimately regulated and closely geared to its context through nonvocal gestures which are very differently distributed from the particular language and subcodes employed by any set of participants—although just where these boundaries of gesture-use *are* to be drawn remains an almost unstudied question.[20]

20. On the geographical boundaries of some nonvocal gestures, see Morris et al. (1979). A useful critique of this work is Kendon (forthcoming).

REFERENCES

Cook-Gumperz, Jenny, and Corsaro, William. 1976. "Social-ecological constraints on children's communicative strategies." In *Papers on Language and Context* (Working Paper 46), edited by Jenny Cook-Gumperz and John Gumperz. Berkeley: Language Behavior Research Laboratory, University of California.

Gopnik, Alison. 1977. "No, there, more, and allgone: Why the first words aren't about things." *Nottingham Linguistic Circular* 6:15–20.

James, Deborah. 1972. "Some aspects of the syntax and semantics of interjections." In *Papers from the Eighth Regional Meeting, Chicago Linguistic Society*, pp. 162–72.

Jefferson, Gail. 1974. "Error correction as an interactional resource." *Language in Society* 3:181–200.

Kendon, Adam. Forthcoming. "Geography of gesture." *Semiotica.*

Kohlberg, Lawrence; Yaeger, Judy; and Hjertholm, Elsie. 1968. "Private speech: Four studies and a review of theories." *Child Development* 39: 691–736.

Morris, Desmond; Collett, Peter; Marsh, Peter; and O'Shaughnessy, Marie. 1979. *Gestures: Their origins and distribution.* New York: Stein and Day.

Piaget, Jean. 1956. The language and thought of the child. 4th ed. Neuchâtel. [Translated by Marjorie Gabain. New York: Meridian, 1974.]

————. 1962. "Comments on Vygotsky's critical remarks concerning *The language and thought of the child,* and *Judgment and reasoning in the child.* " In *Thought and language,* edited by Lev Semenovich Vygotsky. MIT Press and John Wiley and Sons.

Quang Phuc Dong. 1971. "English sentences without overt grammatical subject." In *Studies out in left field,* edited by A. M. Zwicky et al., pp. 3–9. Edmonton: Linguistic Research, Inc.

Quine, W. Van. 1959. *Word and object.* New York: Wiley.

Sudnow, David. 1967. *Passing on: The social organization of dying.* Englewood Cliffs, N.J.: Prentice-Hall.

Trager, George L. 1958. "Paralanguage: A first approximation." *Studies in Linguistics* 13:1–12.

Vygotsky, Lev Semenovich. 1962. *Thought and language.* Translated by Eugenia Hanfmann and Gertrude Vakar. MIT Press and John Wiley and Sons.

3
FOOTING

I

Consider a journalistically reported strip of interaction, a news bureau release of 1973 on presidential doings.[1] The scene is the Oval Office, the participants an assemblage of government officers and newspaper reporters gathered in their professional capacities for a political ritual, the witnessing of the signing of a bill:

> WASHINGTON [UPI]—President Nixon, a gentleman of the old school, teased a newspaper woman yesterday about wearing slacks to the White House and made it clear that he prefers dresses on women.
>
> After a bill-signing ceremony in the Oval Office, the President stood up from his desk and in a teasing voice said to UPI's Helen Thomas: "Helen, are you still wearing slacks? Do you prefer them actually? Every time I see girls in slacks it reminds me of China."
>
> Miss Thomas, somewhat abashed, told the President that Chinese women were moving toward Western dress.
>
> "This is not said in an uncomplimentary way, but slacks can do something for some people and some it can't." He hastened to add, "but I think you do very well. Turn around."
>
> As Nixon, Attorney General Elliott L. Richardson, FBI Director Clarence Kelley and other high-ranking law enforcement officials smiling [*sic*], Miss Thomas did a pirouette for the President. She was wearing white pants, a navy blue jersey shirt, long white beads and navy blue patent leather shoes with red trim.

1. Grateful acknowledgment is made to *Semiotica,* where this paper first appeared (25[1979]:1–29).

> Nixon asked Miss Thomas how her husband, Douglas Cornell, liked her wearing pants outfits.
>
> "He doesn't mind," she replied.
>
> "Do they cost less than gowns?"
>
> "No," said Miss Thomas.
>
> "Then change," commanded the President with a wide grin as other reporters and cameramen roared with laughter. [*The Evening Bulletin* (Philadelphia), 1973]

This incident points to the power of the president to force an individual who is female from her occupational capacity into a sexual, domestic one during an occasion in which she (and the many women who could accord her the role of symbolic representative) might well be very concerned that she be given her full professional due, and that due only. And, of course, the incident points to a moment in gender politics when a president might unthinkingly exert such power. Behind this fact is something much more significant: the contemporary social definition that women must always be ready to receive comments on their "appearance," the chief constraints being that the remarks should be favorable, delivered by someone with whom they are acquainted, and not interpretable as sarcasm. Implied, structurally, is that a woman must ever be ready to change ground, or, rather, have the ground changed for her, by virtue of being subject to becoming momentarily an object of approving attention, not—or not merely—a participant in it.

The Nixon sally can also remind us of some other things. In our society, whenever two acquainted individuals meet for business, professional, or service dealings, a period of "small talk" may well initiate and terminate the transaction—a mini version of the "preplay" and "postplay" that bracket larger social affairs. This small talk will probably invoke matters felt to bear on the "overall" relation of the participants and on what each participant can take to be the perduring concerns of the other (health, family, etc.). During the business proper of the encounter, the two interactants will presumably be in a more segmental relation, ordered by work requirements, functionally specific authority, and the like. Contrariwise, a planning session among the military may begin and end with a formal acknowledgment of rank, and in between a shift into something closer to equalitarian decision-making. In either case, in shifting in and out of the business at hand, a change of tone is involved, and an alteration in the social capacities in which the persons present claim to be active.

Finally, it might be observed that when such change of gears occurs among more than two persons, then a change commonly occurs regarding who is addressed. In the Nixon scene, Ms. Thomas is singled out as a specific recipient the moment that "unserious" activity begins. (A change may also simultaneously occur in posture, here indeed very broadly with Mr. Nixon rising from his desk.)

The obvious candidate for illustrations of the Nixon shift comes from what linguists generally call "code switching," code here referring to language or dialect. The work of John Gumperz and his colleagues provides a central source. A crude example may be cited (Blom and Gumperz 1972:424):

> On one occasion, when we, as outsiders, stepped up to a group of locals engaged in conversation, our arrival caused a significant alteration in the casual posture of the group. Hands were removed from pockets and looks changed. Predictably, our remarks elicited a code switch marked simultaneously by a change in channel cues (i.e., sentence speed, rhythm, more hesitation pauses, etc.) and by a shift from (R) [a regional Norwegian dialect] to (B) [an official, standard form of Norwegian] grammar.

But of course, an outsider isn't essential; the switch can be employed among the ethnically homogeneous (ibid., p. 425):

> Likewise, when residents [in Hemnesberget, northern Norway] step up to a clerk's desk, greetings and inquiries about family affairs tend to be exchanged in the dialect, while the business part of the transaction is carried on in the standard.

Nor need one restrict oneself to the formal, adult world of government and business and its perfunctory service relationships; the schoolroom will do (ibid., p. 424):

> Teachers report that while formal lectures—where interruptions are not encouraged—are delivered in (B) [an official standard form of Norwegian], the speaker will shift to (R) [a regional Norwegian

dialect] when they want to encourage open and free discussion among students.

By 1976, in unpublished work on a community where Slovene and German are in active coexistence, matters are getting more delicate for Gumperz. Scraps of dialogue are collected between mothers and daughters, sisters and sisters, and code shifting is found to be present in almost every corner of conversational life. And Gumperz (1976) makes a stab at identifying what these shifts mark and how they function:

1. direct or reported speech
2. selection of recipient
3. interjections
4. repetitions
5. personal directness or involvement
6. new and old information
7. emphasis
8. separation of topic and subject
9. discourse type, e.g., lecture and discussion

More important for our purposes here, Gumperz and his coworkers now also begin to look at code-switchinglike behavior that doesn't involve a code switch at all. Thus, from reconstituted notes on classroom observations, the Gumperzes provide three sequential statements by a teacher to a group of first-graders, the statements printed in listed form to mark the fact that three different stances were involved: the first a claim on the children's immediate behavior, the second a review of experiences to come, and the third a side remark to a particular child (Cook-Gumperz and Gumperz 1976:8–9):

1. Now listen everybody.
2. At ten o'clock we'll have assembly. We'll all go out together and go to the auditorium and sit in the first two rows. Mr. Dock, the principal, is going to speak to us. When he comes in, sit quietly and listen carefully.
3. Don't wiggle your legs. Pay attention to what I'm saying.

The point being that, without access to bodily orientation and tone of voice, it would be easy to run the three segments into a continuous text and miss the fact that significant shifts in alignment of speaker to hearers were occurring.

I have illustrated through its changes what will be called "footing."[2] In rough summary:

1. Participant's alignment, or set, or stance, or posture, or projected self is somehow at issue.
2. The projection can be held across a strip of behavior that is less long than a grammatical sentence, or longer, so sentence grammar won't help us all that much, although it seems clear that a cognitive unit of some kind is involved, minimally, perhaps, a "phonemic clause." Prosodic, not syntactic, segments are implied.
3. A continuum must be considered, from gross changes in stance to the most subtle shifts in tone that can be perceived.
4. For speakers, code switching is usually involved, and if not this then at least the sound markers that linguists study: pitch, volume, rhythm, stress, tonal quality.
5. The bracketing of a "higher level" phase or episode of interaction is commonly involved, the new footing having a liminal role, serving as a buffer between two more substantially sustained episodes.

A change in footing implies a change in the alignment we take up to ourselves and the others present as expressed in the way we manage the production or reception of an utterance. A change in our footing is another way of talking about a change in our frame for events. This paper is largely concerned with pointing out that participants over the course of their speaking constantly change their footing, these changes being a persistent feature of natural talk.

As suggested, change in footing is very commonly language-linked; if not that, then at least one can claim that the paralinguistic markers of language will figure. Sociolinguists, therefore, can be looked to for help in the study of footing, including the most subtle examples. And if they are to compete in this heretofore literary and psychological area, then presumably they must find a structural means of doing so. In this paper I want to make a pass at analyzing the structural underpinnings of changes in footing. The task will be approached by reexamining the primitive notions of speaker and hearer, and some of our unstated presuppositions about spoken interaction.

2. An initial statement appears in Goffman (1974:496–559).

Traditional analysis of saying and what gets said seems tacitly committed to the following paradigm: Two and only two individuals are engaged together in it. During any moment in time, one will be speaking his own thoughts on a matter and expressing his own feelings, however circumspectly; the other listening. The full concern of the person speaking is given over to speaking and to its reception, the concern of the person listening to what is being said. The discourse, then, would be the main involvement of both of them. And, in effect, these two individuals are the only ones who know who is saying, who is listening, what is being said, or, indeed, that speaking is going on—all aspects of their doings being imperceivable by others, that is, "inaccessible." Over the course of the interaction the roles of speaker and hearer will be interchanged in support of a statement-reply format, the acknowledged current-speaking right—the floor—passing back and forth. Finally, what is going on is said to be conversation or talk.

The two-person arrangement here described seems in fact to be fairly common, and a good thing, too, being the one that informs the underlying imagery we have about face-to-face interaction. And it is an arrangement for which the terms "speaker" and "hearer" fully and neatly apply—lay terms here being perfectly adequate for all technical needs. Thus, it is felt that without requiring a basic change in the terms of the analysis, any modification of conditions can be handled: additional participants can be added, the ensemble can be situated in the immediate presence of nonparticipants, and so forth.

It is my belief that the language that students have drawn on for talking about speaking and hearing is not well adapted to its purpose. And I believe this is so both generally and for a consideration of something like footing. It is too gross to provide us with much of a beginning. It takes global folk categories (like speaker and hearer) for granted instead of decomposing them into smaller, analytically coherent elements.

For example, the terms "speaker" and "hearer" imply that sound alone is at issue, when, in fact, it is obvious that sight is organizationally very significant too, sometimes even touch. In the management of turn-taking, in the assessment of reception through visual back-channel cues, in the paralinguistic function of gesticulation, in the synchrony of gaze shift, in the provision of evidence of attention (as in the middle-distance look), in the assessment of engrossment through evidence of side-involvements and facial expression—in all of these ways it is apparent that sight is crucial, both for the speaker and for the hearer. For the effective conduct of talk, speaker and hearer had best be in a position to *watch* each other. The fact that telephoning can be practicable without the visual channel, and that written transcriptions of talk also seem effective, is not to be taken as a sign that, indeed, conveying words is the only thing that is crucial, but that reconstruction and transformation are very powerful processes.

III

The easiest improvement on the traditional paradigm for talk is to recognize that any given moment of it might always be part of *a* talk, namely, a substantive, naturally bounded stretch of interaction comprising all that relevantly goes on from the moment two (or more) individuals open such dealings between themselves and continuing until they finally close this activity out. The opening will typically be marked by the participants turning from their several disjointed orientations, moving together and bodily addressing one another; the closing by their departing in some physical way from the prior immediacy of copresence. Typically, ritual brackets will also be found, such as greetings and farewells, these establishing and terminating open, official, joint engagement, that is, ratified participation. In summary, a "social encounter." Throughout the course of the encounter the participants will be obliged to sustain involvement in what is being said and ensure that no long stretch occurs when no one (and not more than one) is taking the floor. Thus, at a given moment no talk may be occurring, and yet the participants will still be in a "state of talk." Observe, once one assumes that an encounter will have features of its own—if only an initiation, a termination, and a period marked by neither—then it becomes plain that any cross-sectional perspective, any instantaneous slice focusing on talking, not *a* talk, necessarily misses important features. Certain issues, such as the work done in summonings, the factor of topicality, the building up of an information state known to be common to the participants (with consequent "filling in" of new participants), the role of "preclosings," seem especially dependent on the question of the unit as a whole.

Giving credit to the autonomy of "a talk" as a unit of activity in its own right, a domain *sui generis* for analysis is a crucial step. But, of course, only new questions are opened up. For although it is easy to select for study a stretch of talk that exhibits the properties of a nicely bounded social encounter (and even easier to assume that any selected occasion of talk derives from such a unit), there are apparently lots of moments of talk that cannot be so located. And there are lots of encounters so intertwined with other encounters as to weaken the claim of any of them to autonomy. So I think one must return to a cross-sectional analysis, to examining *moments* of talk, but now bearing in mind that any broad labeling of what one is looking at—such as "conversation," "talk," "discourse"—is very premature. The question of substantive unit is one that will eventually have to be addressed, even though analysis may have to begin by blithely plucking out a moment's talk to talk about, and blithely using labels that might not apply to the whole course of a conversation.

I V

Turn first, then, to the notion of a hearer (or a recipient, or a listener). The process of auditing what a speaker says and following the gist of his remarks—hearing in the communication-system sense—is from the start to be distinguished from the social slot in which this activity usually occurs, namely, official status as a ratified participant in the encounter. For plainly, we might not be listening when indeed we have a ratified social place in the talk, and this in spite of normative expectations on the part of the speaker. Correspondingly, it is evident that when we are not an official participant in the encounter, we might still be following the talk closely, in one of two socially different ways: either we have purposely engineered this, resulting in "eavesdropping," or the opportunity has unintentionally and inadvertently come about, as in "overhearing." In brief, a ratified participant may not be listening, and someone listening may not be a ratified participant.

Now consider that much of talk takes place in the visual and aural range of persons who are not ratified participants and whose access to the encounter, however minimal, is itself perceivable by the official participants. These adventitious participants are "bystanders." Their presence should be considered the rule, not the exception. In some circumstances they can temporarily follow the talk, or catch bits and pieces of it, all without much effort or intent, becoming, thus, overhearers. In other circumstances they may surreptitiously exploit the accessibility they find they have, thus qualifying as eavesdroppers, here not dissimilar to those who secretly listen in on conversations electronically. Ordinarily, however, we bystanders politely disavail ourselves of these latter opportunities, practicing the situational ethic which obliges us to warn those who are, that they are, unknowingly accessible, obliging us also to enact a show of disinterest, and by disattending and withdrawing ecologically to minimize our actual access to the talk. (Much of the etiquette of bystanders can be generated from the basic understanding that they should act so as to maximally encourage the fiction that they aren't present; in brief, that the assumptions of the conversational paradigm are being realized.) But however polite, bystanders will still be able to glean some information; for example, the language spoken, "who" (whether in categorical or biographical terms) is in an encounter with whom, which of the participants is speaker and which are listeners, what the general mood of the conversational circle is, and so forth. Observe, too, that in managing the accessibility of an encounter both its participants and its bystanders will rely heavily on sight, not sound, providing another reason why our initial two-party paradigm is inadequate. (Imagine a deaf person bystanding a conversation; would he not be able to glean considerable social information from what he could see?)

The hearing sustained by our paradigmatic listener turns out to be an ambiguous act in an additional sense. The ratified hearer in two-person talk is necessarily also the "addressed" one, that is, the one to whom the speaker addresses his visual attention and to whom, incidentally, he expects to turn over the speaking role. But obviously two-person encounters, however common, are not the only kind; three or more official participants are often found. In such cases it will often be feasible for the current speaker to address his remarks to the circle as a whole, encompassing all his hearers in his glance, according them something like equal status. But, more likely, the speaker will, at least during periods of his talk, address his remarks to one listener, so that among official hearers one must distinguish the addressed recipient from "unaddressed" ones. Observe again that this structurally important distinction between official recipients is often accomplished exclusively through visual cues, although vocatives are available for managing it through audible ones.

The relation(s) among speaker, addressed recipient, and unaddressed recipient(s) are complicated, significant, and not much explored. An ideal in friendly conversation is that no one participant serve more frequently, or for a longer summation of time, in any one of these three roles, than does any other participant. In practice, such an arrangement is hardly to be found, and every possible variation is met with. Even when a particular pair holds the floor for an extended period, the structural implication can vary; for example, their talk can move to private topics and increasingly chill the involvement of the remaining participants, or it can be played out as a display for the encircling hearers— a miniature version of the arrangement employed in TV talk shows, or a lawyer's examination of a witness before a jury.

Once the dyadic limits of talk are breached, and one admits bystanders and/or more than one ratified recipient to the scene, then "subordinate communication" becomes a recognizable possibility: talk that is manned, timed, and pitched to constitute a perceivedly limited interference to what might be called the "dominating communication" in its vicinity. Indeed, there are a great number of work settings where informal talk is subordinated to the task at hand, the accommodation being not to another conversation but to the exigencies of work in progress.

Those maintaining subordinate communication relative to a dominant state of talk may make no effort to conceal that they are communicating in this selective way, and apparently no pointed effort to conceal what it is they are communicating. Thus "byplay": subordinated communication of a subset of ratified participants; "crossplay": communication between ratified participants and bystanders across the boundaries of the dominant encounter; "sideplay": respectfully hushed words exchanged entirely among bystanders. Nature is a pedant; in our culture each of these three forms of apparently unchallenging communication is managed through gestural markers that are distinctive and well standardized, and I assume that other gesture communities have their own sets of functional equivalents.

When an attempt *is* made to conceal subordinate communication, "collusion" occurs, whether within the boundaries of an encounter (collusive byplay) or across these boundaries (collusive crossplay) or entirely outside the encounter, as when two bystanders surreptitiously editorialize on what they are overhearing (collusive sideplay). Collusion is accomplished variously: by concealing the subordinate communication, by affecting that the words the excolluded can't hear are innocuous, or by using allusive words ostensibly meant for all participants, but whose additional meaning will be caught by only some.

Allied to collusion is "innuendo," whereby a speaker, ostensibly directing words to an addressed recipient, overlays his remarks with a patent but deniable meaning, a meaning that has a target more so than a recipient, is typically disparaging of it, and is meant to be caught by the target, whether this be the addressed recipient or an unaddressed recipient, or even a bystander (Fisher 1976).

A further issue. In recommending earlier that a conversation could be subordinated to an instrumental task at hand, that is, fitted in when and where the task allowed, it was assumed that the participants could desist from their talk at any moment when the requirements of work gave reason, and presumably return to it when the current attention requirements of the task made this palpably feasible. In these circumstances it is imaginable that the usual ritualization of encounters would be muted, and stretches of silence would occur of variable length which aren't nicely definable as either interludes between different encounters or pauses within an encounter. Under these conditions (and many others) an "open state of talk" can develop, participants having the right but not the obligation to initiate a little flurry of talk, then relapse back into silence, all this with no apparent ritual marking, as though adding but another interchange to a chronic conversation in progress. Here something must be addressed that is neither ratified participation nor bystanding, but a peculiar condition between.

There remains to consider the dynamics of ratified participation. Plainly, a distinction must be drawn between opening or closing an encounter, and joining or leaving an ongoing one; conventional practices are to be found for distinguishably accomplishing both. And plainly, two differently manned encounters can occur under conditions of mutual accessibility, each bystanding the other.[3] At point here, however, is another issue: the right to leave and to join, taken together, imply circumstances in which participants will shift from one encounter to another. At a "higher" level, one must also consider the possibility of an encounter of four or more participants splitting, and of separate encounters merging. And it appears that in some microecological social circumstances these various changes are frequent. Thus, at table during convivial dinners of eight or so participants, marked instability of participation is often found. Here a speaker may feel it necessary to police his listenership, not so much to guard against eavesdroppers (for, indeed, at table overhearing hardly needs to be concealed), as to bring back strays and encourage incipient joiners. In such environments, interruption, pitch raising and trunk orientation seem to acquire a special function and significance. (Note how a passenger sitting in the front seat of a taxi can function as a pivot, now addressing his fellow passengers in the back seat, now the driver, effectively trusting the driver to determine whether to act as a nonperson or an addressee, and all this without the driver's taking his eyes off the road or depending on the content of the remark to provide participation instructions.) Another example of structural instability is to be observed when couples meet. What had been two "withs" provide the personnel for a momentarily inclusive encounter, which can then

3. One standard arrangement is mutual modulation presented as equally allocating the available sound space; another (as suggested), is differential muting, whereby those in one of the encounters unilaterally constrain their communication in deference to the other, or even bring it to a respectful close.

bifurcate so that each member of one of the entering withs can personally greet a member of the other with, after which greeting, partners are exchanged and another pair of greeting interchanges follows, and after *this,* a more sustained regrouping can occur.

Consider now that, in dealing with the notion of bystanders, a shift was tacitly made from the encounter as a point of reference to something somewhat wider, namely, the "social situation," defining this as the full physical arena in which persons present are in sight and sound of one another. (These persons, in their aggregate, can be called a "gathering," no implications of any kind being intended concerning the relationships in which they might severally stand to one another.) For it turns out that routinely it is relative to a gathering, not merely to an encounter, that the interactional facts will have to be considered. Plainly, for example, speakers will modify how they speak, if not what they say, by virtue of conducting their talk in visual and aural range of nonparticipants. Indeed, as Joel Sherzer has suggested, when reporting on having heard someone say something, we are likely to feel obliged to make clear whether we heard the words as a ratified participant to the talk of which they were a part or whether we overheard them as a bystander.

Perhaps the clearest evidence of the structural significance of the social situation for talk (and, incidentally, of the limitation of the conventional model of talk) is to be found in our verbal behavior when we are by ourselves yet in the immediate presence of passing strangers. Proscriptive rules of communication oblige us to desist in use of speech and wordlike, articulated sounds. But in fact there is a wide variety of circumstances in which we will audibly address statements to ourselves, blurt out imprecations, and utter "response cries," such as *Oops!, Eek!,* and the like (Goffman, "Response Cries," 1978 and this volume). These vocalizations can be shown to have a self-management function, providing evidence to everyone who can hear that our observable plight is not something that should be taken to define us. To that end the volume of the sounding will be adjusted, so that those in the social situation who can perceive our plight will also hear our comment on it. No doubt, then, that we seek some response from those who can hear us, but not a specific reply. No doubt the intent is to provide information to everyone in range, but without taking the conversational floor to do so. What is sought is not hearers but overhearers, albeit intended ones. Plainly, the substantive natural unit of which self-directed remarks and response cries are a part need not be a conversation, whatever else it might be.

Finally, observe that if one starts with a particular individual in the act of speaking—a cross-sectional instantaneous view—one can describe the role or function of all the several members of the encompassing social gathering from this point of reference (whether they are ratified participants of the talk or not), couching the description in the concepts that have been reviewed. The relation of any one such member to this utterance can be called his "participation status" relative to it, and that of all the persons in the gathering the "participation framework" for that moment of speech. The same two terms can be employed when the point of reference is shifted from a given particular speaker to something wider: all the activity in the situation itself. The point of all this, of course, is that an utterance does not carve up the world beyond the speaker into precisely two parts, recipients and nonrecipients, but rather opens up an array of structurally differentiated possibilities, establishing the participation framework in which the speaker will be guiding his delivery.

V

I have argued that the notion of hearer or recipient is rather crude. In so doing, however, I restricted myself to something akin to ordinary conversation. But conversation is not the only context of talk. Obviously talk can (in modern society) take the form of a platform monologue, as in the case of political addresses, stand-up comedy routines, lectures, dramatic recitations, and poetry readings. These entertainments involve long stretches of words coming from a single speaker who has been given a relatively large set of listeners and exclusive claim to the floor. Talk, after all, can occur at the town podium, as well as the town pump.

And when talk comes from the podium, what does the hearing is an audience, not a set of fellow conversationalists. Audiences hear in a way special to them. Perhaps in conjunction with the fact that audience members are further removed physically from the speaker than a coconversationalist might be, they have the right to examine the speaker directly, with an openness that might be offensive in conversation. And except for those very special circumstances when, for example, the audience can be told to rise and repeat the Lord's Prayer, or to donate money to a cause, actions can only be recommended for later consideration, not current execution. Indeed, and fundamentally, the role of the audience is to appreciate remarks made, not to reply in any direct way. They are to conjure up what a reply might be, but not utter it; "back-channel" response alone is what is meant to be available to them. They give the floor but (except during the question period) rarely get it.

The term "audience" is easily extended to those who hear talks on the radio or TV, but these hearers are different in obvious and important ways from those who are live witnesses to it. Live witnesses are coparticipants in a social occasion, responsive to all the mutual stimulation that that provides; those who audit the talk by listening to their set can only vicariously join the station audience. Further, much radio and TV talk is not addressed (as ordinary podium talk is) to a massed but visible grouping off the stage, but to *imagined* recipients; in fact, broadcasters are under pressure to style their talk as though it were addressed to a single listener. Often, then, broadcast talk involves a conversational mode of address, but, of course, merely a simulated one, the requisite recipients not being there in the flesh to evoke it. And so a broadcast talk may have a "live" audience and a broadcast audience, the speaker now styling his projection mainly for the one, now for the other, and only the music of language can lull us into thinking that the same kind of recipient entity is involved.

Still further multiplicities of meaning must be addressed. Podiums are often placed on a stage; this said, it becomes plain that podiums and their limpets are not the only things one finds there. Stage actors are found there, too, performing speeches to one another in character, all arranged so they can be listened in on by those who are off the stage. We resolutely use one word, "audience," to refer to those who listen to a political speech and those who watch a play; but again the many ways in which these two kinds of hearers are in the same position shouldn't blind one to the very important ways in which their circumstances differ. A town speaker's words are meant for his audience and are spoken to them; were a reply to be made, it would have to come from these listeners, and indeed, as suggested, signs of agreement and disagreement are often in order. It is presumably because there are so many persons in an audience that direct queries and replies must be omitted, or at least postponed to a time when the speech itself can be considered over. Should a member of the audience assay to reply in words to something that a speaker in midspeech says, the latter can elect to answer and, if he knows what he's about, sustain the reality he is engaged in. But the words addressed by one character in a play to another (at least in modern Western dramaturgy) are eternally sealed off from the audience, belonging entirely to a self-enclosed, make-believe realm—although the actors who are performing these characters (and who in a way are also cut off from the dramatic action) might well appreciate signs of audience attentiveness.[4]

I have suggested that orators and actors provide a ready contrast to a conversation's speaker, the former having audiences, the latter fellow conversationalists. But it must be borne in mind that what goes on upon the platform is only incidentally—not analytically—talk. Singing can occur there (this being another way words can be uttered), and doings which don't centrally involve words at all, such as instrument playing, hat tricks, juggling, and all the other guileful acts that have done a turn in vaudeville. The various kinds of audiences are not, analytically speaking, a feature of speech events (to use Hymes's term), but of stage events.

And from here one can go on to still more difficult cases. There are, for example, church congregations of the revivalist type wherein an active interchange is sustained of calls and answers between minister and churchgoers. And there are lots of

4. Maintaining a rigid line between characters and audience is by no means, of course, the only way to organize dramatic productions, Burmese traditional theatre providing one example (Becker 1970), our own burlesqued melodrama almost another.

social arrangements in which a single speaking slot is organizationally central, and yet neither a stage event with its audience, nor a conversation with its participants, is taking place. Rather, something binding is: court trials, auctions, briefing sessions, and course lectures are examples. Although these podium occasions of binding talk can often support participants who are fully in the audience role, they also necessarily support another class of hearers, ones who are more committed by what is said and have more right to be heard than ordinarily occurs in platform entertainments.

Whether one deals with podium events of the recreational, congregational, or binding kind, a participation framework specific to it will be found, and the array of these will be different from, and additional to, the one generic to conversation. The participation framework paradigmatic of two-person talk doesn't tell us very much about participation frameworks as such.

V I

It is claimed that to appreciate how many different kinds of hearers there are, first one must move from the notion of a conversational encounter to the social situation in which the encounter occurs; and then one must see that, instead of being part of a conversation, words can be part of a podium occasion where doings other than talk are often featured, words entering at the beginning and ending of phases of the program, to announce, welcome, and thank. This might still incline one to hold that when words pass among a small number of persons, the prototypical unit to consider is nevertheless a conversation or a chat. However, this assumption must be questioned, too.

In canonical talk, the participants seem to share a focus of cognitive concern—a common subject matter—but less simply so a common focus of visual attention. The subject of attention is clear, the object of it less so. Listeners are obliged to avoid staring directly at the speaker too long lest they violate his territoriality, and yet they are encouraged to direct their visual attention so as to obtain gesticulatory cues to his meaning and provide him with evidence that he is being attended. It is as if they were to look into the speaker's words, which, after all, cannot be seen. It is as if they must look at the speaker, but not see him.[5]

But, of course, it is possible for a speaker to direct the visual attention of his hearers to some passing object—say, a car or a view—in which case for a moment there will be a sharp difference between speaker and both cognitive and visual attention. And the same is true when this focus of both kinds of attention is a person, as when two individuals talking to each other remark on a person whom they see asleep or across the street. And so one must consider another possibility: when a patient shows a physician where something hurts, or a customer points to where a try-on shoe pinches, or a tailor demonstrates how the new jacket fits, the individual who is the object of attention is also a fully qualified participant. The rub—and now to be considered—is that in lots of these latter occasions a conversation is not really the context of the utterance; a physically elaborated, nonlinguistic undertaking is, one in which nonlinguistic events may have the floor. (Indeed, if language is to be traced back to some primal scene, better it is traced back to the occasional need of a grunted signal to help coordinate action in what is already the shared world of a joint task than to a conversation in and through which a common subjective universe is generated.[6])

One standard nonlinguistic context for utterances is the perfunctory service contact, where a server and client come together momentarily in a coordinated transaction, often involving money on one side and goods or services on the other. Another involves those passing contacts between two strangers wherein the time is told, the salt is passed, or a narrow, crowded passageway is negotiated. Although a full-fledged ritual interchange is often found in these moments, physical transactions of some kind form

5. Overlayed on this general pattern is a very wide range of practices bearing on the management of interaction. Frequency, duration, and occasion of mutual and unilateral gaze can mark initiation and termination of turn at talk, physical distance, emphasis, intimacy, gender, and so forth—and, of course, a change in footing. See, for example. Argyle and Dean (1965).

6. A useful review of the arguments may be found in Hewes (1973); a counterview in Falk (1980).

the meaningful context and the relevant unit for analysis; the words spoken, whether by one participant or two, are an integral part of a mutually coordinated physical undertaking, not a talk. Ritual is so often truncated in these settings because it is nonconversational work that is being done. It is the execution of this work, not utterances, that will ordinarily be the chief concern of the participants. And it is when a hitch occurs in what would otherwise have been the routine interdigitation of their acts that a verbal interchange between them is most likely.

A similar picture can be seen in extended service transactions. Take, for example, mother-child pediatric consultations in Scottish public health clinics, as recently reported by Strong (1979, esp. chap. 6). Here a mother's business with a doctor (when she finally gets her turn) is apparently bracketed with little small talk, very little by way of preplay and postplay, although the child itself may be the recipient of a few ritual solicitudes. The mother sits before the doctor's desk and briefly answers such questions as he puts her, waiting patiently, quietly, and attentively between questions. She is on immediate call, poised to speak, but speaking only when spoken to, almost as well behaved as the machine that is of so much use to airline ticketers. The physician, for his part, intersperses his unceremoniously addressed queries with notetaking, note-reading, thoughtful musings, instruction to students, physical manipulation of the child, verbal exchanges with his nurse and colleagues, and movements away from his desk to get at such things as files and equipment—all of which actions appear warranted by his institutional role if not by the current examination. The mother's answers will sometimes lead the doctor to follow up with a next question, but often instead to some other sort of act on his part. For his social and professional status allows him to be very businesslike; he is running through the phases of an examination, or checklist, not a conversation, and only a scattering of items require a mother's verbal contribution. And indeed, the mother may not know with any specificity what any of the doctor's acts are leading up to or getting at, her being "in on" the instrumentally meaningful sequence of events in no way being necessary for her contribution to it. So although she fits her turns at talk, and what she says, to the doctor's questionings (as in the organization of talk), what immediately precedes and what immediately follows these exchanges is not a speech environment. What is being sustained, then, is not a state of talk but a state of inquiry, and it is this latter to which utterances first must be referred if one is to get at their organization significance.

Or take the open state of talk that is commonly found in connection with an extended joint task, as when two mechanics, separately located around a car, exchange the words required to diagnose, repair, and check the repairing of an engine fault. An audio transcription of twenty minutes of such talk might be very little interpretable even if we know about cars; we would have to watch what was being done to the car in question. The tape would contain long stretches with no words, verbal directives answered only by mechanical sounds, and mechanical sounds answered by verbal responses. And rarely might the relevant context of one utterance be another utterance.

So, too, game encounters of the kind, say, that playing bridge provides, where some of the moves are made with cards, and some with voiced avowals which have been transformed into ideal performatives by the rules of the game.

And indeed, in the White House scene presented initially, the colloquy between Mr. Nixon and Ms. Thomas is not an embedded part of a wider conversation, but an embedded part of a ritualized political procedure, the ceremonial signing of a bill.

One clearly finds, then, that coordinated task activity—not conversation—is what lots of words are part of. A presumed common interest in effectively pursuing the activity at hand, in accordance with some sort of overall plan for doing so, is the contextual matrix which renders many utterances, especially brief ones, meaningful. And these are not unimportant words; it takes a linguist to overlook them.

It is apparent, then, that utterances can be an intimate, functionally integrated part of something that involves other words only in a peripheral and functionally optional way. A naturally bounded unit may be implied, but not one that could be called a speech event.

Beginning with the conversational paradigm, I have tried to decompose the global notion of hearer or recipient, and I have incidentally argued that the notion of a conversational encounter does not suffice in dealing with the context in which words are spoken; a social occasion involving a podium may be involved, or no speech event at all, and, in any case, the whole social situation, the whole surround, must always be considered. Provided, thus, has been a lengthy gloss on Hymes's admonition (1974:54): "The common dyadic model of speaker-hearer specifies sometimes too many, sometimes too few, sometimes the wrong participants."

It is necessary now to look at the remaining element of the conversational paradigm, the notion of *speaker*.

In canonical talk, one of the two participants moves his lips up and down to the accompaniment of his own facial (and sometimes bodily) gesticulations, and words can be heard issuing from the locus of his mouth. His is the sounding box in use, albeit in some actual cases he can share this physical function with a loudspeaker system or a telephone. In short, he is the talking machine, a body engaged in acoustic activity, or, if you will, an individual active in the role of utterance production. He is functioning as an "animator." Animator and recipient are part of the same level and mode of analysis, two terms cut from the same cloth, not social roles in the full sense so much as functional nodes in a communication system.

But, of course, when one uses the term "speaker," one very often beclouds the issue, having additional things in mind, this being one reason why "animator" cannot comfortably be termed a social role, merely an analytical one.

Sometimes one has in mind that there is an "author" of the words that are heard, that is, someone who has selected the sentiments that are being expressed and the words in which they are encoded.

Sometimes one has in mind that a "principal" (in the legalistic sense) is involved, that is, someone whose position is established by the words that are spoken, someone whose beliefs have been told, someone who is committed to what the words say.

Note that one deals in this case not so much with a body or mind as with a person active in some particular social identity or role, some special capacity as a member of a group, office, category, relationship, association, or whatever, some socially based source of self-identification. Often this will mean that the individual speaks, explicitly or implicitly, in the name of "we," not "I" (but not for the reasons Queen Victoria or Nixon felt they had), the "we" including more than the self (Spiegelberg 1973:129–56; Moerman 1968:153–69). And, of course, the same individual can rapidly alter the social role in which he is active, even though his capacity as animator and author remains constant—what in committee meetings is called "changing hats." (This, indeed, is what occurs during a considerable amount of code switching, as Gumperz has amply illustrated.) In thus introducing the name or capacity in which he speaks, the speaker goes some distance in establishing a corresponding reciprocal basis of identification for those to whom this stand-taking is addressed. To a degree, then, to select the capacity in which we are to be active is to select (or to attempt to select) the capacity in which the recipients of our action are present (Weinstein and Deutschberger 1963:454–66). All of this work is consolidated by naming practices and, in many languages, through choice among available second-person pronouns.

The notions of animator, author, and principal, taken together, can be said to tell us about the "production format" of an utterance.

When one uses the term "speaker," one often implies that the individual who animates is formulating his own text and staking out his own position through it: animator, author, and principal are one. What could be more natural? So natural indeed that I cannot avoid continuing to use the term "speaker" in this sense, let alone the masculine pronoun as the unmarked singular form.

But, of course, the implied overlaying of roles has extensive institutionalized exceptions. Plainly, *reciting* a fully memorized text or *reading aloud* from a prepared script allows us to animate words we had no hand in formulating, and to express opinions, beliefs, and sentiments we do not hold. We can openly speak *for* someone else and *in* someone else's words, as we do, say, in reading a deposition or providing a simultaneous translation of a speech—the latter an interesting example because so often the original speaker's words, although ones that person commits himself to, are ones that someone else wrote for him. As will later be seen, the tricky problem is that often when we do engage in "fresh talk," that is, the extemporaneous, ongoing formulation of a text under the exigency of immediate response to our current situation,[7] it is not true to say that we always speak our own words and ourself take the position to which these words attest.

A final consideration. Just as we can listen to a conversation without being ratified hearers (or be ratified to listen but fail to do so), so as ratified listeners—participants who don't now have the floor—we can briefly interject our words and feelings into the temporal interstices within or between interchanges sustained by other participants (Goffman 1976:275–76, and this volume, pp. 28–29). Moreover, once others tacitly have given us the promise of floor time to recount a tale or to develop an argument, we may tolerate or even invite kibitzing, knowing that there is a good chance that we can listen for a moment without ceasing to be the speaker, just as others can interrupt for a moment without ceasing to be listeners.

VIII

Given an utterance as a starting point of inquiry, I have recommended that our commonsense notions of hearer and speaker are crude, the first potentially concealing a complex differentiation of participation statuses, and the second, complex questions of production format.

The delineation of participation framework and production format provides a structural basis for analyzing changes in footing. At least it does for the changes in footing described at the beginning of this paper. But the view that results systematically simplifies the bearing of participation frameworks and production formats on the structure of utterances. Sturdy, sober, socio-

7. David Abercrombie (1965:2) divides what I here call fresh talk into conversation, involving a rapid exchange of speaker-hearer roles, and monologue, which involves extended one-person exercises featuring a vaunted style that approaches the formality of a written form.

logical matters are engaged, but the freewheeling, self-referential character of speech receives no place. The essential fancifulness of talk is missed. And for these fluidities linguistics, not sociology, provides the lead. It is these matters that open up the possibility of finding some structural basis for even the subtlest shifts in footing.

A beginning can be made by examining the way statements are constructed, especially in regard to "embedding," a tricky matter made more so by how easy it is to confuse it with an analytically quite different idea, the notion of multiple social roles already considered in connection with "principal."

You hear an individual grunt out an unadorned, naked utterance, hedged and parenthesized with no qualifier or pronoun, such as:

a directive: Shut the window.
an interrogative: Why here?
a declarative: The rain has started.
a commissive: The job will be done by three o'clock.

Commonly the words are heard as representing in some direct way the *current* desire, belief, perception, or intention of whoever animates the utterance. The current self of the person who animates seems inevitably involved in some way—what might be called the "addressing self." So, too, deixis in regard to time and place is commonly involved. One is close here to the expressive communication we think of as the kind an animal could manage through the small vocabulary of sound-gestures available to it. Observe that when such utterances are heard they are still heard as coming from an individual who not only animates the words but is active in a *particular* social capacity, the words taking their authority from this capacity.

Many, if not most, utterances, however, are not constructed in this fashion. Rather, as speaker, we represent ourselves through the offices of a personal pronoun, typically "I," and it is thus a *figure*—a figure in a statement—that serves as the agent, a protagonist in a *described* scene, a "character" in an anecdote, someone, after all, who belongs to the world that is spoken about, not the world in which the speaking occurs. And once this format is employed, an astonishing flexibility is created.

For one thing, hedges and qualifiers introduced in the form of performative modal verbs (I "wish," "think," "could," "hope," etc.) become possible, introducing some distance between the figure and its avowal. Indeed, a double distance is produced, for presumably some part of us unconditionally stands behind our conditional utterance, else we would have to say something like "I think that I think. . . ." Thus, when we slip on a word and elect to further interrupt the flow by interjecting a remedial statement such as, "Whoops! I got that wrong, . . ." or "I meant to say . . .," we are projecting ourselves as animators into the talk. But this is a figure, nonetheless, and not the actual animator; it is merely a figure that comes closer than most to the individual who animates its presentation. And, of course, a point about these apologies for breaks in fluency is that they themselves can be animated fluently, exhibiting a property markedly different from the one they refer to, reminding one that howsoever we feel obliged to describe ourselves, we need not include in this description the capacity and propensity to project such descriptions. (Indeed, we cannot entirely do so.) When we say, "I can't seem to talk clearly today," *that* statement can be very clearly said. When we say, "I'm speechless!", we aren't. (And if we tried to be cute and say, "I'm speechless—but apparently not enough to prevent myself from saying that," our description would embody the cuteness but not refer to it.) In Mead's terms, a "me" that tries to incorporate its "I" requires another "I" to do so.

Second, as Hockett (1963:11) recommends, unrestricted displacement in time and place becomes possible, such that our reference can be to what we did, wanted, thought, etc., at some distant time and place, when, incidentally, we were active in a social capacity we may currently no longer enjoy and an identity we no longer claim. It is perfectly true that when we say:

I said shut the window

we can mean almost exactly what we would have meant had we uttered the unadorned version:

Shut the window

as a repetition of a prior command. But if we happen to be recounting a tale of something that happened many years ago, when we were a person we consider we no longer are, then the "I" in "I said shut the window" is linked to us—the person present—merely through biographical continuity, something that much or little can be made of, and nothing more immediate than that. In which case, two animators can be said to be involved: the one who is physically animating the sounds that are heard, and an embedded animator, a figure in a statement who is present only in a world that is being told about, not in the world in which the current telling takes place. (Embedded authors and principals are also possible.) Following the same argument, one can see that by using second or third person in place of first person we can tell of something someone *else* said, someone present or absent, someone human or mythical. We can embed an entirely different speaker into our utterance. For it is as easy to cite what someone else said as to cite oneself. Indeed, when queried as to precisely what someone said, we can reply quotatively:

Shut the window

and, although quite unadorned, this statement will be understood as something someone other than we, the current and actual animator, said. Presumably, "He (or "she") said" is implied but not necessarily stated.[8]

Once embedding is admitted as a possibility, then it is an easy step to see that multiple embeddings will be possible, as in the following:

To the best of my recollection,
(1) I think that
(2) I said
(3) I once lived that sort of life.

where (1) reflects something that is currently true of the individual who animates (the "addressing self"), (2) an embedded

8. Some generative semanticists have argued that *any* unadorned utterance implies a higher performative verb and a pronoun, e.g., "I say," "aver," "demand," etc., the implication being that all statements are made by figures mentioned or implied, not by living individuals. See, for example, Ross 1970.

animator who is an earlier incarnation of the present speaker and (3) is a doubly embedded figure, namely, a still earlier incarnation of an earlier incarnation.[9]

Although linguists have provided us with very useful treatments of direct and indirect quotation, they have been less helpful in the question of how else, as animators, we can convey words that are not our own. For example, if someone repeatedly tells us to shut the window, we can finally respond by repeating his words in a strident pitch, enacting a satirical version of his utterance ("say-foring"). In a similar way we can mock an accent or dialect, projecting a stereotyped figure more in the manner that stage actors do than in the manner that mere quotation provides. So, too, without much warning, we can corroborate our own words with an adage or saying, the understanding being that fresh talk has momentarily ceased and an anonymous authority wider and different from ourselves is being suddenly invoked (Laberge and Sankoff 1979, esp. sec. 3). If these playful projections are to be thought of in terms of embeddings, then stage acting and recitation must be thought of as forms of embedded action, too. Interestingly, it seems very much the case that in socializing infants linguistically, in introducing them to words and utterances, we from the very beginning teach them to use talk in this self-dissociated, fanciful way.[10]

9. It would be easy to think that "I" had special properties uniquely bridging between the scene in which the talking occurs and the scene about which there is talking, for it refers both to a figure in a statement and to the currently present, live individual who is animating the utterance. But that is not quite so. Second-person pronouns are equally two-faced, referring to figures in statements and currently present, live individuals engaged in hearing what a speaker is saying about them. Moreover, both types of pronoun routinely appear embedded as part of quoted statements:

She said, "I insist you shut the window."

in which case the individual who had served as a live, currently present animator has herself become a figure in a lower-order statement. The bridging power of "I" remains, but what is bridged is an embedded speaker to the figure it describes. The scene in which speaking and hearing is currently and actually occurring does not appear except through implicature: the implication that everyone listening will know who is referred to by "she."

10. In play with a child, a parent tries to ease the child into talk. Using "we" or "I" or "baby" or a term of endearment or the child's name, and a lisping sort of baby talk, the parent makes it apparent that it is the child that is being

It should be clear, then, that the significance of production format cannot be dealt with unless one faces up to the embedding function of much talk. For obviously, when we shift from saying something ourselves to reporting what someone else said, we are changing our footing. And so, too, when we shift from reporting our current feelings, the feelings of the "addressing self," to the feelings we once had but no longer espouse. (Indeed, a code switch sometimes functions as a mark of this shift.)

Final points. As suggested, when as speaker we project ourselves in a current and locally active capacity, then our coparticipants in the encounter are the ones who will have their selves partly determined correspondingly. But in the case of a replay of a past event, the self we select for ourself can only "altercast" the other figures *in the story,* leaving the hearers of the replay undetermined in that regard. *They* are cast into recipients of a bit of narrative, and this will be much the same sort of self whomsoever we people our narrative with, and in whatsoever capacity they are there active. The statuses "narrator" and "story listener," which would seem to be of small significance in terms of the overall social structure, turn out, then, to be of considerable importance in conversation, for they provide a footing to which a very wide range of speakers and hearers can briefly shift.[11] (Ad-

---

talked *for,* not to. In addition, there are sure to be play-beings easy to hand—dolls, teddy bears, and now toy robots—and these the parent will speak for, too. So even as the child learns to speak, it learns to speak for, learns to speak in the name of figures that will never be, or at least aren't yet, the self. George Herbert Mead notwithstanding, the child does not merely learn to refer to itself through a name for itself that others had first chosen; it learns just as early to embed the statements and mannerisms of a zoo-full of beings in its own verbal behavior. It can be argued that it is just this format that will allow the child in later years to describe its own past actions which it no longer feels are characteristic, just as this format will allow the child to use "I" as part of a statement that is quoted as something someone else said. (One might say that Mead had the wrong term: the child does not acquire a "generalized other" so much as a capacity to embed "particularized others"—which others, taken together, form a heterogeneous, accidental collection, a teething ring for utterances and not a ball team.) It strikes me, then, that although a parent's baby talk (and the talk the child first learns) may involve some sort of simplification of syntax and lexicon, its laminative features are anything but childlike. Nor do I think parents should be told about this. A treatment of this issue in another culture is provided by Schieffelin (1974).

11. One example: A few years ago, the BBC did an hour-length TV documentary on backstage at the Royal Household. The show purported to

mittedly, if a listener is also a character in the story he is listening to, as in the millions of mild recriminations communicated between intimates, then he is likely to have more than a mere listener's concern with the tale.)

Storytelling, of course, requires the teller to embed in his own utterances the utterances and actions of the story's characters. And a full-scale story requires that the speaker remove himself for the telling's duration from the alignment he would maintain in ordinary conversational give and take, and for this period of narration maintain another footing, that of a narrator whose extended pauses and utterance completions are not to be understood as signals that he is now ready to give up the floor. But these changes in footing are by no means the only kind that occur during storytelling. For during the telling of a tale (as Livia Polanyi has nicely shown [1977]), the teller is likely to break narrative frame at strategic junctures: to recap for new listeners; to provide (in the raconteur's version of direct address) encouragement to listeners to wait for the punch line, or gratuitous characterizations of various protagonists in the tale; or to backtrack a correction for any felt failure to sustain narrative requirements such as contextual detail, proper temporal sequencing, dramatic build-up, and so forth.[12]

---

display the Queen in her full domestic round, including shopping and picnicking with her Family. Somehow the producers and stars of the program managed to get through the whole show without displaying much that could be deemed inadvertent, revealing, unstaged, or unself-conscious, in part, no doubt, because much of royal life is probably managed this way even in the absence of cameras. But one exception did shine through. The Queen and other members of the Family occasionally reverted to telling family stories or personal experiences to their interlocutor. The stories no doubt were carefully selected (as all stories must be), but in the telling of them the royal personages could not but momentarily slip into the unregal stance of storyteller, allowing their hearers the momentary (relative) intimacy of story listeners. What could be conceived of as "humanity" is thus practically inescapable. For there is a democracy implied in narration; the lowest rank in that activity is not very low by society's standards—the right and obligation to listen to a story from a person to whom we need not be in a position to tell one.

12. Interestingly, the texts that folklorists and sociolinguists provide of everyday stories often systematically omit the narrative frame breaks that very likely occurred throughout the actual tellings. Here the student of stories has tactfully accepted the teller's injunction that the shift in footing required to introduce a correction or some other out-of-frame comment be omitted from the official record. Often omitted, too, is any appreciation of the frequency with

I X

It was recommended that one can get at the structural basis of footing by breaking up the primitive notions of hearer and speaker into more differentiated parts, namely, participation framework and production format. Then it was suggested that this picture must itself be complicated by the concept of embedding and an understanding of the layering effect that seems to be an essential outcome of the production process in speaking. But this complication itself cannot be clearly seen unless one appreciates another aspect of embedding, one that linguistic analysis hasn't much prepared us for, namely, the sense in which participation frameworks are subject to transformation. For it turns out that, in something like the ethological sense, we quite routinely ritualize participation frameworks; that is, we self-consciously transplant the participation arrangement that is natural in one social situation into an interactional environment in which it isn't. In linguistic terms, we not only embed utterances, we embed interaction arrangements.

Take collusion, for example. This arrangement may not itself be common, but common, surely, is apparently unserious collusion broadly played out with winks and elbow nudges in the obviously open presence of the excolluded. Innuendo is also a common candidate for playful transformation, the target of the slight meant to understand that a form is being used unseriously —a practice sometimes employed to convey an opinion that could not safely be conveyed through actual innuendo, let alone direct statement. The shielding of the mouth with the hand, already a ritualized way of marking a byplay during large meetings, is brought into small conversational circles to mark a communication as having the character of an aside but here with no one to be excluded from it. (I have seen an elderly woman in a quiet street talking about neighborhood business to the man next door and then, in termination of the encounter, bisect her mouth with the five stiff fingers of her right hand and out of one side remark on how his geraniums were growing, the use of this gesture,

---

which hearers change footing and inject in passing their own contribution to the tale (Goodwin 1978, esp. chap. 3 and chap. 4, pt. 5).

apparently, marking her appreciation that to play her inquiry straight would be directly to invoke a shared interest and competency, not a particularly masculine one, and hence a similarity her neighbor might be disinclined to confront.) Or witness the way in which the physical contact, focusing tone, and loving endearments appropriate within the privacy of a courtship encounter can be performed in fun to an unsuitable candidate as a set piece to set into the focus of attention of a wider convivial circle. Or, in the same sort of circle, how we can respond to what a speaker says to an addressed recipient as though we weren't ratified coparticipants, but bystanders engaged in irreverent sideplay. Or, even when two individuals are quite alone together and cannot possibly be overheard, how one may mark the confidential and disclosive status of a bit of gossip by switching into a whisper voice. I think there is no doubt that a considerable amount of natural conversation is laminated in the manner these illustrations suggest; in any case, conversation is certainly vulnerable to such lamination. And each increase or decrease in layering—each movement closer to or further from the "literal"—carries with it a change in footing.

Once it is seen that a participation framework can be parenthesized and set into an alien environment, it should be evident that all the participation frameworks earlier described as occurring outside of conversation—that is, arrangements involving an audience or no official recipient at all—are themselves candidates for this reframing process; they, too, can be reset into conversational talk. And, of course, with each such embedding a change of footing occurs. The private, ruminative self-talk we may employ among strangers when our circumstances suddenly require explaining, we can playfully restage in conversation, not so much projecting the words, but projecting a dumbfounded person projecting the words. So, too, on such occasions, we can momentarily affect a podium speech register, or provide a theatrical version (burlesqued, melodramatic) of an aside. All of which, of course, provides extra warrant—indeed, perhaps, the main warrant—for differentiating various participation frameworks in the first place.

It is true, then, that the frameworks in which words are spoken pass far beyond ordinary conversation. But it is just as true that these frameworks are brought back into conversation, acted out in a setting which they initially transcended. What nature divides, talk frivolously embeds, insets, and intermingles. As dramatists can put any world on their stage, so we can enact any participation framework and production format in our conversation.

x

I have dealt till now with *changes* in footing as though the individual were involved merely in switching from one stance or alignment to another. But this image is itself too mechanical and too easy. It is insufficiently responsive to the way embedding and ritualization work. For often it seems that when we change voice —whether to speak for another aspect of ourselves or for someone else, or to lighten our discourse with a darted enactment of some alien interaction arrangement—we are not so much terminating the prior alignment as holding it in abeyance with the understanding that it will almost immediately be reengaged. So, too, when we give up the floor in a conversation, thereby taking up the footing of a recipient (addressed or otherwise), we can be warranted in expecting to reenter the speaker role on the same footing from which we left it. As suggested, this is clearly the case when a narrator allows hearers to "chip in," but such perceivedly temporary foregoing of one's position is also to be found when storytelling isn't featured. So it must be allowed that we can hold the same footing across several of our turns at talk. And within one alignment, another can be fully enclosed. In truth, in talk it seems routine that, while firmly standing on two feet, we jump up and down on another.

Which should prepare us for those institutional niches in which a hard-pressed functionary is constrained to routinely sustain more than one state of talk simultaneously. Thus, throughout an auction, an auctioneer may intersperse the utterances he directs to the bidding audience with several streams of out-of-frame communication—reports on each sale spoken through a microphone to a recording clerk in another room, instructions to assistants on the floor, and (less routinely) greetings to friends and responses to individual buyers who approach with quiet requests for an updating. Nor need there be one dominant state of talk and the rest styled as asides respectfully inserted at junctures. For example, in a medical research/training facility (as reported in a forthcoming paper by Tannen and Wallat), a pediatrician may find she must continuously switch code, now addressing her youthful patient in "motherese," now sustaining a conversation-like exchange with the mother, now turning to the video camera to provide her trainee audience with a running account couched in the register of medical reporting. Here one deals with the capacity of different classes of participants to by-stand the current stream of communication whilst "on hold" for the attention of the pivotal person to reengage them. And one deals with the capacity of a dexterous speaker to jump back and forth, keeping different circles in play.

X I

To end, let us return to the Nixon scene that formed the introduction to this paper. When Helen Thomas pirouetted for the president, she was parenthesizing within her journalistic stance another stance, that of a woman receiving comments on her appearance. No doubt the forces at work are sexism and presidents, but the forces can work in this particular way because of our general capacity to embed the fleeting enactment of one role in the more extended performance of another.

When Helen Thomas pirouetted for the president, she was employing a form of behavior indigenous to the environment of the ballet, a form that has come, by conventional reframing, to be a feature of female modeling in fashion shows, and she was enacting it—of all places—in a news conference. No one present apparently found this transplantation odd. *That* is how experience is laminated.

The news report of this conference itself does not tell us, but from what is known about Nixon as a performer, a guess would be that he switched from the high ritual of signing a bill to the joshing of Ms. Thomas not merely as a bracketing device, a signal that the substantive phase of the ceremony was over, but to show he was a person of spirit, always capable of the common touch.

And I surmise that although his audience dutifully laughed loudly, they may have seen his gesture as forced, wooden, and artificial, separating him from them by a behavioral veil of design and self-consciousness. All of that would have to be understood to gain any close sense of what Nixon was projecting, of his alignment to those present, of his footing. And I believe linguistics provides us with the cues and markers through which such footings become manifest, helping us to find our way to a structural basis for analyzing them.

REFERENCES

Abercrombie, David. 1965. *Conversation and spoken prose: Studies in phonetics and linguistics.* London: Oxford University Press.

Argyle, Michael, and Dean, Janet. 1965. "Eye contact, distance and affiliation." *Sociometry* 28:289–304.

Becker, A. L. 1970. "Journey through the night: Notes on Burmese traditional theatre." *The Drama Review* 15/3:83–87.

Blom, Jan-Peter, and Gumperz, John J. 1972. "Social meaning in linguistic structure: Code-switching in Norway." In *Directions in Sociolinguistics,* edited by John J. Gumperz and Dell H. Hymes. New York: Holt, Rinehart and Winston.

Cook-Gumperz, Jenny, and Gumperz, John. 1976. "Context in children's speech." In *Papers on Language and Context* (Working Paper 46), by Jenny Cook-Gumperz and John Gumperz. Berkeley: Language Behavior Research Laboratory, University of California, Berkeley.

The Evening Bulletin (Philadelphia), August 7, 1973.

Falk, Dean, "Language, handedness, and primate brains: Did the Australopithecines sign? *American Anthropologist* 82 (1980): 78.

Fisher, Lawrence E. 1976. "Dropping remarks and the Barbadian audience." *American Ethnologist* 3/2:227–42.

Goffman, Erving. 1974. *Frame analysis.* New York: Harper and Row.

———. 1976. "Replies and responses." *Language in Society* 5:257–313.

———. 1978. "Response cries." *Language* 54/4.

Goodwin, Marjorie. 1978. "Conversational practices in a peer group of urban black children." Ph.D. dissertation, Department of Anthropology, University of Pennsylvania, Philadelphia, Pennsylvania.

Gossen, Gary H. 1976. "Verbal dueling in Chamula." In *Speech play,* edited by Barbara Kirshenblatt-Gimblett, pp. 121–46. Philadelphia: University of Pennsylvania Press.

Gumperz, John. 1976. "Social network and language shift." In *Papers on Language and Context* (Working Paper 46), by Jenny Cook-Gumperz and John Gumperz. Berkeley: Language Behavior Research Laboratory, University of California, Berkeley.

Hewes, Gordon W. 1973. "Primate communication and the gestural origin of language." *Current Anthropology* 14:5–24.

Hockett, Charles. 1963. "The problem of universals in language." In *Universals of language,* edited by Joseph Greenberg, pp. 1–29. Cambridge: MIT Press.

Hymes, Dell H. 1974. *Foundations in sociolinguistics.* Philadelphia: University of Pennsylvania Press.

Laberge, Suzanne, and Sankoff, Gillian. 1979. "Anything *you* can do." In *Discourse and syntax,* edited by Talmy Givón and Charles Li. New York: Academic Press.

Moerman, Michael. 1968. "Being Lue: Uses and abuses of ethnic identification." In *Essays on the problem of tribe,* edited by June Helm, pp. 153–69. Seattle: University of Washington Press.

Polanyi, Livia. 1977. "Not so false starts." *Working Papers in Sociolinguistics,* no. 41. Austin, Texas: Southwest Educational Development Laboratory.

Ross, John Robert. 1970. "On declarative sentences." In *Readings in English transformational grammar,* edited by Roderick A. Jacobs and Peter S. Rosenbaum, pp. 222–72. Waltham, Mass.: Ginn and Company.

Schieffelin, Bambi B. 1979. "Getting it together: An ethnographic approach to the study of the development of communicative competence." In *Studies in developmental pragmatics,* edited by Elinor O. Keenan. New York: Academic Press.

Spiegelberg, Herbert. 1973. "On the right to say 'we': A linguistic and phenomenological analysis." In *Phenomenological sociology,* edited by George Psathas, pp. 129–56. New York: John Wiley and Sons.

Strong, P. M. 1979. *The ceremonial order of the clinic.* London: Routledge and Kegan Paul.

Tannen, Deborah, and Wallat, Cynthia. Forthcoming. "A sociolinguistic analysis of multiple demands on the pediatrician in doctor/mother/child interaction."

Weinstein, Eugene, and Deutschberger, Paul. 1963. "Some dimensions of altercasting." *Sociometry* 26/4:454–66.

4

The following paper was originally presented as the Katz-New-comb Memorial Lecture, University of Michigan, 1976. It was designed to be spoken, and through its text and delivery to provide an actual instance—not merely a discussion—of some differences between talk and the printed word. Nevertheless, with a modest amount of editorial work, the original format could have been transformed. Reference, laconic and otherwise, to time, place, and occasion could have been omitted; footnotes could have been used to house appropriate bibliography, extended asides, and full identification of sources mentioned in passing; first-person references could have been recast; categoric pronouncements could have been qualified; and other features of the style and syntax appropriate to papers in print could have been imposed. Without this, readers might feel that they had been fobbed off—with a text meant for others and a writer who felt that rewriting was not worth the bother. However, I have refrained almost entirely from making such changes. My hope is that as it stands, this version will make certain framing issues clear by apparent inadvertence, again instantiating the difference between talk and print, this time from the other side, although much less vividly than might be accomplished by publishing an unedited, closely transcribed tape recording of the initial delivery, along with phrase-by-phrase parenthetical exegesis of gesticulation, timing, and elisions. (This latter would be useful, but requires a bit much by way of warrant for public self-dissection.) I venture this plea without confidence, because it provides the obvious (albeit the only valid) excuse for obliging readers to suffer a text that has not been reworked for their mode of apprehending it. Of course, both this abuse of readers and what they can learn about framing from being thus abused are somewhat weakened by the fact that the original speaking was not extemporaneous talk, merely aloud reading from a typed text, and that all spontaneous elaborations added to the script on that occasion (and on others when the paper was reread) have been omitted—a standard practice in almost all conversions from talk to print. The punctuation signs employed are those designed for written grammar, being the same as those employed in the typed text from which the talk was read; however, the version of this order that appeared in sound arises from the original in unspecified ways—at least unspecified here. (For example, quotation marks that appear in the reading typescript appear also in the present text, but the reader is not informed as to how the words so marked were managed in the speaking, whether by prosodic markers, verbal transliteration ["quotes" . . . "unquote"], or/and finger gestures.) Moreover, here and there I have not foreborne to change a word or add a line (indeed, a paragraph or two) to the original, and these modifications are not identified as such. Finally, a prefatory statement has been added, namely, this one, along with the bibliographical references which allow me to acknowledge help from Hymes (1975) and Bauman (1975), all of which is solely part of the printed presentation. Thus, however much the original talk was in bad faith, this edited documentation of it is more so. (For a parallel discussion of the spoken lecture, and a parallel disclaimer regarding the written version, see Frake [1977].)

THE LECTURE

I

My topic and my arguments this afternoon are part of the substantive area I work in, the naturalistic study of human foregatherings and cominglings, that is, the forms and occasions of face-to-face interaction. The particular form in question incidentally provides scope for what I call "frame analysis." No other justifications are offered, but these are. Therefore, I hope you will reserve judgment and will not immediately assume that my selection of the lecture as a topic proves I am yet another self-appointed cut-up, optimistically attempting a podium shuck. I am not trying to wriggle out of my contract with you by using my situation at the podium to talk about something ready to hand, my situation at the podium. To do so would be to occupy a status for purposes other than fulfilling it. Of that sort of puerile opportunism we have had quite enough, whether from classroom practitioners of group dynamics, the left wing of ethnomethodology, or the John Cage school of performance rip-offs. (He who says he is tearing up his prepared address to talk to you extemporaneously about what it is like to address you or what it is like to write talks, or to formulate sentences in the first place, has torn up the wrong prepared address.) That I am transmitting my remarks through a lecture and not, say, in print or during a conversation, I take to be incidental. Indeed, a term like "paper" in its relevant sense can refer equally to something that is printed and something that is delivered.

Surely nothing I can want to say about lectures can have the effect of questioning the opportunity they give to purposely impart a coherent chapter of information, including, in my own case, imparting something about lecturing. One necessary condition for the validity of my analysis is that I cannot avoid its application to this occasion of communicating it to you; another is that this applicability does not, in turn, undermine either the presentation or the arguments. He who lectures on speech error and its correction will inevitably make some of the very errors he analyzes, but such an unintended exhibition attests to the value of the analysis, however it reflects upon the speaking competence of the analyst. More still, he who lectures on discourse presuppositions will be utterly tongue-tied unless unself-consciously he makes as many as anyone else. He who lectures about prefaces and excuses might still be advised to begin his talk with an apologetic introduction. And he who lectures about lectures does not have a special excuse for lecturing badly; his description of delivery faults will be judged according to how well the description is organized and delivered; his failure to engross his listeners cannot be reframed retrospectively as an illustration of the interactional significance of such failure. Should he actually succeed in breaching lecturing's constraints, he becomes a performing speaker, not a speaker performing. (He who attempts such breaching, and succeeds, should have come to the occasion dressed in tights, carrying a lute. He who attempts such evasion and fails—as is likely—is just a plain schmuck, and it would be better had he not come to the occasion at all.) Which is not to say that other sorts of frame break might be as clearly doomed; for example, a reference at this point to the very questionable procedure of my employing "he" in the immediately preceding utterances, carefully mingling a sex-biased word for the indefinite nominal pronoun, and an unobjectionable anaphoric term for someone like myself.

However, it is apparent that lecturing on lectures is nonetheless a little special. To hold forth in an extended fashion on lecturing to persons while they have to sit through one, is to force them to serve double time—a cruel and unusual punishment. To claim authority on lectures before an audience such as this one is to push forward into that zone where presumption shades into idiocy. Moreover, much as I argue that my avowals can, should, and must be firmly contained within the lecture format, something is likely to leak out. Indeed, I know that before this talk is over I will have turned more than once on my own immediately past behavior as an illustration of what is currently being said; for certainly I can inadvertently exhibit a thing better than I can consciously mock up a version for illustrative presentation. But there is a limit to how much of this sort of turning in one's tracks is allowable. Illustrations themselves raise questions. He who reports jokes, in a lecture on humor, has a right, and perhaps the obligation, to tell bad ones, for the punch line is properly to be found in the analysis, not in the story; he can allow data jokes to spark his presentation, but not to burn his thought down. Similarly, lecturing linguists can do a glottal stop or an alveolar flap as an illustration of it, and ornithologists a bird call, without particularly threatening the definition that it is lecturing that is going on. In a lecture on the grey-legged goose, slides of threat behavior are perfectly in order, words and slides being somehow equally insulated from the situation in which they are presented. In fact, medical lecturers can bring in the goose itself, providing it is a human one, and only the goose need be embarrassed. And yet, were the speaker to use the whole of his body to perform an illustration of grey-leg threat behavior—as I have seen Konrad Lorenz do—then something else begins to happen, something of the sort that only Lorenz can get away with doing, and he not without leaving a confirming residue in his reputation.

Trickier still: if an impropriety is enacted as an illustration of an impropriety, the enactment being, as it were, in quotes, how much extra insulation does that provide? In lectures on torture, speakers understandably hesitate to play tapes of actual occurrences; with how much less risk could I play such a tape as an illustration of what can't be played? Would that twice removal from actual events suffice to keep us all within the unkinetic world that lecturing is supposed to sustain? And finally, given that the situation *about* which a lecture deals is insulated in various ways from the situation *in* which the lecturing occurs, and is obliged to be insulated in this way, can an illustrated discussion of this disjunctive condition be carried on without breaching the very line that is under scrutiny? And if all of the presentation which is to follow is a single, extended example of the vulnerability of the line between the process of referring and the subject matter that is referred to, and I so state it to be from the beginning, am I giving a lecture or a lecture-hall exhibition? And is it possible to raise that question directly without ceasing to lecture? In reporting in this way about the goose, don't I become one?

You will note that I have eased you into a discussion of the lecture by talking about the lecturer. Indeed, I will continue to do so. Balance could only come from what I won't provide, an analysis of the intricacies of audience behavior.

I I

A lecture is an institutionalized extended holding of the floor in which one speaker imparts his views on a subject, these thoughts comprising what can be called his "text." The style is typically serious and slightly impersonal, the controlling intent being to generate calmly considered understanding, not mere entertainment, emotional impact, or immediate action. Constituent statements presumably take their warrant from their role in attesting to the truth, truth appearing as something to be cultivated and developed from a distance, coolly, as an end in itself.

A platform arrangement is often involved, underlining the fact that listeners are an "immediate audience." I mean a gathered set of individuals, typically seated, whose numbers can vary greatly without requiring the speaker (typically standing) to change his style, who have the right to hold the whole of the speaker's body in the focus of staring-at attention (as they would an entertainer), and who (initially, at least) have only the back channel through which to convey their response.

Those who present themselves before an audience are said to be "performers" and to provide a "performance"—in the peculiar, theatrical sense of the term. Thereby they tacitly claim those platform skills for lack of which an ordinary person thrust upon the stage would flounder hopelessly—an object to laugh at, be embarrassed for, and have massive impatience with. And they tacitly accept judgment in these terms by those who themselves need never be exposed to such appraisal. The clear contrast is to everyday talk, for there, it is felt, no elevated role is being sought, no special competency is required, and surely only morbid shyness or some other unusual impediment could prevent one from delivering the grunts and eyebrow flashes that will often suffice. (Which is not to say that in conversational settings individuals may not occasionally attempt a set piece that asks to be judged as entertainment, not talk, and unlike talk is *relatively* loosely coupled to the character and size of the listening circle.) In any case, in talk, all those who judge competency know themselves to be thus appraised.

Face-to-face undertakings of the focused kind, be they games, joint tasks, theater performances, or conversations, succeed or fail as interactions in the degree to which participants get caught up by and carried away into the special realm of being that can be generated by these engagements. So, too, lectures. However, unlike games and staged plays, lectures must not be frankly presented as if engrossment were the controlling intent. Indeed, lectures draw on a precarious ideal: certainly the listeners are to be carried away so that time slips by, but because of the speaker's subject matter, not his antics; the subject matter is meant to have its own enduring claims upon the listeners apart from the felicities or infelicities of the presentation. A lecture, then, purports to take the audience right past the auditorium, the occasion, and the speaker into the subject matter upon which the lecture comments. So your lecturer is meant to be a performer, but not merely a performer. Observe, I am not saying that audiences regularly do become involved in the speaker's subject matter, only that they handle whatever they do become involved in so as not to openly embarrass the understanding that it's the text they are involved in. In fact, there is truth in saying that audiences become involved in spite of the text, not because of it; they skip along, dipping in and out of following the lecturer's argument, waiting for the special effects which actually capture them, and topple them momentarily into what is being said—which special effects I need not specify but had better produce.

In the analysis of all occasions in which talk figures largely —what Hymes has called "speech events"—it is common to use the term "speaker," as I will also. But in fact the term "speaker" is very troublesome. It can be shown to have variable and separable functions, and the word itself seems to demand that we use it because of these ambiguities, not in spite of them. In the case of a lecture, one person can be identified as the talking machine, the thing that sound comes out of, the "animator." Typically in lectures, that person is also seen as having "authored" the text, that is, as having formulated and scripted the statements that get made. And he is seen as the "principal," namely, someone who believes personally in what is being said and takes the position that is implied in the remarks. (Of course, the lecturer is likely to assume that right-thinking persons also will take the position he describes.)

I am suggesting that it is characteristic of lectures (in the sense of common to them and important for them) that animator, author, and principal are the same person. Also, it is characteristic that this three-sided functionary is assumed to have "authority" —intellectual, as opposed to institutional. By virtue of reputation or office, he is assumed to have knowledge and experience in textual matters, and of this considerably more than that possessed by the audience. And, as suggested, he does not have to fight to hold the floor—at least for a stipulated block of time— this monopoly being his, automatically, as part of the social arrangements. The floor is his, but, of course, attention may not be. As would also be true if instead of a lecturer at stage center we had a singer, a poet, a juggler, or some other trained seal.

Following the linguist Kenneth Pike, it can be said that lectures belong to that broad class of situational enterprises wherein a difference clearly occurs between game and spectacle, that is, between the business at hand and the custard of interaction in which the business is embedded. (The custard shows up most clearly as "preplay" and "postplay," that is, a squeeze of talk and bustle just before the occasioned proceedings start and just after they have finished.) The term "lecture" itself firmly obscures the matter, sometimes referring to a spoken text, sometimes to the embracing social event in which its delivery occurs—an ambiguity, also, of most terms for other stage activities.

The arrangement we have been looking at—the laminated affair of spectacle and game—itself will come in various formats:

as a one-shot event, or one of a series involving the same arrangements but different speakers, or one session of a course, the latter a sequence of lectures by the same speaker.

The spectacle, the environing social fuss in which a lecture is delivered, sometimes qualifies as a celebrative occasion. By "celebrative occasion" I mean a social affair that is looked forward to and back upon as a festivity of some kind whose business at hand, when any is discernible, is not the only reason for participation; rather import is intendedly given to social intercourse among the participants gathered under the auspices of honoring and commemorating something, if only their own social circle. Moreover, there is a tendency to phrase participation as involving one's total social personality, not merely a specialized segment. (The first and last night of a theatrical run according to this definition could be a celebrative occasion, but not likely the showings in between; a day at the office is not a special occasion, but the Christmas party hopefully is.) One-shot lectures "open to the public" involving a speaker otherwise inaccessible to the audience (and an audience otherwise inaccessible to him) are often embedded in a celebrative occasion, as are talks to private audiences in a serial format. Lectures that are part of a college course delivered by a local person tend to go unmarked in this particular way, except sometimes the opening and closing ones. Course lectures have another marginal feature: listeners can be made officially responsible for learning what is said—a condition that strikes deeply at the ritual character of performances. There note taking can occur, the lecturer accommodating in various ways to facilitate this, the note taker preferring to come away with a summary instead of an experience. (May I add, celebrative occasions seem to be a fundamental organizational form of our public life, yet hardly any study has been given to them as such.)

The recruitment of an audience through advertising, announcements to members, class scheduling, and the like; the selection and payment of the speaker; the provision of requisite housekeeping services—all these presuppose an organizational base which takes and is accorded responsibility, allowing one to speak of the "auspices" or sponsors of the lecture. A committee of some kind, a division of a university, a professional association, a government agency—any of these can serve. Characteristically this sponsoring organization will have a life and a purpose extending beyond the mounting of the lecture itself. Insofar as the lecture is itself embedded in a celebrative occasion, the occasion will celebrate the auspices of the talk even as it celebrates the speaker and his topic. (A rock concert may have auspices whose life is restricted to the mounting of this one event, and the event itself may little celebrate its auspices—in this case its promoters—these persons hoping for rewards of a more palpable kind.) In celebrative occasions in which a lecture is to occur, transition from spectacle to game, from hoopla to business at hand, is routinely divided (as you have recently witnessed) into two parts, the first part enacted by a representative of the auspices introducing the speaker, and the second part by the speaker introducing his topic. Sometimes the introducer's part of the introduction is itself split in two, the introducer himself being introduced, as though the organizers felt that the contribution of this slot to their various concerns could best be used by inserting more than one candidate.

Observe, the interests of the organizers will lie not only with the actual lecture delivery, but also with the photographic, taped, and textual record thereof, for such a record can serve organizational interests as much as or more than the talk itself. (The clear case here is the sort of charity ball that is held for a worthy organization, where commonly the costs of mounting the ball are barely offset by the monies gained from tickets, the real underlying purpose being to give newspapers a warrant for coverage.) Patently, to advertise a lecture is also to advertise its auspices; to obtain coverage of the lecture by the press has the same consequence. (Campus newspapers are interesting in this connection. They are ostensibly designed as independent, if not dissident, expressions of inmate opinion. But they appreciably function as vanity presses for administrations, providing coverage for what might otherwise, mercifully, go unrecorded.)

Here there is an obvious link between formal organizations and the "star system." Sponsoring organizations frequently judge themselves dependent on some degree of public support and approval, some recognition of their presence and their mission, even though their financial resources may have a more circumscribed base. A principal way of bringing the name of the sponsorship before the public is to advertise some commemorative event and to obtain press coverage of it. To make such an event significant to a wide public, it is apparently helpful to schedule one or more well-known names—personages—to make an appearance. This helps give members of the public who are far afield warrant for the journey in to witness the occasion. In a sense, then, an institution's advertising isn't done in response to the anticipated presence of a well-known figure; rather, a well-known figure is useful in order to have something present that warrants wide advertising. So one might also say that large halls aren't built to accommodate large audiences but rather to accommodate wide advertising. Of course, a speaker's prestige is relevant in another way: he lends his weight to the sponsoring organization and to its social occasions, on the assumption, apparently, that worthies only affiliate with what is worthy. For thus lending his name, the speaker receives publicity and an honorarium—rewards apart from a warm reception for his words and the opportunity to spread them. In all of this we see a glimmering of the links between social affairs and social structures, a glimpse of the politics of ceremony—and another way in which preeminence derives less from differential achievement than from the organizational needs of sponsors and their occasions.

There can be, then, between auspices and speaker a tacit, some would say unholy, alliance. And this alliance may be sustained at the expense of the lecture itself—the lecture as a means of transmitting knowledge. The speaker is encouraged to pitch his remarks down to fit the competence of a large audience—an audience large enough to warrant the celebration and cost that is involved. He is encouraged to fit his remarks into the stretch of time that such an audience might be ready to forebear, and to employ mannerisms which ensure audience involvement. And he is encouraged to accept all manner of rampant intrusion from interviewers, photographers, recording specialists, and the like—intrusions that often take place right in the middle of the heat of the occasion. (If at any moment you should get the notion that a speaker really is fully caught up in talking to you, take note of his capacity to treat photographers as though they weren't interrupting his talk. Such apparent obliviousness can, of course, come from his involvement with you, as opposed to his commitment to publicity, but don't count on it.)

Finally it should be said that although a lecture can be the main business of the social occasion in which it is embedded—an arrangement that speakers presumably find ideal—other settings are common. In the United States, for example, there is the institution of the lunch speaker, and the understanding that a membership's regular get-togethers for a meal cannot be complete without a guest speaker; who, or on what topic, need not be a first consideration—anyone in the neighborhood who does talks for a fee will often do. (In many cases, of course, we might find it more natural to speak of such luncheon performances as giving a talk, not a lecture, the critical difference somehow involving the matter of systematic topic development.) And just as an occasion can make a convenience of a speaker, so a speaker can make a convenience of an occasion, as when a political figure graces a local gathering but his main concern is the transmission of his talk to media audiences.

III

What I have said so far about lectures is obvious and requires no special perspective; we move now to more intimate matters.

In our society we recognize three main modes of animating spoken words: *memorization, aloud reading* (such as I had been doing up to now), and *fresh talk.* In the case of fresh talk, the text is formulated by the animator from moment to moment, or at least from clause to clause. This conveys the impression that the formulation is responsive to the current situation in which the words are delivered, including the current content of the auditorium and of the speaker's head, and including, but not merely, what could have been envisaged and anticipated. Memorization is sometimes employed in lectures, but not admittedly. (Theatrical parts present a more complicated picture: they are delivered as though in fresh talk, and although everyone knows they are thoroughly memorized, this knowledge is to be held in abeyance, and fresh talk is to be made-believe.) In lectures, aloud reading is a frequent mode of delivery. Fresh talk is perhaps the general ideal and (with the assistance of notes) quite common.

Memorization, aloud reading, and fresh talk are different production modes. Each presupposes its own special relation between speaker and listener, establishing the speaker on a characteristic "footing" in regard to the audience. Switches from one of the three forms to another, that is, "production shifts," imply for the speaker a change of footing, and, as will be seen, are a crucial part of lecturing. The critical point that will later be addressed is that a great number of lectures (because of my incompetence, not including this one) depend upon a fresh-talk illusion. Radio announcing, I might add, is even more deeply involved in maintaining this precarious effect.

It might be noted that fresh talk itself is something of an illusion of itself, never being as fresh as it seems. Apparently we construct our utterances out of phrase- and clause-length segments, each of which is in some sense formulated mentally and then recited. Whilst delivering one such segment one must be on the way to formulating the next mentally, and the segments must be patched together without exceeding acceptable limits for pauses, restarts, repetitions, redirections, and other linguistically detectable faults. Lecturers mark a natural turning point in the acquisition of fresh-talk competence when they feel they can come close to finishing a segment without knowing yet what in the world the next will be, and yet be confident of being able to come up with (and on time) something that is grammatically and thematically acceptable, and all this without making it evident that a production crisis has been going on. And they mark a natural turning point in fresh talking *or* aloud reading a lecture when they realize they can give thought to how they seem to be doing, where they stand in terms of finishing too soon or too late, and what they plan to do after the talk—without these backstage considerations becoming evident as their concern; for should such preoccupation become evident, the illusion that they are properly involved in communicating will be threatened.

Earlier I recommended that a lecture contains a text that could just as well be imparted through print or informal talk. This being the case, the content of a lecture is not to be understood as something distinctive to and characteristic of lecturing. At best one is left with the special contingencies of delivering any particular text through the lecture medium. At best the interface, the bonding between text and situation of delivery. One is left with the form, the interactional encasement; the box, not the cake. And I believe there is no way to get at these interactional issues without directing full and sustained attention to the question of the speaker's handling of himself—a question that is easy to write about circumspectly but hard to lecture on without abusing one's podium position. I have a right to obtain and direct your attention to some relevant topic, including myself if I can manage to work that particular object into some topical event or opinion. I have the right, indeed the obligation, to back up this communicative process (whether what is said includes me as a protagonist or not) with all due manner of gesticulatory accompaniment and seemly jumping up and down. However, if, because of what I say, you focus your attention on this supportive animation; if, because of what I refer to, you attend the process through which I make references, then something is jeopardized that is structurally crucial in speech events: the partition between the inside and outside of words, between the realm of being sustained through the meaning of a discourse and the mechanics of discoursing. This partition, this membrane, this boundary, is the tickler; what happens to it largely determines the pleasure and displeasure that will be had in the occasion.

I V

Now consider footing and its changes. Differently put, consider the multiple senses in which the self of the speaker can appear, that is, the multiple self-implicatory projections discoverable in what is said and done at the podium.

At the apparent center will be the textual self, that is, the sense of the person that seems to stand behind the textual statements made and which incidentally gives these statements authority. Typically this is a self of relatively long standing, one the speaker was involved in long before the current occasion of talk. This is the self that others will cite as the author of various publications, recognize as the holder of various positions, and so forth. As often the case in these matters, the speaker may use the term "I" or even "we" to refer to the capacity that is involved and the alignment to the audience that this particular self subtends, but this pronominal explicitness need not occur. Allied with this scholarly voice will sometimes be found a relevant historical-experiential one, the one that figures in a replay the speaker may provide of a strip of personal experience from his or her own past during which something of textual relevance occurred. (The lecture that a returning war correspondent or diplomat gives will be full of this sort of thing, as will lectures by elder academicians when they recount their personal dealings with historic personages of their field.) Observe, this textual self, presupposed by and projected through the transmission of either scholarship or historically relevant personal experience, can be displayed entirely through the printable aspects of words; it can appear in full form in a printed version of the lecture's text, an emanation from the text itself and not, say, from the way in which its oral delivery is managed on any occasion. Characteristically, it is this self that can still be projected even though the writer falls sick and a stand-in must deliver his address.

In truth, however, the interesting and analytically relevant point about the lecture as a performance is not the textual stance that is projected in the course of the lecture's delivery, but the additional footings that can be managed at the same time, footings whose whole point is the contrast they provide to what the text itself might otherwise generate. I speak of distance-altering alignments, some quite briefly taken, which appear as a running counterpoint to the text, and of elaborative comments and gestures which do not appear in the substance of the text but in the mechanics of transmitting it on a particular occasion and in a particular setting.

First, there are overlayed "keyings." The published text of a serious paper can contain passages that are not intended to be interpreted "straight," but rather understood as sarcasm, irony, "words from another's mouth," and the like. However, this sort of self-removal from the literal content of what one says seems much more common in spoken papers, for there vocal cues can be employed to ensure that the boundaries and the character of the quotatively intended strip are marked off from the normally intended stream. (Which is not to say that as of now these para-linguistic markers can be satisfactorily identified, let alone tran-scribed.) Thus, a competent lecturer will be able to read a remark with a twinkle in his voice, or stand off from an utterance by slightly raising his vocal eyebrows. Contrariwise, when he enters a particular passage he can collapse the distance he had been maintaining, and allow his voice to resonate with feeling, convic-tion, and even passion. In sensing that these vocally tinted lines could not be delivered this way in print, hearers sense they have preferential access to the mind of the author, that live listening provides the kind of contact that reading doesn't.

Second, consider text brackets. You will note that papers destined to be printed, not spoken, are likely to have some sort of introduction and closing. These bracketing phases will be pre-sented in a slightly different voice from the one employed in the body of the text itself. But nothing elaborate by way of a shift in footing is likely—although such change *is* likely, I might add, in full-length books. In the case of *spoken* papers, however, text brackets are likely to involve some fancy footwork. The intro-duction, as is said, will attempt to put into perspective what is about to be discussed. The speaker lets us know what else he might have chosen to talk about but hasn't, and what reserva-tions he places on what he is about to say, so that should we judge what follows as weak, limited, speculative, presumptuous, lugu-brious, pedantic, or whatever, we can see that the speaker (he hopes) is not to be totally identified thereby; and in addition to the vaunted self implied in addressing a group at considerable length on a sober topic, he is to be seen as having an ordinary side —modest, unassuming, down-to-earth, ready to forego the pomp of presentation, appreciative that, after all, the textual self that is about to emerge is not the only one he wants to be known by, at least so far as the present company is concerned.

Closing comments have a similar flavor, this time bringing speaker back down from his horse, allowing him to fall back from his textual self into one that is intimately responsive to the cur-rent situation, concerned to show that the tack taken in the lec-ture is only one of the tacks he could have taken, and generally bringing him back to the audience as merely another member of it, a person just like ourselves. Comparatively speaking, a conclusion is part way between the curtain call through which a stage actor finally appears outside of the character he has been portraying, and the coda (to use Labov's term) by which a storyteller throws up a bridge between the situation he was in as protagonist in the narrative, and his current situation as someone who stands before his listeners. As part of this down-gearing, the speaker may, of course, shift into the intimacies and informalities of question and answer, through which some members of the audience are allowed to come into direct conversational contact with him, symbolizing that in effect he and all members of the audience are now on changed terms. Responding to questions, after all, requires fresh talk. In other words, question answering requires a production shift from aloud reading to fresh talk, with the speaker often marking the shift by means of bracket rituals, such as lighting a cigarette, changing from a standing to a sitting position, drinking a glass of water, and so forth. As suggested, introductions and closings, that is, bracket expressions, occur at the interface between spectacle and game, in this case, occasion and lecture proper. Question period apart, prefatory and closing comments are likely to be delivered in fresh talk or a more serious simulation of this than the body of the lecture itself provides. And these comments are likely to contain direct reference to what is true only of this current social occasion and its current audience. Observe, when several speakers share the same platform, mini versions of opening and closing brackets can occur *during* a presentation, sometimes with the reengagement of a presiding figure, all this marking the transfer of the speaking role from one person to another.

So there are text brackets. Third, there are text-parenthetical remarks. Again, if one starts from a *printed* text—one meant to be read, not heard—one will find that the author exercises the right to introduce parenthetical statements, qualifying, elaborating, digressing, apologizing, hedging, editorializing, and the like. These passing changes in voice, these momentary changes in footing, may be marked in print through bracketings of some kind—parenthetical signs, dashes, etc. Or the heavy-handed device of footnotes may be employed. (So fully are footnotes institutionalized for this change in voice that someone other than the writer, namely, the editor or translator, can use footnotes, too, to comment on the text in what is patently a voice totally different from the textual one.) Through all of these devices, the writer briefly changes footing relative to his text as a whole, coming to the reader in consequence from a slightly different angle. Observe, these elaborations ordinarily extend the "production base" for the reader, giving him more of a grounding in the writer's circumstances and opinions than the naked text might allow.

Turning from a printed text to a spoken one, aptly printable parenthetical remarks remain, but now much amplified by ones that are unlikely to appear in a printed version of the talk. (Admittedly advertisers sometimes employ the device of adding in the margins of a printed text remarks in print-script that are presumably to be taken as sprightly afterthoughts, and thus providing a keying of a communication not destined for print in the first place, a communication destined to be labored and cute.) In brief, during his talk, the speaker will almost inevitably interject remarks in passing to qualify, amplify, and editorialize on what the text itself carries, extending the parenthetical comments which would appear in a printed version. Although these remarks may be perfectly scholarly and contributed in a serious vein, they nonetheless introduce a somewhat changed alignment of speaker to hearer, a change in footing that in turn implies a facet of self different from the one theretofore projected. What results can only be partly captured through the nearest equivalents available in print, namely, parenthetical sentences and footnotes.

Text parenthetical remarks are of great interactional interest. On one hand, they are oriented to the text; on the other, they intimately fit the mood of the occasion and the special interest and identity of the particular audience. (Observe, unlike lectures, conversations appear to be scripted a phrase or clause at a time, allowing the speaker to build sensitivity to the immediately current circumstances through the very words selected to realize the main text itself.) Text-parenthetical remarks convey qualifying thoughts that the speaker appears to have arrived at just at the very moment. It is as if the speaker here functioned as a broker of his own statements, a mediator between text and audience, a resource capable of picking up on the nonverbally conveyed concerns of the listeners and responding to them in the light of the text and everything else known and experienced by the speaker.

More so even than bracketing comments, text-parenthetical ones had best be delivered in fresh talk, for by what other means could the speaker expect to respond to the trajectory of the *current* situation? Note that although only politicians and other desperadoes of the podium simulate fresh-talk replies to questions that they themselves have planted in the audience, a great number of speakers simulate fresh talk in conveying text-parenthetical remarks. The speaker will have reviewed some of these remarks beforehand and may even have inscribed them in his reading copy in note form as a reminder of the footing to be employed in delivering them. In all of this, observe, lectures are like stories or jokes: a teller can (and is encouraged to) throw himself into his telling as if this telling were occurring for the first and only time. The only constraint is that no one in the audience should have already heard his performance. And, in fact, every communication fosters a little of this "first and only" illusion.

There is an irony here. There are moments in a lecture when the speaker seems most alive to the ambience of the occasion and is particularly ready with wit and extemporaneous response to show how fully he has mobilized his spirit and mind for the moment at hand. Yet these inspired moments will often be ones to most suspect. For during them the speaker is quite likely to be delivering something he memorized some time ago, having happened upon an utterance that fits so well that he cannot resist reusing it in that particular slot whenever he gives the talk in question. Or take as a heavy-handed example the parenthetically interjected anecdote. It is told in a manner to imply that its telling was not planned, but that the story has now become so apropos that the speaker can't forebear recounting it even at the cost of a minor digression. At this moment of obvious relevance it is rarely appreciated that anecdotes are specialized for aptness. As with pat comebacks, standard excuses, and other universal joints of discourse, relevance is to be found not so much in the situation as in the intrinsic organization of the anecdote itself. The little narratives we allow ourselves to interject in a current talk we are likely to have interjected in other talks, too, let alone other presentations of the current one.

May I digress for a moment? Parenthetical elaboration is found in all communication, albeit with differing roles across differing forms. During conversation, a raconteur, lodged in the telling of a story, is likely to kibitz his own telling, breaking narrative frame throughout to interject initially overlooked detail, or provide background whose relevance is only now evident, or warn hearers that a climactic event is imminent. Between songs, pop singers in recital commonly switch into direct address, providing out-of-frame comments as a bridge between offerings, presenting themselves in their "own" name instead of characters in sung dramas. Indeed, they are sometimes so concerned about the figure that they cut while not singing that they develop a stand-up comic's routine in order to linger on the bridges. Giving readings of one's own poetry provides a different sort of case. As with singing, parenthetical transitions from one unit to the next are more or less required by virtue of the segmented character of the offering, but poets must allow themselves less room for what they project during these transitions. Poetry is itself an exploration of the elaborations and asides that the poet can manage in regard to some stated theme; compressed in the text itself there should be allusions to most of what a live commentator might parenthetically elect to say, and preferably this should be rendered to sound spontaneous. To cut a figure talking about a poem is to have failed to cut that figure in the poem.

To return. Bracketing and parenthetical remarks, along with keyings imposed on the ongoing text, seem to bear more than the text does on the situation *in* which the lecture is given, as opposed to the situation *about* which the lecture is given. These remarks can, incidentally, also draw on the biography of experience of the speaker-author in a way that depends upon *this* particular speaker being present, not just *a* particular speaker. And here, of course, is the reason why the printed version of a spoken text is unlikely to contain the introductory and textual asides that enlivened the spoken presentation; what is engagingly relevant for a physically present audience is not likely to be so snugly suitable for a readership. It is not so much that an immediately present audience and a readership are differently circumstanced —although they are—but that a speaker can directly perceive the circumstances of his recipients and a writer cannot. Topical and local matters that a speaker can cite and otherwise respond to are precisely what cannot be addressed in print. And, of course, it is just through such response that the social occasion can be made palpable.

Consider now some words speakers use to describe audiences, words which also happen to be much like those employed by any other type of platform performer. An audience sensed by the speaker to be "unresponsive," an audience that does not pick up on the talker's little gems and doesn't back-channel a chuckle or offer some other sign of appreciation, will tend to freeze him to his script. An audience that is "good" or "warm," that is, one that is audibly quick on the uptake, showing a ready, approving responsiveness, a willingness to take his innuendoes and sarcasms as he intended them to be taken, is likely to induce the speaker to extend each response-evoking phrase or phrasing: he will continue along for a moment extemporaneously where gestured feedback from the audience suggests he has touched home —a playing-by-ear that Albert Lord tells us singers of epic poetry also manage. (If an audience is to be warm, it may have to be "warmed up," a process that is consciously engineered in variety programs, but ordinarily given little thought in lecturing.) Again, note, fresh-talk elaborations that are themselves a response to audience response can little find a place in the printed version of the talk; for where could the writer find the response to trigger these remarks?

One can become aware of the situational work of overlayed keyings, text bracketing, and parenthetical utterances by examining the disphoric effects which result when circumstances require someone other than its author to read the author's talk. Such pinch-hitting can be studded with as many "I's" and other self-references as a normally delivered talk. It can even follow the text in employing a style that is for speaking, not reading. And yet what it can't do is provide the usual kind of keying, bracketing, and parenthetical elaboration. A nonauthorial speaker, that is, someone filling in, can preface his reading with an account of why he is doing it, avow at the beginning that the "I" of the text is obviously not himself (but that he will use it anyway), and even during the reading, break frame and parenthetically add a comment of his own, as does an editor of printed text in an editor's footnote. But to speak a passage with irony or passion would be confusing. Whose irony? Whose passion? To employ parenthetical expressions introduces the same dilemma; for fresh-talk asides can here only encode the thoughts of a second author. And the stand-in who stands off from a particular passage must appreciate that he will be seen as having too easy a shot. In any case, all of these changes in footing cut too deep; they project the self of the animator all right, but this time not the author of the text, thereby widening a split that is just the one that successful lecturing heals. Such an arrangement, then, strikes at the ritual elements of the presentation. (Understandably this tack is principally found in professional meetings where a session may provide reports on the work of three to five authors who are not eminent, so that the failure of one or two to appear in person does not much reduce the ritual density of the occasion.)

Three places for alternate footings have been mentioned: keyed passages, text brackets, and parenthetical remarks. Finally consider—at the cost of a lengthy digression—a fourth location, this one connected with the management of performance contingencies.

Every transmission of signals through a channel is necessarily subject to "noise," namely, transmissions that aren't part of the intended signal and reduce its clarity. In telephonic communication, this interference will involve sound; in TV, by easy extension of the term, sound and sight. (I suppose those who read braille can also suffer noise by touch.)

To those who watch TV it is abundantly clear that a disturbance to reception can come from radically different sources: from the studio's transmission; from malfunction in one's own set; from neighborhood electronic effects, such as spark-coil transmissions; and so on. There are, of course, quite practical reasons why source discrimination should be made; indeed, when a station is at fault it may employ a special visual or sound signal to so inform audiences. Now look at the telephone. In ordinary telephonic communication, the fit of the earpiece to the ear is such that a concern for noise at that interface in the system is unnecessary; at worst, one need only cover the other ear. With TV (and speaker phones) it becomes evident that considerable noise can enter the communication system between the point of signal output and the receiver, as when one tries to listen to a car radio over the noise of an uninsulated engine, or tries to tape radio programs "on air." It is also evident that speaker and hearer can fail to effectively communicate over the phone for physical reasons internal to either, as when the one has laryngitis or the other is hard of hearing. By extending the term "noise," all such constraints on transmission can also be included for consideration.

I elaborate these obvious points to warrant the following formulation: that when communication occurs, noise will also; that a communication system can be seen as a layered composite structure—electronic, physical, biological, and so forth; and that effective communication is vulnerable to noise sources from different layerings in the structure of the system that sustains it.

The next point to note is that the recipients in every communication system develop tolerance for a range of noise, in the sense that they can disattend such sound with little distraction. Recipients doing so, senders can afford to follow their lead. In addition, both recipients and senders deal with some noise by affecting unconcern, treating it as if it were not present even though they are distracted by it. Further, whether a particular source of noise is distracting or not, participants in the communication system can elect to engage in physical actions calculated to improve reception.

To complete the picture it need only be said that senders have another course of action open to them. Whether or not they make a physical effort to improve transmission, they can directly mention the disturbance and their remedial action (if any), employing parenthetical remarks to do so. These remarks necessarily break frame, for instead of transmitting the anticipated text, the sender transmits comments about the transmission. Senders have various motives for such actions. They may not wish the disruption to stand without introducing an account or apology for what has happened to communication, the hope presumably being that they then won't be judged by these failures. Or they may feel that to maintain the appearances of disattendance is itself too distracting for everyone concerned, and that open reference to the difficulty will release hearers from having to fake unconcern. Or they may feel compelled to forestall other interpretations of the disturbance.

Return now to the particular communication system under

consideration—the lecture. It is apparent that the noise associated with lecturing can involve sound or sight, and that its source may be variably located, say in the outside environment surrounding the auditorium, or the interior shell itself, or the audience, or the podium. This latter location is particularly important because noise coming from the podium area will be much more difficult to ignore than noise coming from places where the audience is not obliged to pinpoint its attention.

As a source of potential noise, the podium itself is a many-layered thing. One source we owe to the fact that lecturers come equipped with bodies, and bodies can easily introduce visual and audio effects unconnected with the speech stream, and these may be distracting. A speaker must breathe, fidget a little, scratch occasionally, and may feel cause to cough, brush back his hair, straighten her skirt, sniffle, take a drink of water, finger her pearls, clean his glasses, burp, shift from one foot to another, sway, manneristically button and unbutton a jacket, turn the pages and square them off, and so forth—not to mention tripping over the carpet or appearing not to be entirely zipped up. Observe that these bodily faults can equally plague full-fledged entertainers such as singers, mentalists, and comedians.

Another structural source of noise can be located even closer to the source of transmission: those minor peculiarities of human sound equipment that affect speech production across the board —for example, lisps, harelips, laryngitis, affected speech, "thick accent," a stiff neck, denture whistles, and so forth. One can think here of equipment faults, the human, not the electronic kind. These faults are to be compared to what an improperly tuned instrument brings to a recital, what a wall-eyed person brings to two-person conversation, what misalignment of type brings to the communication occurring on the printed page, what bad lighting brings to the showing of slides, and, of course, to what a malfunctioning microphone brings to any podium.

Human sound-equipment faults as a class have not been much studied systematically, but a closely related source of trouble has: encoding faults bearing differentially on elements of the speech flow itself. Speaking inevitably contains what can be linguistically defined as faults: pauses (filled and otherwise), restarts, redirections, repetitions, mispronunciations, unintended double meanings, word searches, lost lines, and so forth. What will obtrude as a fault varies markedly according to which of the speech forms is involved—fresh, memorized, or read.

During lectures, some equipment and encoding faults are inevitable; they imply that a living body is behind the communication and, correspondingly, a self in terms of which the speaker is present and active, although not relevantly so. A place is made for this self. It is okay to self-correct a word one has begun to mispronounce. It is okay to clear one's throat or even take a drink of water, providing that these side-involvements are performed in speech-segment junctures—except, uniquely, this one, this being the only juncture when so minor a deflection would not be that, but some overcute theatricality, of merit only as a frame-analytical illustration of how to go wrong in performances. In sum, such attention as these various maneuvers get either from speaker or hearer is meant to be dissociated from the main concern. The proper place of this self is a very limited one.

You will note that what is here defined as equipment and encoding noise is meant to be disattended and usually is. Occasionally, however, disturbances from these sources do occur, both visual and aural, which the audience cannot easily ignore, the less so for obligatorily trying to do so. More to the point, there will be noise that the speaker correctly or incorrectly *feels* the audience cannot easily disattend, or shouldn't be allowed to. (This latter occurs, for example, when the speaker misstates a fact that would get by were he not to correct matters.) In response, the speaker may be inclined to briefly introduce accounts, excuses, and apologies. These remedial remarks will have an obvious parenthetical character, something split off from the mainstream of official textual communication yet comprehended nonetheless. One has, then, not merely a disattended stream of events, but sometimes a dissociated stream of verbal communication, too. And this stream of communication, just like the equipment and encoding faults to which it is a response, implies a self, one indeed that has claims upon the audience even if this means minor overridings of other selves that are being projected at the time. After all, an animator not only has a right to cough, but under certain circumstances, to extend the interruption by excusing himself. Indeed, someone serving as a substitute reader (or a language translator) can make precisely the same sort of mistakes, and project the same self in the process of apologizing for them.

Plainly, then, speakers are necessarily in a structural position to betray their obligation to transmit their texts; they can choose instead to intrude comments on the contingencies of transmitting it. Observe that comments on such difficulties, as well as remedial remarks consequent on failing to avoid them, are likely to entail use of the pronouns "I" and "me," but one must be very careful to see that now these terms refer to an individual in his capacity as animator, not the individual in his capacity as author of a prepared text. The fact that the same pronouns are employed, and that indeed they ordinarily refer to the same person makes it very easy to neglect critical differences. When a speaker says, "Excuse me" or, "Let me try that once more" or, "There, I think that will stop the feedback," the author of these remarks is an individual in his capacity as animator, and not an individual in his text-authorial capacity. The person hasn't changed, but his footing certainly has, no less than would be the case were a substitute reader to make a mistake and apologize for it.

I have suggested that when a speaker senses that equipment or encoding troubles have occurred, he may intrude a comment about the difficulty and about any effort to physically correct matters he may undertake. The minor change in footing that ensues as the speaker ceases to transmit his text and instead transmits open reference to his plight as an animator will often be quite acceptable, characteristically attended in a dissociated way. But there are format-specific limits. It is a structurally significant fact of friendly conversations that they are set up to allow for a vast amount of this reflexive frame breaking, and, contrariwise, a crucial condition of prime-time broadcasting to allow for extremely little. Lecturing falls somewhere between. Interestingly, speakers can be optimistic here. Sensing that time is running short, a speaker may change voice and let the hearers in on the fact that the pages he is now turning over are ones he has now decided to summarize in fresh talk or even skip, projecting the rather touching plea that he be given credit for what he *could* have imparted. Finding a page out of order in the script, he may hunt for the right one while candidly describing that this is what he is doing. Reaching for the book he planned to quote from, he may assay a little quip, confiding that he hopes he brought the right one. I believe that once the show has seriously begun, these efforts to frankly project oneself exclusively in one's capacity as an animator are not likely to come off—at least not as frequently as speakers believe. Nonetheless the liberty is often taken.

v

We can now try to put the pieces together. As suggested, from one perspective a lecture is a means through which an author can impart a text to recipients and (from this point of view) is very much like what occurs when any other method of imparting is employed, such as conversational talk or the printed page. The relevant differences among the available methods would presumably have to do with cost, distribution, and the like, that is, constraints on access to the message. But if this imparting were the main point about lecturing, we might only have the university course kind, and even there the matter is in doubt; other means of transmission would probably displace it. Audiences in fact attend because a lecture is more than text transmission; indeed, as suggested, they may feel that listening to text transmission is the price they have to pay for listening to the transmitter. They attend—in part—because of something that is infused into the speaking on the occasion of the text's transmission, an infusion that ties the text into the occasion. Plainly, noise here is a very limited notion. For what is noise from the perspective of the text as such can be the music of the interaction—the very source of the auditors' satisfaction in the occasion, the very difference between reading a lecture at home and attending one. Let me review two aspects of this attendance.

First, there is the issue of access. In any printed work, the writer exposes himself in various ways. Through writing style, biographical detail, intellectual assumptions, mode of publication, and so forth, information about the writer becomes available to readers. Indeed, a book is likely to contain a brief biographical sketch of the author and even a picture on the dust jacket. What readers here learn about the author, they can cross-reference to what, if anything, they had already known

186

about him. Thus, in making himself accessible, and in facilitating their familiarity with him, the writer encourages readers to form something like a one-way social relationship to him.

In the case of live lecturing, all these sources of accessibility (or their equivalent) are present, plus a large number of others. This is especially clear when a speaker is known to his audience through his writings or other activities. Whatever view they may have had of him, this view will be modified when they can see him in the flesh and watch and listen to him handle the transmission of his text over the course of its delivery. Furthermore, however candid and revealing a speaker's written text may be, he can easily render its spoken delivery much more so (or less not so); for vocal keyings and parenthetical admissions not in the text can be added throughout. And all of this opening up and exposing of the self will mean accessibility *only* to the members of the listening audience, a much more exclusive claim than ordinarily can be made by a readership.

To the degree that the speaker is a significant figure in some relevant world or other, to that degree this access has a ritual character, in the Durkheimian, not ethological, sense of affording supplicants preferential contact with an entity held to be of value. May I add that in thus gaining access to an authority, the audience also gains ritual access to the subject matter over which the speaker has command. (Substantive access is quite another matter.) And indeed, this sort of access is the basis of the talk-circuit business. Individuals who come to the attention of the media public because of their association with something in the news can make themselves available in person through a lecture tour. Here authority is not a prerequisite, or the thoughtful development of an academic topic, only association. The subject matter of these talks is exactly and as fully diverse as are the fleeting directions of public attention, the various speakers sharing only the agents and bureaus that arrange their appearances. It is thus that a very heterogeneous band of the famed and ill-famed serve to vivify what is or has recently been noteworthy, each celebrity touching audiences with what he or she has been touched by, each selling association.

So there is the issue of access. (I have mercifully omitted consideration of its final form, the little sociable gathering held by the sponsors for select members of the audience after the talk to "meet" the speaker.) Second, there is the matter of celebrative occasion. The difference between the text as such and the verbal delivery of the text not only supports a sense of preferential access to the speaker, but also gives weight to the uniqueness, the here and now, once only character of the occasion in which the delivery takes place. In thus committing himself to the particular occasion at hand, in thus mobilizing his resources to pay it mind, the speaker is conferring himself on those who are participants.

It might now be worth reviewing and detailing how a printed text that is available to any competent reader can be transformed into a talk that is responsive to the local situation in which it is delivered. Consider, then, some "contextualizing" devices.

First, there is the tacit assumption, an assumption carefully preserved, that what the audience hears was formulated just for them and for this current occasion. A crude token here is the topical reference through which the speaker shows that at least one of his sentences belongs entirely to the particular setting in which the current delivery is taking place. (This is a device of traveling performers which probably antedates even Bob Hope's camp visits.) Introductions, it turns out, are especially likely to be seeded with these topicality tokens.

But there are less obvious devices for producing the effect of responsiveness. When a lecture is given in fresh talk or a simulation of fresh talk, then responsiveness to the current scene seems apparent. And so another kind of tokenism becomes possible. As suggested, bracketing comments and parenthetical remarks delivered in fresh talk can be used to give a coloration of freshness to the whole script. (Where these remarks are not actually in fresh talk, fresh talk can easily be simulated out of memorized bits, simply because only short strips are necessary.)

Another simulation method, standard in aloud reading, is to scan a small chunk and then address the audience with one's eyes while reciting what has just been scanned.

Then there is the effect of "hypersmooth" delivery. As suggested, conversational talk is full of minor hitches—hesitations, repetitions, restarts—that are rarely oriented to as such by speaker or hearers; these little disruptions are simply passed by. On the other hand, it is just such minor hitches that are noticeable when they occur in aloud reading, crudely reminding us that it is aloud reading that is going on. Paradoxically, then, by managing to read aloud without these routine blemishes, we can give the impression that something more than merely aloud reading is occurring, something closer to fresh talk. (Hyperfluency, I might add, is crucial in the illusion of fresh talk that broadcasters achieve.)

Finally, consider the effect of "high style," even if issuing from a patently read address. Elegance of language—turns of phrase, metaphor, parallel structures, aphoristic formulations—can be taken as evidence not only of the speaker's intelligence (which presumably is worth gaining access to), but also of his giving his mind and ability over to the job he is now performing. Indeed, one could argue that "expressive" writing is precisely that which allows a consumer of the text to feel that its producer has lent himself fully to this particular occasion of communication.

Underlying all these devices for localizing or indexicalizing a text is the style or register of spoken discourse itself. What makes for "good" writing is systematically different from what makes for "good" speaking, and the degree to which the lecturer uses the normative spoken form marks the degree to which it will appear he has delivered himself to a speaking event. Some of the differences between written prose and spoken prose are these:

1. In general, writers can use editors' instructions, style sheets of journals, and college writing manuals as a guide for what will and won't be ambiguous, as though the reader, as well as the writer, had an obligation to apply these standards. Readers accept the responsibility of rereading a passage to catch its sense, and seem to be ready to tolerate the difficult more than the "grammatically incorrect." And, of course, readers can reread a passage, whereas hearers can't rehear an utterance—except from a tape. Also, spelling helps to disambiguate what in speech would be homonymous. The reader is further helped by punctuation marks having fixed sets of meanings; most of these marks, observe, have only very rough, ambiguous equivalents in sound. In consequence, a sentence whose head is far away from its feet is much easier to use effectively in print than in speech. In brief, for talk, clauses may have to be changed into sentences. But in compensation, contraction and deletion are favored, as are "left displacement" forms and deictic terms.

2. Print conventions for laying out a text provide for coherence in ways unavailable to oral delivery. Talk has no obvious paragraph markers or section headings. In printed texts, footnotes allow a sharp break in thematic development and can thus accommodate acknowledgments, scholarly elaboration, and parallelisms. (For example, it would be hard for me here, in the speaking that I am doing, to bring in the fact that spoken prose in turn differs very considerably from what occurs in natural conversation, and to cite the source, David Abercrombie's "Studies in Phonetics and Linguistics," but this would be easy and apt as a footnote in the printed form.)

3. Ordinarily, liberties that can be taken with an audience can't be taken with a readership. A speaker correctly senses that there are colloquialisms, irreverences, and the like he can use with his current audience that he would censor in a printed text. In talk, he is likely to feel that he can exaggerate, be dogmatic, say things that obviously aren't quite fully true, and omit documentation. He can employ figures of speech he might feel uncomfortable about in print. For he can rely on people he can see getting the spirit of his remarks, not merely the literal words that carry them. He can also use sarcasm, *sotto voce* asides, and other crude devices which cast him and his audience in some sort of collusion against absent figures, sometimes with the effect of "getting a laugh" (and he can further milk the audience when he gets one) —something that print cannot quite get from a reader. And a speaker can interrupt his own sentence almost anywhere, and with the help of an audible change in voice, interject something that is flagrantly irrelevant.

I need only add that in preparing a text for oral delivery, an author can make an effort to write in spoken prose; indeed he had better. Speakers do sometimes read a chapter from a book or a paper that is ready to be sent to the printer, but they don't keep audiences awake when doing so—at least in contemporary platform performances. Your effective speaker is someone who has written his reading text in the spoken register; he has tied himself in advance to his upcoming audience with a typewriter ribbon.

To write a text in spoken prose and to read it "expertly" is, then, to foster the feeling that something like fresh talk is occurring. But, of course, with illusion goes vulnerability. The prosodic shaping a fresh talker gives to a phrase, clause, or brief sentence is closely guided by his knowing the general drift, if not thematic development, of the argument to follow. So although he may botch a word, or lose one, he remains pointed in the right direction. The worst that can happen is that he can be stopped short momentarily for want of a usable word or because of having lost the point of his own current remark. In aloud reading, however, the speaker tends to commit himself to a particular syntactical interpretation (and therefore prosodic punctuation) of his current phrase by reference mainly to the immediately visible, upcoming line of his text. The sense that informs a fuller portion of his script—the sense that must inevitably emerge—does not much serve the speaker as a check upon what he is currently saying. A simple mistake in perceiving a word or a punctuation mark can therefore send the speaker off on a radically misconstrued aloud reading of his upcoming text. The eventual, and necessary, correction of that reading will expose the speaker as having all along faked the appearance of being in touch with the thoughts his utterances were conveying. As all of you know, this can be a little embarrassing.

VI

Now let me take another try at saying what it is that a speaker brings to the podium. Of course, there is his text. But whatever the intrinsic merit of the text, this would be available to readers of a printed version—as would the reputation of its author. What a lecturer brings to hearers in addition to all this is added access to himself and a commitment to the particular occasion at hand. He exposes himself to the audience. He addresses the occasion. In both ways he gives himself up to the situation. And this ritual work is done under cover of conveying his text. No one need feel that ritual has become an end in itself. As the manifest content of a dream allows a latent meaning to be tolerated, so the transmission of a text allows for the ritual of performance.

Through evident scholarship and fluent delivery the speaker -author demonstrates that such claims to authority as his office, reputation, and auspices imply are warranted. Thus a link is provided between institutional status, reputation, and the occasion at hand. Given warranted claims, parenthetical embroidery provides an example to the audience of how such authority can be worn lightly. The distance that status can exact is here relaxed; the respect that authority can demand is unobtrusively declined. Indeed, the speaker-author shows that although he has external claim to an elevated view of himself, and some currently demonstrated warrant for the claim, he chooses instead to be unimpressed by his own quality. He elects to present himself as just another member of the gathering that is present, someone no different from you or me. He thus provides not only vicarious access to himself but also a model of how to handle oneself in the matter of one's own claims to position (as well as how to cope with performance contingencies). In many ways, this modeling may be the most important thing a speaker does—aligning him, I might say, with TV personalities who provide the same sort of model, but for a wider public. (I only wish such authority existed in the field of face-to-face interaction, and that I had it to handle unassumingly. What I can treat modestly and offhandedly, alas, might not even merit that.)

So the person who delivers a talk can meld himself into the occasion by how, as a speaker, he extemporaneously (or apparently extemporaneously) embellishes his text, using his text as a basis for a situationally sensitive rendition, mingling the living and the read. And in consequence of the way he handles himself, he can render his subject matter something that his listeners feel they can handle. (Which is not to say that he need use anything more broad than donnish vocal qualifiers to gently remove himself from occasional passages.)

But a deeper understanding is to be drawn, an understanding that speaks to the ultimate claims that society makes upon a person who performs. What the audience will sense in an esteemed speaker as intelligence, wit, and charm, what the audience will impute to him as his own internally encompassed character —all this turns out to be generated through what he does to effectively put himself at the disposal of an occasion and hence its participants, opening himself up to it and to them, counting the rest of himself as something to be subordinated for the purpose. If, then, a speaker would encourage the imputation to himself of sterling attributes, he would be advised to display in the way he stands off from his topic and from its textual self that he has rendered both up to the audience. The animator invites the audience to take up this alignment to the text, too — an invitation carried in the intimate and comradely way in which he talks about his material. And lo and behold, this posture to his text is one that members of his audience find they can readily take up, for it gives credit to the world of the text, while showing that people like them are fully equal to the task of appreciation and are not themselves depreciated thereby. And surely this stance to the text is respectful enough, for the speaker himself has modeled it. He who delivers a talk, then, is obliged to be his own go-between, splitting off a self-as-animator who can speak with the voice of the audience although the audience itself is allowed only a rudimentary one. (Indeed, it turns out that the only thing some members of the audience may actually comprehend—let alone take an interest in—is this attitude that has been struck up on their behalf in regard to what is being delivered.) And, to repeat, it isn't merely that the speaker's side-comments are designed for the current context; the self that would utter such comments must be designed for the context, too.

It is here that we can begin to learn about a basic feature of all face-to-face interactions, namely, how the wider world of structures and positions is bled into these occasions. The pre-determined text (and its implied authorial self) that the speaker brings to a podium is somewhat like other external matters that present themselves to a local situation: the age, sex, and socio-economic status that a conversationalist brings to a sociable encounter; the academic and associational credentials that a professional brings to an interview with clients; the corporative organization that a deputy brings to the bargaining table. In all these cases, a translation problem exists. Externally grounded properties whose shape and form have nothing to do with face-to-face interaction must be identified and mapped with such ingredients as are available to and in local settings. The external must be melded to the internal, coupled in some way, if only to be systematically disattended. And just as diplomatic protocol is a transformation function for mapping official position into cele-brative occasions, and just as everyday civility is a formula for giving recognition to age, sex, and office in passing social contacts, so, in a deeper way, an author's speaking personality maps his text and his status into a speaking engagement. Observe, no one can better provide a situationally usable construing of the individual than that individual himself. For if liberties must be taken with him, or with what he is identified with, he alone can cause no offense in taking them. If the shoe is to pinch, it is the wearer himself who had best ease it on.

So the individual who has prepared a lecture trumps up an audience-usable self to do the speaking. He performs this self-construing at the podium. Indeed, he can model this self-management for interaction in general. Of course, as any platform performer might remind you, although he is obliged to put out in this way for his audience, he doesn't have to put out for any particular member of it—as he might in personal communication—although, admittedly, at the little reception held in his honor after the talk he will find it more difficult to avoid these person-to-person involvement penalties. And in exchange for this comic song and dance, this stage-limited performance of approachability, this illusion of personal access—in exchange for this, he gets honor, attention, applause, and a fee. For which I thank you.

But that, ladies and gentlemen, is not the end of it. Some there are who would press a final argument.

A text allows a speaker a cover for the rituals of performance. Fair enough. But his shenanigans could be said to produce a reward for him and for the audience that is greater than the ones so far described. For the performance leads the audience and the speaker to treat lecturing, and what is lectured about, as serious, real matters, not less so even when the talk is covertly designed hopefully to be amusing.

The lecturer and the audience join in affirming a single proposition. They join in affirming that organized talking can reflect, express, delineate, portray—if not come to grips with—the real world, and that, finally, there is a real, structured, somewhat unitary world out there to comprehend. (After all, that's what distinguishes lectures from stints at the podium openly designed as entertainments.) And here, surely, we have the lecturer's real contract. Whatever his substantive domain, whatever his school of thought, and whatever his inclination to piety or impiety, he signs the same agreement and he serves the same cause: to protect us from the wind, to stand up and seriously project the assumption that through lecturing, a meaningful picture of some part of the world can be conveyed, and that the talker can have access to a picture worth conveying.

It is in this sense that every lecturer, merely by presuming to lecture before an audience, is a functionary of the cognitive establishment, actively supporting the same position: I repeat, that there is structure to the world, that this structure can be perceived and reported, and therefore, that speaking before an audience and listening to a speaker are reasonable things to be doing, and incidentally, of course, that the auspices of the occasion had warrant for making the whole thing possible. Even when the speaker is tacitly claiming that only *his* academic discipline, *his* methodology, or *his* access to the data can produce a valid picture, the tacit claim behind this tacit claim is that valid pictures are possible.

No doubt some public speakers have broken from the fold, but these, of course, cease to have the opportunity to lecture— although presumably other kinds of podium work might become available to them. Those who remain to speak must claim some kind of intellectual authority in speaking; and however valid or invalid their claim to a specialized authority, their speaking presupposes and supports the notion of intellectual authority in general: that through the statements of a lecturer we can be informed about the world. Give some thought to the possibility that this shared presupposition is only that, and that after a speech, the speaker and the audience rightfully return to the flickering, cross-purposed, messy irresolution of their unknowable circumstances.

REFERENCES

Bauman, Richard. 1975. "Verbal art as performance." *American Anthropologist* 77(2):290–311.

Frake, Charles O. 1977. "Plying frames can be dangerous: Some reflections on methodology in cognitive anthropology." *Quarterly Newsletter of the Institute for Comparative Human Development* 1(3):1–15.

Hymes, Dell. 1975. "Breakthrough into performance." In *Folklore: Communication and performance,* edited by Dan Ben-Amos and Kenneth Goldstein, pp. 9–74. The Hague: Mouton.

5

RADIO TALK
A STUDY OF THE WAYS OF OUR ERRORS

In this paper I want to consider a form of talk that is the central work of a trade—radio announcing—and to consider this talk (and this trade) mainly from the perspective of what audiences can glean by merely listening closely. This allows me to try to bring sociolinguistic concerns to ethnographic ones, all in the name of microsociology.

For the student of talk, the broadcast kind has much to recommend it. It is everywhere available, particularly easy to record, and, because publicly transmitted words are involved, no prior permission for scholarly use seems necessary.[1] Further,

1. The study draws on the following sources: eight of the LP records and three of the books produced by Kermit Schafer from his recording (Jubilee Records) of radio bloopers (to which I am much indebted and for which I offer much thanks); twenty hours of taped programs from two local stations in Philadelphia and one in the San Francisco Bay area; a brief period of observation and interviewing of a classical DJ at work; and informal note-taking from broadcasts over a three-year period. I am grateful to Lee Ann Draud for taping and editing, and to John Carey for reediting the LP recordings. Gillian Sankoff, Anthony Kroch, and Jason Ditton provided critical suggestions, but not enough.

The Schafer sources will be cited as follows: *PB,* for *Pardon My Blooper* (Greenwich, Conn.: Fawcett Crest Books, 1959); *SB,* for *Super Bloopers* (Greenwich, Conn.: Fawcett Gold Medal Books, 1963); *Pr.,* for *Prize Bloopers* (Greenwich, Conn.: Fawcett Gold Medal Books, 1965). I have used the transcriptions presented in the three published books, but where possible have checked them against the LP recordings of the originals. Brackets are employed to mark off my version of Schafer's editorial leads when for brevity I supply only a summary of his own. In a few cases brackets are also used to mark my hearing of

there is no question of the subjects modifying their behavior because they know or suspect they are under study; for after all, announcers in any case are normally very careful to put their best foot forward. Their routine conduct on the air is already wary and self-conscious.

The key contingency in radio announcing (I take it) is to produce the effect of a spontaneous, fluent flow of words—if not a forceful, pleasing personality—under conditions that lay speakers would be unable to manage. What these circumstances are and how they are responded to provide the focus of this study. To properly site the arguments, however, I want to begin very far back in some traditional doctrines of sociology (as enumerated below), work by slow degree through linguistic concerns, and only then consider the problem at hand.

I

1. Once students of social life begin to understand the number of constraints and ends governing each of an individual's acts on every occasion and moment of execution, it becomes natural to shift from considering social practices to considering social competencies. In this way, presumably, appropriate respect can be paid for all the things an individual is managing to do, with or without awareness, on purpose or in effect, when he performs (in the sense of executes) an ordinary act.

A competency, then, can be defined as the capacity to routinely accomplish a given complicated end. An implication is that this end could not have been achieved were the actor unable to accomplish a whole set of slightly different ones, all in the same domain of expertise.

Given this perspective, one can take the traditional line that any occasion of an individual's effort has a double consequence: *substantive,* in terms of the contribution a competent performance would make to some extraneous system of ongoing

---

"tone of voice" in the recordings when no specification is provided in Schafer's printed transcriptions. No station, times, and dates are provided for transcriptions from my own corpus, although these identifications are available, and announcers' names have been changed.

activity, especially when this activity directly involves the interests of other actors; and *expressive,* in terms of the consequent judgment that failure or success produces concerning the individual's competency and his moral character as a claimant to competency.

Failure at competent execution of an act can initiate the workings of social control, the prospect of which is itself, of course, a means of social control. The failing person ordinarily initiates remedial action of some kind, and if not, others may well remind him to do so.

As might be expected from this formulation, remedial action itself takes two directions. First, there are substantive, restitutive acts of an instrumental sort, sometimes codified in civil law, involving repair, replacement, or monetary compensation—all calculated to restore material matters as much as possible to the way they were before the failure. Here the sentiments of the inept actor are not at issue, merely his reparations. Second, there are ritualistic acts (in the anthropological, not ethological, sense), these being commentarylike and self-referring, designed by the doer to redefine the expressive implications of his own maladroit performance. Through gestural and verbal displays, sentimental relief is attempted; the offender typically tries to establish through disclaimers, excuses, apologies, and accounts that the failing performance is not characteristic, or if it was, that it is no longer, or if it is, that the offender is at least alive to his deficiencies and supports social standards in spirit, if not in deed. In brief, misperformance "expresses" a definition of the actor, one he presumably finds inimical, and the remedial ritual pleads a more favorable way of reading the event.

Ritualistic remedies, more so than substantive ones, have a variable temporal relation to what they comment on. Very crudely speaking, they may be retrospective, occurring immediately after what they are designed to modify the meaning of; or prospective and disclamatory, aimed at controlling the possible implications of something that has not yet occurred; or, finally, concurrent, appearing as an overlay on the ongoing dubious activity.

Observe also that remedial rituals tend to be dialogic in character. Once such a remedy is provided, the provider typically requires some response from recipients so that he can be sure his message has been correctly received and is deemed adequate, effectively redefining the breach. Substantive remedy can also have something of a dialogic flavor, for the individual who provides restitution may need to know that what he has offered is deemed sufficient.

The substantive and ritualistic, of course, can be closely connected. The sequestering of learning from scenes of seriously committed effort allows failure to occur without substantive *or* reputational loss—except, of course, as failure may reflect on rate and prospects of learning. Also, faced with an actor's defective performance, his others will need to know whether this is what can be anticipated from him—ofttimes a very practical concern —and his heartfelt accounting and apology can serve to allay this concern even though at the time the expression itself accomplishes nothing by way of physical restitution for the current loss. Of course, evident effort to restore matters substantively— whether effective or not—provides a ready vehicle for eloquently expressing good intentions.

2. Even at the outset, the application made here of the social control model to competencies must be questioned, at least in one particular. Competencies do indeed fall under the management of normative expectations, but in a special way. Favorable and unfavorable appraisals are certainly involved, but less so moral approval and disapproval. Or, if moral judgment is involved, it is so only in a blunted sense. It is not merely that competence deals with the manner of the performance of an act, rather than its end or purpose; it is that competence is a feature of acts (on the face of it) that is not seen as something intentionally realized. An incompetent act—from the perspective of its incompetency—is in the first instance not something done or do-able against someone with the intent of doing them harm. Of course, falsely claiming a competency whose exercise is vital to the interests of another can seem to qualify; but here in the final analysis the offense is not in the consequence of the incompetent act, but in the false claim to competency. So, too, there is the incompetency sometimes engineered (and more often thought to be) by an actor himself as a cover for insubordinate intent, but this ruse could

hardly serve if we thought an actor should be made responsible in every way for an incompetent endeavor. Thus, although failures to sustain standards of competency can lead to demands for restitution and certainly to disapproving appraisals, failures as such are not standard, full-fledged offenses. In appearance, at least, no wicked intent, no malice, is to be found. *Actus non facit reum nisi mens sit rea.*

3. There is a special family of competencies seen to be common to the human estate by virtue of involving ongoing requisites for living in society: the ability, for example, to walk, see, hear, dress appropriately, manipulate small physical objects and, in literate societies, write, read, and compute with numbers. As a class these abilities exhibit the following properties:

   a. Except for the abilities associated with literacy, they are felt to be pancultural.
   b. They are in continuous, if not unremittant, exercise throughout the day.
   c. With reservations regarding sight and hearing, their acquisition is developmental in character, a product of early socialization.
   d. After initial acquisition, they are exercised without apparent effort or focal attention.
   e. Their possession is uncredited, lack alone is noteworthy—i.e., "negatively eventful."
   f. They are subject to what are perceived as biologically based defects.
   g. With reservations for sight, their execution is vulnerable to stress. "Loss of control," "nervousness," "getting rattled," are fundamental possibilities.
   h. They are subject to what is seen as incidental, accidental failure in the sense that the foot, hand, and tongue can be said to slip.

As suggested of competencies in general, the anticipation that the individual will perform adequately in these only-human matters can be said to have two different sides. First is the substantive side: failure here can trip up the smooth operation of the business at hand—not merely the actor's, but also the doings of those with whom he is immediately collaborating. Delay, misinformation, confusion, breakage can result. (These substantive costs, as such costs go, tend to be minor on any one occasion of occurrence, but because the capacities involved are exercised repeatedly throughout the course of the day, the summation of cost can be very considerable.) Second, there is the expressive side. Competency in regard to common-human abilities is something we tacitly allot to all adults we meet with, an achievement and qualification they are taken to start with, credit for which they receive in advance. An individual's failure to sustain these "normal" standards is thus taken as evidence not only that he doesn't (or might not) measure up in these respects, but also that as a claimant he has tacitly presented himself in a false light. With reappraisal goes discrediting and an imputation of bad faith.

Speech, of course, is a common-human ability, and to be examined as a competency, as Hymes (1973) has suggested. Moreover, the division between substance and expression applies, albeit the application must be carefully made. When, for example, we unintentionally misinform by emitting *fourteen* instead of *fifteen,* substantive repair for the verbal slip will necessarily be verbal in character, but substantive nonetheless, and not less so because a ritualistic remedy may accompany the substantive one, it, too, involving words.

4. The treatment of speech as just another common-human competency itself raises some questions, one of which bears mentioning now. As suggested, when an actor muffs a nonlinguistic doing in the immediate presence of others, he is likely to shift into words (typically accompanied by gestures) to account, apologize, assure, and (often) avow that restitution or repair will be forthcoming. So words, then, have a special role in the remedial process. Moreover, a well-designed accommodation is implied between the ongoing activity in which the fault occurred (and in which the substantive remedy, if any, will take place), and the activity through which the ritual elements of the remedy are realized; for the latter can be performed without interfering with the nonlinguistic activity at hand. When, however, the fault itself is verbal in character, then a place will have to be found for the remedial action (both substantive and ritualistic) within the very stream of activity in which the fault has occurred. As will be seen, remedy itself can then add to what must be remedied.

1. I have argued that competency in speech production would seem to be the proper central concern in the study of announcing. Speech competency itself was placed in the class to which it appears to belong—our constantly exercised mundane abilities. The latter were described in terms of the traditional perspective of social control. This is, I believe, the frame of reference (sometimes well buried) that informs both lay and professional views of speech error; indeed, it is such a framework that gives to speech error its status as a subject matter.

Certainly in our society, competency in speaking, like most other common human competencies, is a matter for lay as well as professional concern. As in the case of other common human capacities, we have a folk notion that speech production will ordinarily be faultless, occurring without hitch. Of the difficulties that do occur, some will strike the hearer as characteristic of the speaker—as when the individual is thought to over- or under-employ the opportunity to take the floor, or is heard to exhibit a lisp or a hesitation in the same phonetic environment across all his words or phrases. Some imperfections will appear to be intermittent, as when a given word is always "misused" or "mispronounced" by a particular individual. And some faults will appear to be accidental or even uncharacteristic, as when a particular word on a particular occasion is tripped over.

We employ a set of fairly well-known folk terms to refer to problems in speech production: speech lapse, stutter, speech defect, speech impediment, gaffe, malapropism, spoonerism, slip of the tongue, and so forth. Students of language behavior have refined these identificatory practices somewhat with such terms as silent pause, filled pause, false start (sentence redirection), dangling sentence, prolongation, influency, sound intrusion, transposition, word change, word repetition, word-segment repetition (stuttering), and the like.

2. Linguistically inclined students have some interesting points to make about imperfections of speech production. For example:

a. "Speech lapses are most likely to occur where conditions of excitement, haste, external distraction, mental confusion, or fatigue are present" (Simonini 1956:253).

b. The production of faults can be progressive. The occurrence of one imperfection increases the chance of another, and that in turn increases the chance of consequent ones—as if, indeed, there were such a thing as getting rattled (ibid.).

c. The mangling that spoken words can suffer turns out to have some orderly linguistic properties characteristic of "normal" speech production (Fromkin 1971). Below the level of the word, one finds that misstating takes the form of the interchange, substitution, addition, or loss of phonemes or groups of phonemes, with retention of syllabic place and stress (Boomer and Laver 1968). Thus, varieties of "phonological disturbance," whether involving consonants or vowels and whether generating nonwords or standard words:

i.	anticipatory interference:	John dropped his cuff of coffee.
ii.	preservative interference:	Spanish-speaping hotel.
iii.	exchange or transposition:	flesh crean water, torn the curner, Hoobert Heever.
iv.	omissions:	He had a fat—flat.[2]

And at a higher level, where whole words are interchanged, the transposition is made in conformance with grammatical constraints ("We now bring you 'Mr. Keene, loser of traced persons'" [*PB:* 12]). Moreover, it has been observed that the vocalization *uh,* used to fill a pause, is partway given the status of a legitimate word, for it induces a preceding *thee* instead of a *the* following the rule for managing vowels in initial position (Jefferson 1974:183–85). And substitution itself is most likely to occur in connection with the stressed, informing word (Boomer and Laver 1968:8) late in what will here be

2. In their "Malapropisms and the Structure of the Mental Lexicon," Fay and Cutler (1977:506) suggest an additional possibility, a "blend" arising when two synonyms are merged, resulting in either a nonword or a real word, as when (to use their examples), gripping is merged with grasping to form grisping, or heritage is merged with legacy to form heresy.

referred to as the "sentential utterance"—or "utterance" for short.[3]

d. Then there is the issue of encoding. Apparently almost all pauses occur at word boundaries, suggesting that words are encoded from thought into speech in whole word clumps (Maclay and Osgood 1959). And because phonological disturbance can be traced forward as well as backward in an utterance, one can only conclude that speakers formulate their upcoming statements before they make them, premonitoring what is formulated. (There is general confirmation for this argument. As Laver [1970:69] suggests, intonational and syntactic choices made at the beginning of an utterance can depend on the choices that will be manifest later, and so must in some way have had prior access to them. A specific phonological example is that thee-the concordance with initial vowels and consonants can apparently be invoked by a word that the speaker does not speak instead of the word that appears as his alternative on occasions of self-censoring [Jefferson 1974:188–89].) Furthermore, because hesitations tend to occur near the beginning of sentential utterances, one can say that the decision work for what is to be said is done here, and once done, a speaking chunk is ready for presentation (Boomer 1965; Dittmann and Llewellyn 1967; but see Beattie 1979:75–76). So, too, when interference or interchange errors occur, the interfering and the interfered-with usually fall within an utterance, not across utterance boundaries (Boomer and Laver 1968:8). Also, hesitation is more likely when novel, thought-requiring formulations are to be employed than when pat, stereotyped phrases are used (Goldman-Eisler 1968).

3. By the term "sentential utterance," I mean to refer to what appears to be a basic unit of speech production, but one for which there are established competing names and overlapping definitions. The American version is the "phonemic clause" (Trager and Smith 1951), definable as a "phonologically marked macrosegment" containing "one and only one stress" and ending in a terminal juncture (Boomer 1965:150). The British version, upon which most current work in the area is being done, is the "tone group" (Halliday 1967): a pause-bounded stretch of speech carrying one major change of pitch, whole units of rhythm, an intended unit of new information, and usually, but not necessarily, coinciding with a syntactic clause (Laver 1970:68–69). The term "sentence fragment" (Morgan 1973) is another candidate.

In pursuing their work on speech error, linguistically oriented students have refined lay notions of imperfection and have evoked a tacit notion of perfect speech production, namely, speech with which a linguistically trained observer could not find fault even when in a position to repeatedly examine an audio tape of the strip of talk in question. At the same time students have come to recognize that lay participants in talk seem to be oblivious to a wide range and number of technically detectable faults which occur during any appreciable period of talk.[4] Thus Boomer and Laver (1968:2) suggest:

> It is important to recognize that in speech "normal" does not mean "perfect." The norm for spontaneous speech is demonstrably imperfect. Conversation is characterized by frequent pauses, hesitation sounds, false starts, misarticulations and corrections. . . .
> In everyday circumstances we simply do not hear many of our own tongue-slips nor those made by others. They can be discerned in running speech only by adopting a specialized "proofreader" mode of listening. In ordinary conversation it is as though we were bound by a shared, tacit, social agreement, both as listeners and as speakers, to keep the occurrence of tongue-slips out of conscious awareness, to look beyond them, as it were, to the regularized, idealized utterance.

And Patricia Clancy (1972:84):

> One of these factors [influences on the internal structure of sentences] is the speaker's tendency to repeat words or phrases within a sentence. This repetition is extremely difficult to hear without practice. My transcription failed to record almost every one of these repetitions, since at first I did not even hear them. My experience was confirmed by others, who, listening to the recording for the first time, also failed to detect the repetitions. This leads to the hypothesis that the hearer is probably unaware of such repetitions consciously, screening them out unconsciously so that he hears only the message itself.

Accordingly, it would seem reasonable to employ a variant of the term "technical" to qualify references to imperfections a linguistically attuned student would feel he was uncovering by closely

---

4. George F. Mahl (1956; cited in Kasl and Mahl 1965:425) recommends that, "In terms of absolute frequencies, one of the disturbances occurs, on the average, for every sixteen 'words' spoken; this is equivalent to one disturbance for every 4.6 seconds the individual spends talking."

examining a replayable tape of a strip of talk, this being partly an etic discrimination belonging to the world of linguists. Similarly, a variant of the term "perceived" might be used in referring to the judgment a lay producer or recipient of words makes in orienting to a particular passage as faulty or as unnoteworthy in this respect. (Presumably all perceived faults would be technical ones, too, but not the reverse.) An implication is that a lay listener could be brought along to see that what he heard as talk without imperfections "really" possessed a great number of them, and these he could be trained to detect. Note that insofar as ordinary talk is indeed studded with minor, unnoticed faults, speech competency is different from other common human competencies, for these latter do not seem to incorporate anything like a constancy of minor failings.

3. To these fairly well-established points a few qualifications might be added.

a. There is the tricky issue of how much of a strip of speech is thought to be contaminated by the fault or faults occurring within it—whether these be faults perceived as such by laypersons or merely by linguists. Somehow or other, particular flaws are used as bases for characterizing strips that include more than the actual fault itself, the extension certainly being to the word involved, often to the utterance, and even to the entire stream of words emitted during a turn at talk. But I can say nothing about the conventions involved.

b. Faults should be sorted according to whether they pertain to individual speech production (in the sense of something that occurs once an individual has taken the floor and before he has relinquished it, something that does not appear to directly involve the action of the other participants in the talk) or to turn processing, to be seen, in the first instance at least, as properties of conversations, not conversational utterances. Turn processing faults would include such matters as:

i.   overlap—the initiation of next speaker's utterance slightly before the current speaker comes to the ending he was coming to

ii.   interruption—the stridently voiced attempt at takeover by a candidate speaker while the current one is still lodged in his utterance

iii. interruption override
iv. interturn gap
v. double uptake
vi. double backoff
vii. double speaking

As with individual speech imperfections, turn processing faults that can be detected by students often are not oriented to as such by participants:

> The most remarkable and frequent occurrence in the change from one speaker to the next is the new speaker's tendency to begin talking before the previous speaker has finished. This causes broken-off unfinished sentences on the part of the previous speaker as well as situations in which the previous speaker completes his sentence while the new speaker is already beginning his. In cases of overlap, the words of both speakers can usually be heard, and the hearer unconsciously interprets the sentences sequentially. In my original transcript, these overlaps were not marked, since I automatically heard them as the first speaker finishing and then the next beginning with no overlap. Other people who listened to the tape also did not hear any overlapping at first. It took much practice to detect this surprisingly frequent occurrence, and numerous replays to hear at what points it actually began. Having detected this pattern, I found that in my own conversations it was impossible for me to listen for or try to refrain from making overlapping interruptions since the effort required made me too tense to continue a normal relaxed conversation. [Clancy 1972:83]

In the case of radio talk, I might add, it is largely individual, not conversational, faults that are at issue.

    c. It appears that a working classification of faults can be made—if, indeed, one is not implied in the literature.[5] I divide them into two broad classes, "knows better" and "doesn't know better," according to whether or not the speaker's own hearing (on this or other like occasions) would be likely to inform him of his error, causing him to consider a remedy, which, in turn, he would be competent to provide.

    Among "knows better" faults, the following:

5. An earlier version of my own, with team performance as a point of reference, can be found in Goffman (1959:208–12).

i. *Influencies,* namely, hitches in the smooth flow of syntactically connected words, as with restarts, filled pauses, stuttering.

ii. *Slips,* by which I mean words or their parts that have gotten mixed up, or mis-uttered, as in word transposition, phonological disturbance, and the like. I also include those breaches of the canons of "proper" grammar, pronunciation, and word usage that the speaker himself would ordinarily avoid automatically; so, too, one-shot failures of normally rapid access to the corpus of information one would ordinarily be expected to have. Thus, slips are to be seen as a consequence of confused production, accident, carelessness, and one-time muffings—not as ignorance of official standards or underlying incompetence.

Influencies and slips, then, pertain to speech production in a narrow, formal sense—the capacity to draw effectively on the words one knows, put them together in a syntactically acceptable way, and encode them smoothly into well-articulated sound. These are the faults that linguists have tended to focus on. The two classes of faults are obviously allied; I distinguish between them because slips can be, and often are, produced fluently.

There is one type of slip that deserves special attention: utterances which allow for a construing or framing—a reading—that the speaker apparently did not intend. The implication is that the speaker has failed to select sound punctuation, words, phrases, or clauses with an ear to excluding alternative readings. (Examples will be considered later.)

Among "doesn't know better" faults, I include the following:

iii. *Boners,* namely, evidence of some failing in the intellectual grasp and achievement required within official or otherwise cultivated circles, this evidence implied in words spoken or others' words not comprehended. Ignorance of the world (it is felt) may thus be demonstrated, or unfamiliarity with the lore of some specific, prestigeful domain. Language capacity in its own right may be involved—general vocabulary, pronunciation, the fine points of grammar, and the like.

Now it turns out that subgroups of individuals, at least in our complex society, may among themselves employ a speech practice (or fail to) which they ordinarily never attend to as a fault, yet in the face of a cultivated hearer's remarks, are vulnerable to criticism regarding it. The extreme case here is the "incorrect" use of a word (especially a "long" one carrying tacit claims to the user's learnedness)[6] or the formulation of a conversational reply that patently indicates a failure to understand prior speaker's use of a "difficult" word.[7] Nationwide schooling and media-inspired sophistication have given such faults a coercive force in wide populations, in the sense that almost anyone breaching the standards in question can be made to feel ashamed for having done so.[8] With respect to wide coerciveness, then, these faults are like influencies and slips; but unlike these latter, the speaker's own hearing cannot inform him of his error: listeners must tell him—and, in some cases, prove to him with a dictionary—that he is "wrong." Of course, there are boners so subtle that standard-bearing hearers may not be able to specify exactly what they sense to be wrong, and only a specialist—a linguist— may be able clearly to score the point, of which the great example is Labov's (1972) examination of phonological "hypercorrection."

iv. *Gaffes,* that is, unintended and unknowing breaches in "manners" or some norm of "good" conduct—breaches of the kind that are here realized in speech, but can also be perpetrated through other modes of activity. Thus: indiscretions, tactlessness, indelicacy, irreverence, immodesty, intrusiveness, etc.[9] A very

---

6. The term for it is "malapropism," taking this to refer to the introduction of a whole, meaningful word that is unrelated in meaning to the one apparently intended but sounds somewhat like it (Fay and Cutler, 1977:505), and gives the impression that the speaker is attempting to rise above his lexical station—to use Zwicky's phrase (1978–79:341), but not his argument that the last is not an essential attribute.

7. Although malapropistic speaking has been considered in the literature, malapropistic hearing has not. In the first case, the speaker disavails himself of the opportunity to employ a substitute he can use "properly," and in the second he fails to ask candidly for clarification.)

8. A basic general treatment of the shaming power of prestigeful speech usage is provided by Bourdieu (1975). A useful historical treatment of notions of "proper" English is available in Finegan (1980).

9. See Goffman (1967:36–37). The point has recently been remade well by Lakoff (1973:303):

> One thing I would like to note briefly in passing: the rules of politeness function for speech and actions alike. A polite action is such because it is in accord with the dictates of one or more of Rules 1, 2, 3 [don't impose, give options, be friendly] as in a polite utterance. So covering my mouth when I cough is polite because it prevents me from imposing my

special ignorance is inadvertently displayed, namely, ignorance of what one would have to know about the rights and biography of one's coparticipants in order to conduct oneself with moral sensibility in regard to them.

It is possible, then, to discriminate roughly four kinds of speech faults: influencies, slips, boners, and gaffes.[10] Although these mishaps cover a very wide range of standards and constraints, it appears that somewhat the same sort of embarrassment and chagrin can be felt by the speaker when he discovers he has committed any one of the four, and something of the same sort of spoken corrective action can be taken by him to remedy the matter, the classes of faults merging together as far as their immediate consequences are concerned.

d. In a very useful analysis of error correction, Schegloff et

---

own personal excreta on someone else (quite apart from germs); and standing aside as someone enters a door I am in front of is polite because it leaves him his options, that is, his freedom of movement. This suggests that the rules of language and the rules for other types of cooperative human transactions are all parts of the same system; it is futile to set linguistic behavior apart from other forms of human behavior.

10. Corresponding to the various kinds of speech faults, one finds functionally equivalent handwriting faults. But, of course, there are differences. Speakers can't misspell, writers can't mispronounce. Sentence grammar itself is more strict in the written than the spoken form. No "invisible mending" is possible in the spoken form, some is in the written form. (Taped TV and radio talk, however, does allow for invisible patching.) Multiply interpretable sentences in written texts come under the jurisdiction of formal grammar, and it is my impression that they are held to be an expression of writing incompetency, and thus more to be seen as boners than as slips. The same in the spoken form seem better able to pass as mere slips.

Typing, like handwriting, displays spelling mistakes. Typing mistakes in general seem easier studied than those associated with handwriting. Allowably sloppy penmanship obscures all kinds of errors, whereas typing provides a clear record of mistakes. Typing is learned relatively late in life by learners who can report on themselves with adult sophistication, Interestingly, typing exhibits kinds of faults that are more commonly found in speech than in handwritten texts, perhaps because of the speed of production. One finds lots of misspacing (the equivalent of speech influencies), and the sort of spelling error that corresponds precisely to phonological disturbance—slips which seem much less prevalent in handwriting. In contrast, the misforming of letters in handwriting does not seem to have a close analogue in speech, nor, of course, is this much of a problem ordinarily in typing. (The thorough work on typing errors is due from David Sudnow: the world awaits.)

al. (1977) argue for a distinction between correction as such and the "initiation of a reparative segment" (p. 364), that is, the notification that a correction is or might be called for. And further, that "other-correction" is very rare, "other-initiation" less so ("self-correction" and "self-initiation" being preferred), that remedial work overwhelmingly occurs in one of four possible positions: faulted turn, faulted turn's "transition space," third turn, and (in the case of other-initiation) second turn.[11] In radio talk, of course, "other" has very little direct role in the remedial process, although hearers are sometimes stirred enough to write or phone in a correction.

Taking the lead from Schegloff et al., then, it can be said that upon discovering he has committed what he takes to be a speech fault, a speaker's overt response to his own speech seems to be divisible into two parts: "reaction" (in the form of exhibited

11. Schegloff et al. give much weight to the thesis that there is a preference for self-initiation over other-initiation, and that other-correction is very rare. They recommend the interesting argument that other-initiation can pass as a request for clarification, a side-sequence that does not alter the projected sequence of turn-takings, whereas other-correction among other things can be confused with disagreement (p. 380). They also claim that when other-initiation does occur it is likely to occur after speaker has been given an opportunity during the completion of the turn in which the trouble occurred to initiate and complete his own correcting. Underlying these arguments (insofar as they are valid) would seem to be a general rule of politeness, namely, that the individual be given a chance to correct his own mistakes first, this presumably entailing less threat, less loss of face, than if he must be rescued entirely by other. To which should be added the fact that in many cases the recipient *can't* provide a correction or even a hint that one might be required; not knowing what the speaker had wanted to say (or "should" have said), he may not know that a fault has occurred, or, if he does, what the intended statement was.

Schegloff et al. use "repair" as a covering term for all corrective action. I have not followed their practice because "repair" strikes me as implying the fixing of something that has been broken, and although this nicely covers the substantive reconstructing of a word or phrase, it less happily fits a range of other kinds of work performed in the remedial process. (Of course, no lay term is likely to be satisfactory on all counts.) I have stronger reservations about "initiation" (as a label but not as a concept), for this term can too easily imply the beginning of an actual correction, when in fact—as Schegloff et al. are themselves at pains to point out—no correction at all may follow. What is involved, surely, is a giving of notice that some remedial work might be called for and/or is to be anticipated. "Notification" is a possible choice. Perhaps a better one is the term used by Jordan and Fuller (1975:12): "flag," as in "a trouble-flag."

embarrassment, chagrin, consternation, and the like, externalized as notification or flagging) and "remedy" (in the form of some corrective effort, both substantive and ritualistic).[12]

e. Given a social control perspective—however deeply buried—it seems rather arbitrary to study speech faults without studying the standard techniques for avoiding their occurrence and for remedying the trouble once it has occurred. (As a matter of fact, it seems just as arbitrary to examine production faults and their remedies without also considering the quite parallel subject of speech mishearings,[13] my excuse for which is that the study of radio talk only incidentally raises questions about actual mishearings.) When this more inclusive (and more natural) approach is taken, one can, following Schegloff et al., begin to appreciate that sequences of elements or segments will be involved, and that their delineation is strictly an empirical matter.

In this light consider some of the elementary remedial practices employed by a speaker in response to the issue of speech fault.

First is the simple avoidance of what he assumes might cause trouble. Unsure of the meaning of a word or of his own ability to "properly" pronounce it, he routinely seeks out and employs a safe alternative. Knowing his listener has a particular failing, he tactfully avoids mention of the subject. Speaking in front of a child, he may censor talk of sex and money.

Next the troubles the speaker fails to avert. Some of these neither he nor his listeners catch, and so long as one appreciates

12. I do not mean to imply that this two-part division—reaction and correction—is somehow a "natural" feature of behavior, a reflection of universal human nature. Whatever is biological in this pattern, certainly an important part of the matter consists of individuals acting so as to affirm in their own behavior their own folk theory of human nature.

13. The central work here is Garnes and Bond (1975), where it is shown that hearing errors fairly closely follow speaking ones, that, for example, hearers can: misplace consonantal point of articulation; substitute voicing for stops and fricatives, and l's for r's; delete, add, or shift word boundaries; fail to recover various phonological deletions, simplifications, and neutralizations, or recover these where in fact none had been lost. As typically with speech errors, in all of these hearing errors, only low-level syntactic processes are involved: "Inflectional morphemes are supplied or deleted, as required, and the sentence usually remains intact in terms of NP-VP configuration" (ibid., p. 223). Interestingly, as in production errors, metatheses are commonly found.

that speaker and hearers are subject to realizing or being made to realize what has happened, one need consider the matter no further.

Some problems the speaker will not appreciate but his hearers will. (Doing so, they may tactfully try to give no notice of having done so, or they may flag the fault, or, in some cases, introduce an actual correction.)

Or, knowing that he has gotten himself into trouble, the speaker may try to continue on as though nothing wrong has happened, whether thinking the listeners have not noticed anything wrong (allowing him to sneak by), or that they have noticed, and that drawing attention to the trouble can only make matters worse. The speaker *drives through.* Driving through can be accomplished effectively so that the hearers are unaware of the error (when they hadn't otherwise been); or, being aware, are left not knowing whether the speaker was; or, being aware and sensing that the speaker is, too, are grateful for not having to address the matter further.

It should be immediately apparent that a tricky (and characteristic) problem of interpretation and proof exists here. For in many (but not all) cases there may be no easy way to distinguish between a speaker driving through when this is a strategem, and his driving through "in effect" because he is in fact unaware of his mistake. But I don't think the dilemma is crucial, a question of idiographic, not social analysis. The point is that regardless of the difficulty (or even impossibility) of confidently discriminating the two possibilities in *particular* cases, the two nonetheless occur. As does the possibility that hearers will be left with ambiguity as to actual or feigned obliviousness, as I was in hearing an announcer unfalteringly say:

> She'll be performing selections from the Bach Well-tempered Caviar, Book Two, and also from Beethoven, Sonata in G minor.

Of course, whether a hearer feels sure or unsure of what he has heard, he may be mishearing—a possibility he may appreciate on the occasion.

Sometimes when the speaker essays to drive through, he does not seem to completely believe that the tack is workable or that it should be worked, and during its execution betrays himself with a pause and self-conscious overtone to his voice. (The hesitation or pause can constitute a *negative* notification, as it were: a blank is left where the speaker otherwise would have drawn attention to his error, the slot filled with what can be heard as silent indecision.) The implication is that the speaker is intensely concerned with his predicament and is not in complete control of himself. It is as if he cannot contain his concern for whether or not he will manage himself as he would like; potential disaster seems to be in his mind. Or a speaker may discover a fault in mid-production, pause for a startled moment, give the impression that he is thinking about how to get out of his difficulty, and then make a stab at driving through, as though the other alternative (to frankly draw attention to the embarrassing reading through an apology) had been considered but was found even less acceptable:

> Cooking Show: "So ladies, there is no safer way to insure perfect apple pie each and every time than to use canned sliced apples. . . . So the next time you decide to bake apple pie, go to the can . . . (PAUSE) . . . and you will really enjoy sliced piced apples!" [SB:102]

And throughout, there is the sense that should hearers turn on the speaker and remark on his error, he will have begun to show appropriate shame. The picture, in short, can be one of an individual who isn't really prepared to commit himself fully to appearing to sense that nothing is wrong, and it will always be a close question as to how fully intent the speaker is on concealing *that* impression.

Once the speaker tacitly accepts the strategy of addressing his fault openly, then a standard set of practices—"correction formats"—becomes available to him, these often appearing in combination in various sequences following a notification (if any), the notification itself often taking the form of a nonlexicalized vocal segregate, such as *Uh-oh!* or *Whoops!* Thus, for example, word searches (often associated with filled pauses or prolongation of syllables), restarts, redirections, and perfunctory ritual tags.

These various explicit remedies fall along a continuum with *flat* correction at one end and *strident* correction at the other. In the first extreme, the remedial act is performed apparently unselfconsciously and with no change in pace, as though the correction (and an apology when one is offered) is itself nothing to be ashamed of, nothing to require focal attention. In the other extreme, the speaker gives the impression of suddenly stopping in midstream because of being struck by what he has just heard himself say. Voice is raised and tempo increased. He then seems to redirect his attention to the single-minded task of establishing a corrected statement, as if this could (done quickly and forcefully enough) somehow grind the error into the ground, erase it, obliterate it, and substitute a correct version. If the correction comes in fast and hard enough, presumably the hearer will be saved from registering the mistake and will be able to proceed directly on with the correct version, having been, as it were, overtaken in the receiving process. (The parallel is dropping a breakable pot: move quickly enough and a catch can totally erase the upcoming loss.) The speaker in the act of making such a save often appears momentarily to lose his distance and reserve, flooding into his corrective act. And placed immediately before or after the corrective restatement may be a special tag: *I beg your pardon, I mean, that is,* etc.—the tag itself rendered rapidly so as to minimize the break in what would otherwise be the timing and tempo of the utterance in progress. The stress and rapidity of the correction appears to demonstrate that although the speaker may have been asleep at the switch, he is now more than sufficiently on his toes, fully mobilized to prove that such indiscipline is not characteristic of him, indeed almost as much a surprise to himself as a misguidance to others. I might add that whatever such a save does or doesn't do for what might otherwise have been expressed about the speaker, his text is at least substantively restored to what he had meant it to be:

> "So all you do when you are on your way home is, stop by at Korvette's and leave your odor. . . . ORDER!!!" [*Pr.:* 126]

> Educational Channel: "To me English is an enema . . . enigma!" [*Pr.:* 14]

> Newscaster: "And the Arkansas Senator was injured in a fall when he participated in a turkey toot . . . shoot!" [*Pr.:*111][14]

14. Whole-word correction is ordinarily treated as a simple editing procedure, much the same as restarts involving self-interruption part-way through a word, followed by a new attempt at providing a whole acceptable word; and I have here done so. But another interpretation is possible. A speaker may wait

. . . performing in nude—in *numerous* musicals . . .

. . . sentenced to one year abortion—*probation* . . .

I I I

With a few exceptions, the picture sketched of the state of the art regarding speech production faults seems modest in the matter of supplying us with anything of general interest. Pearls are buried here, but linguists and psychologists chiefly undertake to look for strings. (The bearing of error on the issue of how thought is encoded into speech is perhaps the most significant line of inquiry.) A broader approach, it seems to me, can be developed by addressing the social control model that appears to underlie current analyses. For, as suggested, the limits of this model seem especially crucial in the study of speech faults. Consider some of the issues:

1. It appears that the difference between technical faults and perceived ones is not innocent; it is not the difference between trained ears and unconcerned ones; it is not the difference between "picking up" minor blemishes or letting them go by; it is not the difference between careful listening and lax participation. Nor is the difference between radio talk and informal talk the difference between high standards of speech perfection and low. To think simply in terms of differing social norms or sensitivity regarding error is to preserve error as an easily identifiable thing.

---

until he has completed a sentential utterance before providing a redoing of the problematic word, in which case it becomes clear that he might be introducing a new sentential utterance (or something expandable into one), one he had not planned on:

> Disc Jockey: "And now a record by Little Willie John . . . here's 'Sleep-Sleep-Sleep' . . . By the way, did you get any last night? . . . (PAUSE) . . . SLEEP, that is!" (*Pr.:*44)

In hearing these corrections, we automatically read back to their point of application, unconcerned that the surface structure of the new segment may not make grammatical or discursive sense. Of course, what does make sense of the corrective utterance is not the immediately prior discourse, but the *fault* in the prior utterance and the assumption that the speaker's sudden overriding concern would be to correct it. Obviously, it is the mistake, not the discourse, which here provides a meaningful context for the remedy.

In fact, the basic terms employed to designate some sort of imperfection, such as "fault" or "error" (and, of course, "imperfection" itself), cover behavior so heterogeneous as to undermine any unself-conscious analysis of incidental instances, in spite of commonalities of response. This heterogeneity itself must first be addressed before there can be hope that anything analytically coherent will emerge. Thus the need for distinctions such as those among influencies, slips, boners, and gaffes.

2. The two principal responses to a fault—reaction and remedy—can themselves function as faults, indeed are a major source of them. The display of a "reasonable" amount of startle, consternation, and shame over having committed a speech error, and the provision of an appropriate ritual remedy to demonstrate proper aliveness to how matters should have gone, can but add an extraneous note; and if the speaker at the time happens to be obliged to stick to a prescribed text (as in the case of announcing), then this remedial work itself must introduce more to apologize for. So here the very processes of social control must create problems of social control, the workings of social control working against itself. Plainly, in these matters the standard social control approach misses.[15] Thus, for example, a filled pause to cover a word search for an "apt" expression, or a restart to correct a "wrong" choice of word, syllable, or pronunciation must itself constitute a break in presentation, and thus a technical influency, if nothing else.

An underlying issue here is that faults reflect speech production problems, and speech production is apparently not a homogeneous matter. Accessing one's memory for what it is one wants to say seems a different process from encoding accessed thoughts into acceptable speech sounds; but the two are intimately related functionally, in consequence of which a failing in the first will

15. The musical stream presents a more obvious case than the speech stream. While practicing, a musician can stop and start at will and repeat a phrase a thousand times in order to get it right. But during an actual performance, especially in an ensemble, constraints abound. A second violinist in a quartet, missing the moment when he was to reenter the musical stream, cannot hammer home a rapid correction without adding wrong notes to missed ones; for by the time his belated entry occurs, its notes will not fit with the passage the other musicians have come to.

show up as a fault in the second. Given that the speaker will be obliged to have rapid, easy access to a particular corpus of information (in the sense that this corpus will be assumed to be constantly available as a resource for his utterances), his momentary inability to achieve such access will surface as an influency, and this particular source of influency, signalled as such, will be treated as a speech fault. Clearly, then, our subject matter is not speech error but speech *production* error. And admittedly, all that is to be included under "production" cannot readily be itemized.

Perceived influency is itself a special matter in regard to remedy. There is an important sense in which influency is something for which *no* substantive remedy is possible—the best the speaker can hope for is that his remedy itself will be fluently articulated. Some holes, after all, can't be filled, merely dug deeper. (All of this, it will be seen, is a central concern in radio talk.)

3. To say that there are various classes of faults is also to say that quite disparate standards constrain the behavior of speakers; and saying this, it is hardly a step to seeing that these standards need not always be compatible with one another. It should be understandable, then, that the speaker may have a speech task for which *no* unfaultable rendition is possible. The pronunciation of foreign words and names is an example. If a speaker attempts pronunciation native to the foreign word he is employing and has the linguistic capacity to succeed, he can give the impression of immodestly displaying his cultivation and in any case may require a slight break in ordinary rhythm. If he fully anglicizes the term, or translates it, he can give the impression of ignorance. So instead he may elect to compromise—how much, depending on his audience. But how can such a compromise be perfect? And how can it succeed if the audience is itself of mixed degrees of sophistication?[16]

4. Before an action can be treated by speaker or hearer as a fault, it must be regarded as the kind that the speaker would alter

16. Apparently the BBC currently has what is called the Pronunciation Unit (successor to the BBC's Advisory Committee on Spoken English), which establishes desirable compromises between foreign and Anglo-Saxon pronunciation for various foreign place and personal names. On the pronunciation dilemma in general in broadcasting, see Hyde (1959:90).

were he aware of the impression he was creating and was positioned to start anew—the chief distinction being between faults the speaker perceives as such upon committing them and ones he would never see as such unless attention were drawn to them by someone whose judgment is of concern to him. Many gaffes, however, involve actions that at other times are performed with serious intent to affront, or with knowing unconcern, such that the actor cannot be made to feel abashed when the offensive consequences of his deed are brought to his attention. A common example involves breaches of those standards of behavior that apply to the management of conversations as such, as with interruption, turn persistence, unwelcome encounter initiation, unwillingness to close out the talk, abuse by a nonparticipant of accessibility to the talk, and the like. Hearer response to such behavior may start with polite notification of what could be interpreted as an inadvertent lapse, but then be forced to move from there to frank negative sanctions. One is thus required to see that error and its correction can lead imperceptibly to another topic, the social control of full-fledged offense (Humphrey 1978). Similarly, it has been suggested that other notification and correction can become intermingled with the expression of disagreement and argument, so that once again what is available for interpretation as response to error can develop into something else (Pomerantz 1977). In truth, it appears that "error" correction, especially of the other-contributed kind, is part of a complex social control process providing participants with considerable opportunity to negotiate direction, to define and redefine what it is that has been going on.

5. Faults can fade into something else going in the other direction. The format doesn't change, it is just extended. Thus, a speaker who holds up the talk while he fishes for just the right word can be answering to a private ideal, a vaunted expectation regarding self, not necessarily a standard obligation. So, too, a speaker who audibly stops himself from making an erroneous statement in connection with a matter so specialized and recondite that he alone in the present company could possibly catch it; and so, too, the speaker who retracts a thought that had not quite been encoded in speech, alluding to the thought so we will know what it is we were saved from hearing.

6. Now consider the convenience that can be made of the remedial process. Take a speaker who must utter a foreign word in the tortuous circumstances already described. A standard recourse is to break frame and guy the pronunciation, either by affecting an uneducated hyper-Anglicization, or by an articulation flourish that mimics a fully authentic version—in either case providing a response that isn't merely remedial and can't quite be seen simply as corrective social control. Here the danger of making a mistake is not merely avoided, it is "worked," exploited, turned to advantage in the apparent cause of fun.

Or take a speaker who extracts—sometimes by brute force —an unintentional pun from his own discourse in order to break frame and make a little joke. He has found something he can get away with treating as a fault, something he can construe as allowing corrective attention, and simple error correction is no longer an apt description. Even more, the speaker who purposely puns, his sally intoned with prosodic markers to ensure we appreciate that the breach of single-mindedness is under his control: we follow with an answering groan that too openly expresses disgust to be serious, clearing the books, as it were, counterbalancing one deviation with another and thereby presumably returning everyone to the serious business at hand. Here the obligation to speak unambiguously, and the repertoire of standard flutterings and apologies for failing to do so, become something to draw on for play, not serious realization. One deals in all these cases with self-actionable utterances, with bits of what we have said or tried to say that can serve us under pressure as a subject of some sort of remedial-like action. Social control is operative here, but merely as a background model, determining not the ends of actions but the unserious guise in which actions are presented.

7. I have argued that some faults, such as phonemic reversals, are wholly a matter of speech production (although admittedly there are functionally equivalent troubles in nonlinguistic doings), and that other faults, such as tactlessness, are more a matter of *what* is said (fluently and without a slip), as opposed to *getting* it said; and yet that in both cases the fault can be followed by a reaction and correction which can end up as speech faults in their own right.

Now observe that events that lead to verbal fault-flagging reaction and then to verbal correction need not themselves have anything to do with the speech stream, even merely in its capacity as a medium. Being struck silent by what we have just *seen* interferes with smooth speech production in much the same way as being struck silent because of realizing what we have just *said*. Tripping over a companion's feet can cause us to interrupt our talk with a blurted apology, exactly as we might when we trip interruptively over another's turn to talk. And although the list of failings associated intrinsically with speech production might be tractable, the list of those nonlinguistic failings which can occur while we happen to be in talk with others is endless— failings that lead us to feel shame and to interrupt with an apologetic interjection, the interruption itself then constituting a speech fault in its own right. (Indeed, as suggested, it is a central feature of speech that hitches in the nonlinguistic activity of persons who are "together," but not in conversation at the time, produce a shift to speech as the medium for articulating a remedy.)

And, of course, competencies themselves may not be involved, merely unavoidable or unforeseen contingencies, as when, in seeing that the very person we are gossiping about has suddenly and unexpectedly come within earshot, we become acutely embarrassed and our words suffer disarray.

8. Technically perceivable faults not perceived by the speaker may or may not be perceived by his hearers as faults. When speaker and hearer together both fail to perceive a technical fault, it may be because their norms fully sanction the behavior, as in the case of "minor" restarts and certain pronunciations that are contrary to "educated" practice. But in other cases, especially when filled pauses and other sources of technical influency occur, another factor must be considered. Faults not perceived as such by natural talkers can nonetheless be perceived by them in some way (and in ways different from the perception of a technically unfaulted passage) and, thus perceived, can serve a multitude of functions—important ones—unconnected with the notion of speech error itself. It is defined as natural that all of an individual's concerns show up in his speech; and when some of these particular concerns involve him in, say, vacillation or emo-

tional anguish or (as already suggested) the need for sudden apology, then these states will have to be given expression. And one consequence of (if not resource for) this expression is disturbance in the speech stream. Consequently, this disturbance is not to be seen, necessarily, as something that the speaker might want in this context to avoid. After all, in some circumstances calm speech production might impress listeners as evidence that the speaker was, for example, cold or unfeeling or brazen or shameless. We apparently feel there are times when an individual "should" be upset, and speech disturbances are a prime means of "doing" such states. The general point, of course, is that obligations to one's conversation and to one's coparticipants (in their capacity as conversationalists) can hardly be the only claim that we or they recognize as binding on us—and rarely the deepest one. All of which provide good reason why speech is so full of faults, whereas the products of our other everyday competencies are so little faulted. Here, incidentally, radio announcing provides something of a limiting case, for it would appear that the job requires the performer to set aside all other claims upon himself except that of smoothly presenting the script. He is intended to be a perfect speech machine and that alone.

I have suggested that a particular kind of remedial work may itself produce a speech fault, that this work may be occasioned by breaches that are only incidentally manifest in speech, or even not at all. Also that unrepentant offensiveness and intransigently formulated opinions may be greeted initially with the responses that faults generate, the question of just what is to be seen as going on, being a matter of negotiation. Further, that otherwise passable speech production may be canvassed for opportunities it might provide to introduce a remedial format for "fun." So, too, that on occasion, speech fault may be an inevitable result of incompatible constraints on behavior, and that speech disturbances have functions that speaker would be disinclined to forego. Once all of this is accepted, one is in a position to suspect that speech error and speech error correction may not themselves provide us with a neatly circumscribed subject matter for study —a suspicion that would harden were one to proceed to include the entangling effects of mishearings.

Starting, then, with the notion of speech fault and its correction, forms of behavior must be examined that speak to a larger domain; they speak to elements of an individual's verbal performance that he chooses not to be identified with, something he can elect to find fault with, something he finds reasons to take action against. And this can be *almost* anything.[17] And one finds it necessary to take as an initial point of reference not error in any obvious sense but any bit of speech behavior to which the speaker or listener applies a remedy—substantive and/or ritualistic—and to take also any strip that its producer might be or can be made doubtful about, whether through his own hearing or the response of his listeners or by exemplars of socially approved speech whose judgment might carry some weight with him. In a

17. The notion of reserving judgment on the "objective" character of speech error, and attending instead only to how behavior addressed in this way functions in the speech stream was first pressed on me by Emanuel Schegloff. Thus, Schegloff et al. (1977:363) recommend: "In view of the point about repair being initiated with no apparent error, it appears that nothing is, in principle, excludable from the class 'repairable.' " This is a particular example of the basic procedure that the Sacks-Schegloff-Jefferson group of conversation analysts has promoted, a variant of the topic-not-resource theme in ethnomethodology, which principle has, I think, great heuristic value in microanalysis, being perhaps *the* principle of microanalysis. The way to obtain a corpus of errors is not to start with an intuition as to what a quintessential error is and then seek for some prime examples, but to force oneself to collect what gets treated as an error, whatever that might be. But that does not mean that the items in the collection will necessarily share *only* that fact, or that, for example, there are no other qualifications for inclusion in the set. Some errors, for example, will in this way be systematically omitted, such as those that the actual speaker and hearers fail to perceive as such, but which many other individuals in the speech community might; so also the more important errors that speaker and/or hearer perceive but decided to treat as though not happening, and do so effectively. In any case, the argument that anything in principle *can* be defined by speaker or hearer as warranting remedial action, does not, solely in itself, undermine the notion that there are "objective" speech faults, because it does not speak to another issue, namely, whether or not there are phrasings that for all practical purposes *must* be considered to be errors. Such phrasings will be considered later.

A similar set of issues occurs in regard to mishearing, and similar arguments can be made. But there is a further complication—to be considered later. Put crudely, a hearer's hearing of something a speaker did not intend may not only be due to a misspeaking *or* a mishearing, but also, on occasion, to some mixture of both—especially, I believe, in connection with misplaced word boundaries. Discovering an apparent fault, a hearer may try to attribute responsibility, doing so "correctly" or "incorrectly," and if the latter, thereby contributing another fault to the communication stream.

word: *faultables.* [18] As suggested, all technical faults are faultables, if only by virtue of the prestige of grammarians; but not all faultables are technical faults.

Even accepting, then, a focus on individual speech production instead of joint conversational enterprise, and even taking speech producers who are specifically employed to restrict themselves to speech production, speech error can, I claim, carry us far afield in a sociological direction: the microanalysis of how a speaker uses faultables during the course of his speaking, this being an entirely open question that can begin to be closed only by looking to his actual behavior. And for this endeavor the traditional framework of role and social control will be somewhat restrictive.[19] A more microscopic approach is required.

18. My version of Schegloff et al. (1977:363): "We will refer to that which the repair addresses as the 'repairable' or the 'trouble source.' "

19. A purportedly far-reaching critique of the social control model has been introduced as part of the doctrine of ethnomethodology, arguing that the "normative paradigm" should be replaced by the "evaluative" one. The argument is that the social control process is not something that somehow occurs in nature, but rather that participants intentionally perform their roles to produce the effect of there being normative constraints and reactions to breaching them. This requires, among other things, a tacit agreement to perceive the event at hand in terms of that perspective in which a deviant act (or a corrective one) will be isolated as the defining one in the circumstances (Wilson 1970). In brief, participants tacitly collaborate to uphold a *model,* not a norm.

The argument is not persuasive. There is always an issue as to what perspective, what frame, individuals will employ in perceiving an event, but this choosing does not thereby become all that is relevant to study. Similarly, if wide agreement exists about what aspect of events to abstract out for concern (as in games), a consideration of how this consensus is arrived at is not all that need concern the student. So, too, although the social-control perspective can certainly become a conscious framework for some set of individuals—such as those processed by social workers, therapists, enlightened jailers, and sociology textbooks—thereby entering action differently from social control in general, there will remain the fact that these indoctrinated people themselves will be guided by norms and constraints, merely ones that the critic of the social control model has not had the wit, patience, or interest to uncover. And should the "evaluative model" ever become popular as a conscious basis of orientation and brought through that route into everyday action, then its use will itself be subject to the normative framework, an expression of people doing what they feel is "proper," "meaningful," "persuasive," and so forth.

IV

1. The term "speaker" is central to any discussion of word production, and yet the term is used in several senses, often simultaneously and (when so) in varying combinations, with no consistency from use to use. One meaning, perhaps the dominant, is that of *animator,* that is, the sounding box from which utterances come. A second is *author,* the agent who puts together, composes, or scripts the lines that are uttered. A third is that of *principal,* the party to whose position, stand, and belief the words attest. In this latter case, a particular individual is not so much involved as an individual active in some recognized social role or capacity or identity, an identity which may lead him to speak inclusively for an entity of which he is only a part. Now although it is natural to think of these three functions—animator, author, principal—locked together, as when an individual speaks lines that he has composed and which attest to his own position, in fact such congruence will often not be found. In radio talk, for example, although the announcer typically allows the (typically unwarranted) impression to be formed that he himself is the author of his script, usually his words and tone imply that he is speaking not merely in his own name, but for wider principals, such as the station, the sponsor, right-thinking people, Americans-at-large, and so forth, he himself being merely a small, composite part of a larger whole. (A qualification is that on the hours and half-hours, the announcer is likely to announce his own name, identifying himself when he identifies the station, this involving a slight change in stance as he momentarily switches from a voice that speaks for something larger than himself to a voice that speaks—and properly so—in his own name or that of the station, narrowly defined.)

Animator, author, principal together comprise what can be called the production format of an utterance. This basic element in the structure of an utterance is to be distinguished from another: the participation framework, namely, the circle, ratified and unratified, in which the utterance is variously received, and in which individuals have various participation statuses, one of which is that of animator. Just as the character of the production format of a discourse can shift markedly from moment to moment, so, too, can its participation framework, and in fact, the two elements often shift simultaneously. The alignment of an individual to a particular utterance, whether involving a production format, as in the case of the speaker, or solely a participation status, as in the case of a hearer, can be referred to as his *footing* (Goffman 1974:542–44; 1979 and this volume, chap. 3).

The question of footing is systematically complicated by the possibility of embedding. For example, a speaker can quote himself or another directly or indirectly, thereby setting into an utterance with one production format another utterance with its own production format, albeit now merely an embedded one.

2. Singing, chanting, and speaking appear to be the main forms of vocal production. In literate society this production seems to have three bases:

a. memorization
b. reading off from a written text or score that has not itself been memorized
c. the extemporaneous, ongoing assembly and encoding of text under the exigency of immediate response to one's current situation and audience, in a word, "fresh production."

Our concern will not be with singing or chanting, but with speaking, the three production bases of which can be referred to as "recitation," "aloud reading," and "fresh talk."[20] Note, stage acting accordingly involves the open simulation of fresh talk (and very occasionally, of aloud reading), on the basis of a memorized script.

Some qualification of these discriminations is necessary. Insofar as a speaker formulates discourse units such as a sentential utterance before encoding them into sound, then all fresh talk is, in that degree, reciting a prepared text, albeit a very short one prepared a moment ago by the speaker himself. (Observe, just as

---

20. In *Discourse across Time and Space* (Keenan and Bennett 1977), beginning with Keenan's "Why Look at Unplanned and Planned Discourse" (pp. 1–41), the term "unplanned" is used to refer to spontaneous conversational speech, the contrast being to the various forms of discourse that are thought through before transmission and realized in grammatically formal sentence (and sentence-sequence) structures. This view would seem to slight the "spoken prose" of those practiced public speakers who can provide extemporaneous remarks (and certainly rejoinders) in fluent, well-formed, coherently linked sentences. In any case, it might be argued that the critical issue is scripting, not planning.

we can forget a next line in a memorized text—with the possibility of total derailment—so we can get lodged in uttering a fresh-talk sentence and forget the preformulated strip that was to come next, losing, as is said, our train of thought [Yngve 1973, esp. p. 689].) In the main, however, in fresh talk, what we can do is become "tongue-tied," which is to be at a loss for *any* words, not —as in preformulated texts—*the* words. In aloud reading, of course, we can hardly forget what to say; the worst that can occur (in this connection) is to lose our place.

More important, in some lecturing, aloud reading is closely interwoven with fresh-talked, exegetical asides, which incidentally provide the speaker with a means of heightened responsiveness to the particularities of the occasion of delivery. And of course public addresses can be made from notes, these providing the speaker with a track to stay on and principal stations to pass through, but with little by way of a literal script to repeat. Here the text is in fresh talk and only the thematic development is preformulated. These two styles—elaborated aloud reading and talk from an outline—can be mixed in every proportion.

Finally, many folk traditions provide significant and typical ways in which memorized materials are intermingled with fresh production during audience performances. Prose narratives, songs, and oral poetry can be improvisationally composed during presentation from a blend of formulaic segments, set themes, and traditional plots, the whole artfully tailored to suit the temper of the audience and the specificities of the locale.[21] In which case there is no original or standard text, only a family of equally authentic renditions.

Apparently, then, fresh talk, aloud reading, and recitation can be produced in various blends, with rapid and continuous switching from one form to another, and even mingled with song and recitative. However, it is just in such cases that one most needs to identify and separate out the mingled bases of speech production, for it is likely that the hearers themselves there will obtain an uncertain view of the ingredients.

Just as one can say that there are three bases for speech

21. The classic formulation is by Lord (1960) out of Parry (1971). A critical appraisal of it is available in Finnegan (1977, esp. chap. 3, pp. 52–87).

production, so one might want to argue that there are three types of speech production competency. Plainly, an individual who has one of these competencies may not have another. (An example is the ability of some fresh-talk stutterers to recite or stage-act impeccably.) However, it appears that each of the bases of production is not itself homogeneous with respect to the possession of competency. For example, a speaker's ability with the fresh talk of conversation tells us little about his ability at extemporaneous speech-making. Presumably differences in competency reflect differences in the process of acquiring competency—a comparative subject about which not much seems to be known.

Further, normally competent speech production—that is, speech which strikes the speaker and listeners as something not notably imperfect—will be subject to markedly different standards depending on whether memorization, aloud reading, or fresh talk is involved. The point can be nicely seen when a platform speaker engages in a "production shift," switching, say, from aloud reading to a variety of fresh talk, such as parenthetical elaboration, questions and answers, and so forth. On these occasions it is common for hearers to sense no increase or decrease in competency, and yet examination of a recording is likely to show that a sudden increase in technical faults occurred with the shift. Obviously, corresponding to an increase in fumbling was a decline in defining it as such, but this says very little about what is really involved.

On the face of it, each of the three bases of speech production involves its own characteristic production format. Fresh talk *commonly* presents congruence among animator, author, and principal. Aloud reading can, too, except that in such cases, the person who is author can at best be the "same," in a limited way, as the person who is animator. (After all, the person who was the author necessarily is some past realization of the person who is now the animator.) Memorization seems likely to present an animator who is not the author or principal, although poets (and singers) can present their own work, and moreover be taken to stand behind what gets said. In sum, each of the three bases of speech production is likely to involve a different production format, each such format supporting different grounds for the speaker's relation to his hearers.

A final point. In selecting a phrasing during fresh talk, or managing a scripted phrasing in aloud reading, we seem to have some leeway, some safety margin, with respect to timing, stress, intonation, and so forth. We can therefore find ourselves momentarily distracted or uncertain of what to say or unsure of pronunciation or otherwise needful of special effort at a particular juncture, and yet manage this emergency without the consequent speech flow becoming degraded to technically faulted (when it was technically unfaulted before) or perceivedly faulted (when it was perceivedly unfaulted before). Indeed, this sort of getting things in order in time must be a constant feature of talk not noted for speech faults. One might think here of "production tolerance." Thus, becoming a proficient platform speaker does not so much involve knowing what we are going to say as being able to manage our uncertainties discreetly, that is, within our production tolerance.

3. The various production formats provide a speaker with different relationships to the words he utters, providing, thus, a set of interpretive frameworks in terms of which his words can be understood. (Recitation, aloud reading, and fresh talk are but broad divisions of this potential.) These different possibilities in conjunction with the participation statuses he could enjoy comprise what might be called his *frame space.* In brief, when the individual speaks, he avails himself of certain options and foregoes others, operating within a frame space, but with any moment's footing uses only some of this space. He speaks words formulated by someone in the name of someone, directing these remarks to some set of others in some one of their capacities, and for the moment abjures speaking in all the other ways his resources would allow. And, of course, frame space will be normatively allocated. To speak acceptably is to stay within the frame space allowed one; to speak unacceptably is to take up an alignment that falls outside this space. (A similar statement can be made about the hearer and his frame space.)

As a crude example, take perfunctory accounts and apologies for verbal difficulties, whether presented as disclaimers before an anticipated fault, or, as seems more usual, after. Thus the perfunctory rituals: *Excuse me, I beg your pardon, Let me try that again,* etc.

Such interjections can certainly function as bracket markers, telling listeners where a strip that will be defined as needing attention begins or ends; but apart from this, nothing immediately substantive would seem to be gained. Presumably an aim here is to show, for example, that any deviation from proper standards offends the perpetrator's own sense of propriety and is not to be heard as characteristic of him or as an intended offense to hearers.

Clearly these remedies can be introduced into the stream of talk and executed with utter fluency, aplomb, and unself-consciousness (which is not to say that in some circumstances they can't have an anxious, blurted character); and in a great deal of verbal interaction, such interjections are hardly noticed at all, by implication being well within the rights of the speaker. Nonetheless, these little rituals require a change in footing. Instead of maintaining the prior blend of animator, principal, and author, the speaker suddenly presents his plight as an animator into his discourse, speaking for himself in his capacity as animator, this capacity typically becoming a protagonist, a character or "figure" in his statement, not merely the engine of its production. At the same time, he becomes (if he wasn't already) the sole principal, and certainly the actual author, of his words—often a sharp contrast to what went before, especially if aloud reading or reciting had been in progress.

As suggested, in much informal talk such changes in footing are perfectly in order, hardly to be oriented to as an event. Nonetheless, there are lots of occasions for animating words where such maneuvers can call attention to themselves, a violation of frame space. When (as, for example, in radio announcing) the individual is speaking in the name of an entity more inclusive than himself, his sudden thrusting of himself (and how he is doing in his animation) as a topic upon our attention, pressing himself thus upon us, can intrude him upon our senses in a way we may not have bargained for. Such remedial work, then, can presume, can strike the hearer as improper. Similarly, even the most perfunctory of hedges—such as "in my opinion" or "I think"—may be perceived as a little self-centering, a little aggrandizing, a little self-intruding, even though apparently the speaker actually hopes in this way to minimize the demands he makes by his expression of opinion.[22] Here, then, a glimpse of another way in which a remedy can itself be an offense, a glimpse of inherent difficulties with the social control model.

v

With the foregoing sketch of sociological and linguistic background and some hints of limitations associated with the social control model, turn finally to a special form of talk: TV and (especially) radio announcing—here using "announcing" broadly to cover all routine talk into a microphone.

1. Announcing comes in different modes, each placing the speaker on a distinctive footing.

First, "action override." At social spectacles of various sorts, an on-the-spot announcer is in a position to observe unfoldings that members of the radio audience can't (or can't as knowledgeably), and can undertake to give a running account of "what" is happening immediately following its happening.[23] Fresh talk is a requisite, if only because in the case of blow-by-blow accounts, presumably no one knows how the blows are going to fall before

22. It is as though speaker believes that by bracketing an assertion with a self-reference and an embedding verb, both the encounter and his reputation can be insulated from any trouble the assertion otherwise might create. Instead of taking up the position implied in the embedded portion of his utterance, the speaker (he can feel) takes the more innocuous position: that it is acceptable to report views including, incidentally, his own. And although hearers might sharply disagree with his view, they are likely to be much less in disagreement with his right to express views circumspectly. Paradoxically enough, then, a self-referencing hedge that thrusts a first-person pronoun before listeners may not strike them as self-centering (at least the speaker feels), for presumably this linguistic device allows them to stand back from the opinion expressed (as the speaker is proving he can), and to relate primarily to that sense of the speaker that is the easiest to accept, being fully shared, the self as a conversationalist offering up an opinion.

23. An interesting contrast and limiting case is the bomb-defuser's performance. He broadcasts a running account, too, but he himself is physically executing the actions that are being covered. His use of "I," then (as in: "I am unscrewing the base and I see that . . ."), has nothing to do with himself as animator, except, say, when first checking out microphonic transmission. So, too, the surgeon who explains to students in the surgical theater what he is doing as he does it.

they do—although admittedly in the case of public rituals, the sequence of events is planned beforehand in detail and ordinarily proceeds accordingly. In consequence, the announcer is in something like a "slave" relation to the events he is reporting. He is free to pick his own phrases, as in other kinds of fresh talk, but not free to stray appreciably from what participants and those familiar with the reported world would see as "what is going on."[24] If the activity in question suddenly breaks down because of fights, assassination, the collapse of physical structures, a cloudburst, or whatever, then this too must be reported as if the announcer were chained to the events before him and obliged to

24. Recently it has been argued that a decision as to what is going on cannot be made apart from understandings of what to attend and what to disattend and how to construe what is attended. Notwithstanding, most public spectacles seem to be put together with a prior agreement about what is to come to be defined as "really" going on, and so perhaps agreement is only to be expected. In any case, remote audience and actual participants are locked together in a common relation to a set of unfolding events—to outcomes—which initiates of the activity would tend to agree were the ones that were occurring. It turns out, then, that different announcers do not select greatly different aspects of what is occurring to describe, nor do they describe them very differently. Whatever arbitrariness is thus exhibited in what is defined as the "thing" going on at the time, whatever selectivity, participants in the occasion tend to concur as to what this should be. They can similarly agree that, for example, a particular announcer has intentionally failed to report something that "actually" occurred, a claim that can be valid even though an infinite number of things could occur which no announcer would bother to report on. And to say that the event as we see it is actually going on is to speak with real meaning, for it is relative to this reality that we can judge descriptions of a less "literal" kind and see them to be fictions—as when advertisers sponsor the delayed relay of a boxing match, mounting a show in which the ultimate outcome is not disclosed until the end, and each round is described sequentially in equivalent amounts of real time, so that listeners will have to sit through the same number of advertisements they would have had to, were the actual match broadcast. Whatever the sense in which a live broadcast is not the real thing, these mock-ups are unreal in an important additional sense.

Admittedly games do have a special status in regard to consensus as to what it is that is going on. The reports provided in hourly news broadcasts offer a considerable contrast; for here from nation to nation, interest group to interest group, and region to region, there is very appreciably difference of opinion as to the kinds of things that are worth reporting on and what should be said about them. And within a nation (or region), most participants are passive, in that they themselves would not necessarily hit upon such topics to report were they determining the matter. Games are designed to bring observers and participants into something of the same world; news broadcasts have to help create these circumstances in the name of reporting "significant" events.

provide live coverage of whatever has become of what he started out describing. In the face of quite unexpected tragedies and shocking surprises, the announcer is obliged to maintain enough composure to continue some sort of reporting, and if (as we might feel reasonable and proper) he does flood into "personal" register, breaching the standard distance between himself and us, we are likely to expect him to reestablish evidence of "full control" rather quickly.

In all these cases, the action in question—presumably something that goes on whether or not a remote audience can follow it—is the primary concern of the audience; the talk of the announcer is only a means to that end, required because the audience would not otherwise be able to follow the action effectively. (In television commentary, only explication and elaboration may be required; in radio announcing, verbal portraiture will be needed.) In consequence, the announcer sustains with his audience something that is equivalent to a "subordinate" encounter —subordinate, that is, to the action being reported—an illusion fostered by the announcer's tone of voice. For example, in reported golf matches, the hush that allows a putter to give undivided attention to his shot is rendered—albeit often with no objective reason—by the announcer's use of a hushed voice. Thus, announcing as action override.

Next, consider the "three-way" mode of announcing. In talk shows and guest interview formats, the master of ceremonies sustains a conversation—ostensibly fresh talk—with one or more others in the studio whilst the remote (and studio) audience is treated as if it were a ratified participant, albeit one that cannot assume the speaking role. Something the same can be said of "on the spot" interviewing. In all these cases, as in ordinarily situated face-to-face talk, the announcer may turn from his fellow participants at the microphone and acquaint the audience with background matters. He may even go so far as to let the audience know what has already transpired between the talkers just prior to the broadcast, thus apparently avoiding the need to fake conversational inquiries concerning matters the guest has already told him about. In these ways the audience can appear to be brought into the conversation as it unfolds, knowing enough to follow the talk, in principle no less knowledgeable than the platform listeners themselves as to what is about to be said. Should the announcer want the guest to repeat a particular story the announcer has already heard, this, too, can be made evident—as it is in natural, multiparty, face-to-face conversation. Thus, instead of saying, "Did you ever meet a shark when you were collecting coral?", the interviewer may say, "We were talking earlier in the green room about the time you met a shark. Would you tell our listeners the story?" (Indeed, in an effort to generate a sense of spontaneity, interviewers recently have been foregoing arranging with their guests beforehand what they are going to cover, reversing ordinary precautions.)

In any case, note that guests and panelists can be said to be present as persons, not officials, and will often be in a position to respond to a statement by an avowal of personal belief, a report of feeling, a review of own experience, and so forth; nor need these interjections be considered in any way a departure from prescribed role. Also, a considerable discrepancy can be sustained between technically faulted and perceivedly faulted discourse—almost as in the case of ordinary conversation.

I have touched on two basic modes of announcing: action override and three-way. Consider now a third, and no doubt the basic kind: "direct" announcing. Here the announcer ostensibly speaks to the audience alone, and, in a sense, speaks as if each individual hearer were the only one. A simulation of two-person conversation is thus attempted, something like a telephone conversation except that no one can answer from the other end of the line. (In television announcing, the simulation is strengthened, of course, by the speaker affecting to look directly at his hearers.) Although we individual remote listeners would certainly allow that persons other than ourselves are listening, these others are for the most part unperceivable and have the same status as we do, having no more access to the speaker than we ourselves. And all of us will ordinarily be kept in the dark about the fact that support personnel are likely to be in close touch with the proceedings. Note, should an announcer address a live studio audience, he will have to change footing, giving up the pretense of talking to an individual for the reality of group focus. (Another variant is found in phone-in shows, where the remote audience is made privy to one or both sides of colloquies that the announcer intermittently has with callers, these two-party talks conducted in the encompassing encounter the announcer is maintaining with his wider audience.)

Given the three modes of announcing—action override, three-way, and direct—it is possible to say that recitation is little used (although short commercials are frequently memorized), the main ingredients being aloud reading and fresh talk. In the case of direct announcing, which is our main concern, aloud reading is principally involved.

2. By the very character of their duties one can anticipate that announcers will be required to change footing frequently. Three-way announcing provides some gross examples. An M.C. maintaining a conversation with a guest must attempt to place the topic, mood, and pace "on hold" during station breaks (much as an interviewer must when he changes tapes, or we all do when we have to leave a telephone conversation for a moment), which can involve addressing a few bridging remarks to the station announcer, thus shifting from one three-party talk to another through temporarily excluding the guest. So, too, there is a special form of ratified by-play: finding official cause to communicate with a member of the off-mike production crew, the announcer holds off his on-mike guests and the remote audience to do so, in no way allowing his voice to suggest that anything furtive or irregular is occurring. Characteristically the addressed recipient of these managerial remarks responds in words that can't be heard by the audience, albeit the announcer may repeat the words, after the bit of business is over, in the interests of "bringing the audience in." Direct announcing involves similar changes in footing. In addition to carrying his "own" show, an M.C. may have the job of helping to switch from the show that was in progress to the one that he will do, and, in turn, from this one to the show that follows. And he will have to hold up his own proceedings with set periodicity for station breaks (call letters, frequency identification), public service announcements, and commercials—interludes which he will have to bridge at both ends, not the least precariously when he himself must do the spot "live." In all of these cases, a momentary change in footing is required.

Less gross changes in footing are easy to cite. It is known, for example, that in reading the news, a practiced announcer will rapidly change tone of voice—along with mood—to reflect sequential changes in subject matter, and even, at the end of the newscast, when he recaps what has been covered, attempt a corresponding run-through of the differential stances he employed. But although this is known, how to transcribe it isn't quite; no convenient notation system is available to enable close description.

3. At the very beginning of this paper it was suggested that the critical task of the announcer is to produce an effect of spontaneous, fluent speech. Here some elaboration is in order.

First, with some systematic exceptions, announcers give the impression that they have a personal belief in what they are saying. The way in which commercials are announced provides the most obvious example.[25]Indeed, the professional literature provides rationalizations for this institutionalized lying (Hyde 1959:35):

> Because the commercial announcer is, after all, a salesman, he has the same problem which has confronted salesmen of all times —to be effective, he must believe in his product. This is not really as difficult as one might expect. Most nationally advertised pro-

25. The western theatrical frame provides that an actor staging a character is himself not to be taken to espouse whatever the part calls for him to avow or do, and this insulation is presumably granted by the audience no matter how convincing and thoroughgoing his performance is. In the reading of commercials something else prevails. The radio or TV announcer may himself believe that such insulation is part of the frame in which he operates, but the audience doesn't necessarily agree. And this applies also to celebrities who appear under their "own" name to endorse a product. (Announcers and especially celebrities can, however, feel doubtful about throwing conviction behind what they say about a product, and [as will be illustrated later] can even betray in various ways their commitment to the sponsor.) In any case, it seems to me that radio and TV audiences are much more likely to assume that the announcer is saying what he himself actually believes than that a stage actor is. After all, actors appear in character in a time, place, role, and costume patently not their "own"; announcers, on the other hand, present themselves in the same guise and name they use in their "own" everyday life. (Professional actors who do commercials but who do not appear in their own name for the occasion are a marginal case. They seem to assume all the rights of self-dissociation from one's character enjoyed by ordinary actors, but they find themselves selling a product, not a dramatist's ideas; therein, of course, lies a very considerable moral difference, albeit one that actors have been able to rise above.

ducts are of good quality, and although mass production and fair-trade practices have tended to standardize many competing products, each will have some advantages, small or large, over its competitors. The announcer should begin to develop a belief in the products he advertises by buying and trying them. If possible, he should get to know the people who make the products, and should learn how the product is made and what it is made of. As a feeling of kinship is built up between the announcer and the product or the manufacturer, an honest enthusiasm will almost inevitably arise. If, on the other hand, experience with the product and familiarity with the manufacturer work to the opposite result, the announcer is faced with a difficult choice: he must either give up his job, or else attempt to be enthusiastic and convincing about a product in which he does not believe. This is a matter of conscience and must be settled on an individual basis.[26]

Second, if aloud reading is involved, the fact that it is will be somehow downplayed, rendering it easy for the audience to fall into feeling that fresh talk is occurring:

Even though he works from a script, and even though the audience knows he does, there is yet no worse crime that an announcer can commit than to *sound* as though he is reading. The audience willingly suspends its awareness of the fact that the announcer is reading, but in order to do so, the announcer must play his part. He must *talk* his lines, he must deliver them as though they were thoughts which had just occurred to him. [Ibid.:33]

26. A special problem arises when the same announcer must read the news *and* do the commercials that precede and/or follow. The factual character of the news (such as it is) can carry over to the commercials, which may give to commercial claims even greater credibility than the announcer is comfortable with:

A question that always arises is the newsman's involvement with commercials. Should a newscaster be permitted to deliver a live commercial within the body of his newscast? Some feel that the newsman's credibility is destroyed when he goes along with heavy world news and then reads a commercial, which obviously must be considered as a partial endorsement at least. [Hoffer 1974:40]

The BBC solves the problem by prohibiting TV announcers from *appearing* in commercials, although they are apparently allowed to do voice-overs.

The implication is that the individual animating has authored his own remarks, indeed, is doing so currently, for fresh talk entails such authorship—except, say, for brief strips of quotation of others' words embedded in the text. All of this can be illustrated by the work that announcers do in obscuring production changes. Thus, the "text-locked" voice: in switching from ordinary text to a strip that is *intended* to be heard as aloud reading (a news quote, author-identified program notes, etc.), the ostensible purpose being to relay the material instead of fully animating it, announcers can employ a voice suggesting that they themselves do not currently figure in any way as author or principal, merely as a voicing machine. In brief, instead of concealing or at least downplaying the preformulated source of what is said, the actual source is played up, its identification openly shared with the audience. (The same text-locked effect can be projected in ordinary talk when relaying what someone else has said or when "bringing to mind" what is presumably contained below the surface of one's memory.) In brief, what is merely a switch from one read text the announcer did not write to another is presented as something more than this. And, of course, the opposite impression can be created. Thus, when changing from a prerecorded spot featuring his own voice to live broadcasting, the announcer may attempt to conceal the production shift, apparently taking some pride in an ability to do this.[27]

I want to add, finally, that stations employ a pattern of "subediting" rules, whereby the surface form of sentences deriving from texts destined for print can be transformed into utterances "easy" to understand when read aloud.[28] And it turns out that sentence structures easy to understand when heard are ones that give a sense of fresh talk.

Two techniques through which the announcer produces a sense of spontaneity have been described: the projection of apparent personal belief in what is said, and the simulation of fresh

27. Reported by Marc Friedman (personal communication). It is, of course, also possible for the announcer to simulate aloud reading when, in fact, he has memorized the text, this being a standard ruse for actors in stage plays when the script calls for the ostensible aloud reading of a text.

28. The leading source here, and probably the most extensive current linguistic examination of radio talk, is Bell (1977).

talk. As a third, consider that characteristically, prime-time national network announcers—newscasters, disc jockeys, program M.C.s—deliver lines that technically speaking are almost flawless, and that they operate under a special obligation to do so, whether fresh talk, aloud reading, or memorization is involved. Indeed, although ordinary talk is full of technical faults that go unnoticed as faults, broadcasters seem to be schooled to realize our cultural stereotypes about speech production, namely, that ordinarily it will be without influencies, slips, boners, and gaffes, i.e., unfaultable. Interestingly, these professional obligations, once established, seem to generate their own underlying norms for hearers as well as speakers, so that faults we would have to be trained linguistically to hear in ordinary talk can be glaringly evident to the untrained ear when encountered in broadcast talk. May I add that what one may here gloss as a "difference in norms" is what I claim to be a difference in prescribed frame space.

Another factor is editorial elaboration. Small additions to a prescribed text, if allowable and if handled under the tonal auspices established for the prescribed text, provide means of giving the whole a fresh-talk feel. More interesting, some printed sources of information can be drawn on quickly—even during the announcer's production tolerance time—thereby allowing the announcer to produce something that is a sort of fresh talk and also to project an impression of considerable knowledgeability. Liner notes provide such a source of material on music programs. In classical music broadcasts, the Schwann catalogue and such books as the *Penguin Dictionary of Music* may also serve, although the announcer may have to cull his information a few minutes before it is to be used. Here the format in which he inserts dates and places will be fresh talk (however oft used as a formula), so the listener tends to hear it all as extemporaneous. Something the same can be said of the use of little formulae preceding the final item in a series (for example, "And last but not least . . ."), which can give a sense that the whole series is one the announcer is more than merely mechanically involved with. In news broadcasts, there is the "kicker," an item that can be read with a change in footing as a funny human interest story upon which a passing (even unscripted) comment may be made, consequently giving the whole news spot (if faintly) a fresh-talk character. Observe, too, that when an announcer openly quotes a text as a means of elaborating his own, he can omit from expression the fact that what he culled was *itself* quoted in liner notes or another source. A lamination is slipped, and an impression of both authority and freshness results.

Finally, consider that whatever else an announcer does, he must talk to listeners who are not there in the flesh. Because talk is learned, developed, and ordinarily practiced in connection with the visual and audible response of immediately present recipients, a radio announcer must inevitably talk *as if* responsive others were before his eyes and ears. (Television announcers are even more deeply committed to this condition than are radio announcers.) In brief, announcers must conjure up in their mind's eye the notion of listeners, and act as though these phantoms were physically present to be addressed through gaze, body orientation, voice calibrated for distance, and the like. In a fundamental sense, then, broadcasting (whether announcing news, giving a political address, or whatever) involves self-constructed talk projected under the demands, gaze, and responsiveness of listeners who aren't there. Of course, here a live studio audience can help, but often (in radio, at least) its presence must be downplayed or acknowledged as a second audience different from the invisible one.

So announcers must not only watch the birdie; they must talk to it. Under these circumstances, it is understandable that they will often slip into a simulation of talking *with* it. Thus, after a suitable pause, an announcer can verbally respond to what he can assume is the response his prior statement evoked, his prior statement itself having been selected as one to which a particular response was only to be expected. Or, by switching voices, he himself can reply to his own statement and then respond to the reply, thereby shifting from monologue to the enactment of dialogue. In both cases the timing characteristics of dialogue are simulated. In short (and to be considered later), announcing is response constructive,[29] and this apart from the fact that ordinar-

---

29. Stage acting employs a somewhat different timing adjustment. Ostensibly exhibiting the temporal sequencing of natural conversation, actors in fact

ily a relatively "formal" style is sustained, one that is characteristic of public addresses, not intimate conversation.

VI

One starts, then, with the announcer's commitment to maintaining what is heard as fresh talk no more than ordinarily unfaulted, but which is nearly unfaultable aloud reading. This work obligation distinguishes announcers' delivery from that of laypersons in ordinary day-to-day talk. Announcers must not only face many of the contingencies of everyday speech production (and, as will be seen, at greater cost), but also many contingencies specific to broadcasting. Consider now the special features of broadcasting work insofar as they condition the realization of the broadcaster's central task—the production of seemingly faultless fresh talk.[30]

It should be said first that it is true of radio broadcasting, as it is true of any communication system, that trouble enters from different points, these points located at different levels or layers in the organizational structure of the undertaking. For example, a power failure and a voice failure can equally lead to a breakdown in transmission, but obviously these two possibilities should be traced back to different layers in the structure of the communication system, here reflected in the kind of remedial work that is undertaken. Indeed, one of the values of examining troubles is as a reminder that communication systems are vulnerable from different layerings of their structure.

1. Consider first the special character of broadcast audiences. Plainly, the announcer has little specific control over who joins his audience, and often little knowledge of who has elected to do so. So, except in the case of "special-interest" stations and programs, and, say, the age/sex slant of morning and afternoon TV shows, the audience must be addressed as though it were the public-at-large. And, of course, broadcast audiences are typically

---

inhibit the overlapping found in such talk and build in pauses between turns to allow audiences to "respond" without this response interfering with audibility.

30. Here, for want of proper field work, I draw mainly on the Kermit Schafer corpus of troubles that broadcasters have gotten into.

large compared to auditorium audiences. It follows that any display of faultable conduct will be very widely witnessed, thereby
constituting a threat unique to the electronic age. Influencies and
slips will disseminate a picture of incompetency. Any factual
error that is imparted can mislead a vast number, such that however small the cost to the individual listener, the sum across all
listeners can be enormous. (Thus, a strong imperative to provide
factual corrections no matter what this does to text delivery.) Any
gaffe, any lapse from appropriate respect for ordinary sensibilities
—religious, moral, political, etc.—can be considered an impiety at
a national level. Any boner, any failure to sustain educational
standards, any failure to indicate possession of a respectable corpus of knowledge attesting to familiarity with the world, awareness of recent public events, historical knowledgeability, and so
forth, is not likely to be missed; and even ones that aren't fully
"obvious" will be caught by some, if only Kermit Schafer:[31]

> [Madison Square Garden announcer just before fight]: "May the
> winner emerge victorious." [*PB:*53]

Moreover, radio and television audiences are not only large but
also heterogeneous in regard to "sensitivities": ethnicity, race,
religion, political belief, gender, regional loyalties, and all the
physical and mental stigmata. The announcer's inadvertent or
intended disparagement of almost any category of person or almost any article of belief is likely to find some angry ears. And,
of course, an announcer cannot offend his audience without also
incurring the displeasure of the station management and the
sponsor (if any). In consequence, announcers—like politicians—
have traditionally maintained strict decorum in mentioning sex,
motherhood, the lame, the blind, and, not the least, the station
and its sponsors.

Further, the delicacy of the announcer's position is not accounted for by patently faulted strips or even technically faultable ones. It is as if the sensitivities of sectionalist audiences,
special-interest groups, and presumably the station management

---

31. And apparently not only Kermit Schafer. The British magazine *Private
Eye*, in response to the blooperisms of David Coleman (a sports TV commentator), has established a regular column called "Colemanballs" to record such on
the part of both radio and TV announcers.

and sponsors provided the general listener with a discovery device for uncovering risible mistakes. As though the audience sympathized with the position of the announcer merely to find out what he would find embarrassing. The issue, then, is not what *offends* the listener, but what a listener assumes *might* offend *some* listener or other. Furthermore, error in any obvious sense—lay or linguistic—need not be involved. It appears that listeners seem primed for and oriented to alternative readings of what is said, that is, to the reframing of texts, and in this an obvious "error" is not essential. What is required is listeners skilled in, and oriented to, rereadings.[32] And where an announcer falls short is not only in failing to maintain the usual requirements of word production, but also in failing to canvas every possible reading of his words and phrases before uttering them, thereby correcting for potential alternatives, no matter how far-fetched. Thus, the progression from faults to faultables must be extended to the risibly interpretable, and this last appears to be the broadest category of all. And yet, however "forced" a second reading, it introduces much the same sort of issues for the announcer as do obvious faults. Thus lexically based ambiguity:

> "Men, when it's time to shave, you have a date with our two-headed model." [*PB:* 10]

> "Stay tuned to this station for your evening's entertainment. Immediately following Walter Winchell, hear the current dope in Hollywood—Listen to Louella Parsons." [*SB:* 134]

Contextual "unfreezing" of formulaic figurative phrases:

> Announcer: "Folks, try our comfortable beds. I personally stand behind every bed we sell." [*PB:* 128]

> [Jim McKay, describing the World Barrel-Jumping Championship on ABC's "Wide World of Sports"]: Leo Lebel has been competing with a pulled stomach muscle, showing a lot of guts!" [*Pr.:* 42]

---

32. A parallel is to be marked here to the practice in informal talk of punning playfulness in which participants vie with one another to see who can best transform the other's innocent words into ones with a "suggestive," unintended meaning. On unintended puns in general, see Sherzer (1978).

Pragmatic referential ambiguity bearing on the elision of noun or verb:

> "And just received is a new stock of Ries Sanforized Sports Shirts for men with 15 or 17 necks." [*PB:* 19]

> Commercial: "So, friends, if you're looking for frequent deliveries direct to your home, their driver will deliver as many cases of bottled water as you wish. Think of the many conveniences this service offers . . . no empty bottles to return to the store. Look for the nearest delivery man in the yellow pages of your phone book . . . you'll find him under water!" [*Pr.:* 81]

> "It's a nine pound boy born at Memorial Hospital for Mr. and Mrs. Jack Jason of Elm Road. Mrs. Jason was the former Susan Mulhaney. Services will be held tomorrow at 2 P.M. at Morton's Funeral Chapel for Jasper Howard, age 91, who passed on in his sleep yesterday. I'm sorry, our time is running out, so several deaths and births will have to be postponed until next week at the same time." [*PB:* 69]

Questions of syntactic structure—anaphoric reference, word order, and the like:

> Newscaster: "The loot and the car were listed as stolen by the Los Angeles Police Department." [*SB:* 30]

> "Your Masterwork Concert Hour will now present Boris Goudonov, the only opera Mussorgsky ever wrote on Friday evening." [*PB:* 100]

> Want Ads of the Air: "Our next TV want ad comes from a Mrs. Agnes Cooper. She is an elderly single lady looking for a small room where she can bake herself on a small electric stove." [*SB:* 64]

> Louella Parsons: "And here in Hollywood it is rumored that the former movie starlet is expecting her fifth child in a month!" [*Pr.:* 59]

> Local News: "And here is an item of local interest. Calvin Johnson, age 47, was booked for drunken driving in the county jail!" [*SB:* 31]

Ambiguities such as these would ordinarily go unnoticed in everyday face-to-face talk. The "context" would ordinarily make the speaker's intent clear, and speaker's intent would somehow be allowed to inhibit competing interpretations. But it seems that broadcast talk (as with some written discourse) cannot rely on hearers' good will as a means of discouraging alternate framings. Whereas in conversation ambiguity ordinarily seems to be an issue only when listeners are actually uncertain as to how the speaker meant his words to be taken, in broadcast talk there is a different issue. As suggested, it is not that the audience is left unclear about what could possibly be meant, or uncertain as to which of two possible meanings was correct, or whether or not the announcer wanted a double meaning to be taken. Almost always the audience is certain enough as to how the broadcaster meant his references to be interpreted and his remarks framed. (Nor is there a question of "keying," that is, a correct assessment of what was "literally" said, but a misjudgment of how the speaker intended this to be taken—for example, jokingly, sarcastically, quotatively, theatrically, and so forth; for it seems that in radio talk, actual miskeying is rather effectively guarded against.) Indeed, without this understanding there could be no fun and games, no pleasure taken in vicariously twitting the speaker.[33] It is the announcer's failure to arrange his words so that no obviously unintended, additional reading is discoverable that is at point. (Which is not to say, of course, that in some environments, such as schoolrooms and prisons, alternate readings, especially of a sexual kind, aren't even more imaginatively construed than is the case in public broadcasting.) Frame ambiguities, then, even more than other kinds of faults, must be defined in terms of the tendency of various audiences to look for such possibilities, and by and large (at least in the case of ambiguities) it is only

33. It should be apparent that risible announcer faultables could be treated as one department of a general subject matter—the effects, functions, and uses of multiple framings—another department of which is the riddles and jokes intentionally set up in the language play of children. (In this connection, see the useful linguistic classification of sources of ambiguity—to which I am much indebted—in Hirsh-Pasek, Gleitman, and Gleitman [1978:118]: phonological, lexical, surface structure, deep structure, morpheme boundary without phonological distortion, morpheme boundary with distortion. See also Shultz and Horibe [1974] and Shultz and Pilon [1973].) Indeed, as will be illustrated later, upon discovering that he has inadvertently allowed a risible framing to occur, an announcer may try to save a little face by following up with a remark that is to be perceived as intentionally continuing in the same interpretive frame.

relative to such tendencies that one can refer to objective faults.

I have suggested that broadcast audiences are not only personally offendable by faults, but that they actively seek out faults that might be offensive to someone. Typically this means that once attention is focused, say, on a slip, an alternate framing of what was intended will be searched out simultaneously. Nor need the audience wait for an "obvious" fault to occur; by a stretch of interpretation, a well-delivered, apparently innocent, utterance will often do. It should now be obvious that very often what is found in these various circumstances will not be just *any* alternative—an alternative, such as the ones illustrated, that takes its significance from the sheer fact that it *is* an alternative—but one which calls up meanings that are specifically embarrassing in their own right to the line the announcer is obliged to sustain. And announcers occasionally appear to help in this connection. Perhaps a psychoanalytical argument is sometimes warranted here, namely, that what the announcer would be most embarrassed to say he somehow feels compelled to say in spite of himself. Certainly some members of the audience are alive to this "overdetermination" interpretation of slips (whether believing it or not), and having it in mind leave the announcer needful of having it in mind, too. Two matters are to be considered here.

First, the unintended reading can be seen, occasionally, as "only too true," discrediting not merely the assumption that the announcer will control for a single course of meaning, but also the very sentiments it was his duty to convey. The audience may be generally suspicious that the announcer is in league with the station's commercial interests and is mouthing statements he could not himself believe; in any case, second readings can ironically belie innocent, intended ones.[34]

Thus, whole-word reversal can be involved with retention of original structure:

34. Slips that are seen as all too meaningful cause risible notice during informal talk, but it appears that such occurrences are not frequent, the fit having to be too good. I might add that some ironic reversals depend upon a shift from the "dominant" meaning of a word to a vernacular one, thereby involving two principles, not one:

Religious Program: "In closing our TV CHURCH OF THE AIR, let me remind all of our listeners that time wounds all heals!" [*SB:* 126]

Commercial: "Summer is here, and with it those lazy days at the beach; and don't forget your Tartan sun lotion. Tartan is the lotion that lets you burn but never lets you tan." [*SB:66*]

Station Break: "This is Station WELL, Battle Creek, where listening is by chance, not by choice." [*SB:25*]

Announcer: Try this lovely four-piece starter set in your home for seven days. If you are not satisfied, return it to us. So you see you have everything to lose and nothing to gain. [*PB:44*]

"It's low overhead that does it, so always shop at Robert Hall where prices are high and quality is low." [*PB:126*]

Commercial: "For the best in glass work, metal work or upholstering, see Hastin Glass, where every department is a sideline, not a business!" [*Pr.:39*]

Or whole word substitution (or whole word change due to phonological distortion of one segment of the original), again without structural change:

"Viceroys—if you want a good choke." [*PB:49*]

Sportscaster: "And now coming into the ball game for the Reds is number forty-four, Frank Fuller, futility infielder." [*SB:76*]

[Local Newscast]: "Credit for the discovery of the stolen automobile was given to Lieutenant Blank, a defective of the Los Angeles force." [*PB:92*]

[NBC News]: "Word comes to us from usually reliable White House Souses." [*PB:93*]

"You are listening to the mucous of Clyde Lucas." [*PB:33*]

Or matters of word order involving agents in passivization, adverbial phrases modifying an understood higher sentence, placement of adverbs and of adverbial phrases, or other such sources of structural ambiguity:

"Here's a house for sale that won't last long." [*PB:86*]

Commercial: "So drive your old car down to our showroom, come in, and we will show you how little you need to own a brand-new car." [*SB:82*]

Sportscaster: "Jack Kachave, with a bad knee, limps back to the huddle. He wants to play this game in the worst way . . . and that's exactly what he is doing!" [*Pr.:* 8]

Or pragmatically based referential ambiguity:

Newsman: "And it is felt in Washington that we have been most fortunate in having Nikita Khrushchev with us, and when he leaves we will be most grateful!" [*SB:* 98]

"We note with regrettable sorrow that Mrs. Vandermeer is recovering from a bad fall on the ice." [*PB:* 95]

[Laundry Commercial]: "When your clothing is returned there is little left to iron." [*PB:* 89]

Second, observe that listeners will not only be on the lookout for ironically apt readings, but also of course for prurient, "off-color" ones. Thus, phonological distortion resulting in a conventional word, but an inopportune one:

Local News: "Tonight will be the last night of the charity card party and bridge tournament. As of Friday night, Mrs. Updyke of the Springfield Women's Club is ahead by two pints." [*SB:* 83]

Louella Parsons: "It is rumored here in Hollywood that the film company bought the rights to a new navel for Audrey Hepburn!" [*Pr.:* 16]

"Word has just reached us that a home-made blonde exploded in the Roxy Theater this morning." [*PB:* 139]

"And Dad will love Wonder Bread's delicious flavor too. Remember it's Wonder Bread for the breast in bed." [*PB:* 9]

Or phonological disturbance resulting in a "suggestive" nonword —often along with an inopportune real one:

"This is KTIW, Sexas Titty er, Texas City." [*PB:* 74]

"This is the Dominion network of the Canadian Broad Corping Castration." [*PB:* 105]

Or lexical ambiguity:

Announcer: "Ladies who care to drive by and drop off their clothes will receive prompt attention." [*PB:* 48]

Commercial: "And all you women will love these sheer stockings. This hosiery is dressy enough for any fancy wear, and is so service-able for every day that many women wear nothing else!" [*SB:*109]

[Mutual Network announcer]: "The nation was glad to learn that, in the cold of winter, John L. Lewis dropped his union suit." [*PB:* 94]

Commercial: "Ladies, go to Richard's Variety Store today. . . . Richard is cleaning out ladies' panties for 29¢—be sure to get in on this special deal." [*SB:*32]

Or structural ambiguity:

Announcer: "At Heitman's you will find a variety of fine foods, expertly served by experienced waitresses in appetizing forms." [*PB:*56]

"Good afternoon, this is your department store TV counselor— Here's news for those who have little time for your Christmas shopping. Tonight, after working hours on the sixth floor, models will display gowns half off." [*PB:*72]

Less commonly, prurient readings may be allowed by inopportune word boundaries:[35]

[Louis Armstrong, on the Dorsey's "Stage Show"]: "Okay, you cats, now just play the simple mustard jazz not too slow and not too fast . . . just half fast." [*PB:*132]

[BBC]: "Here's an all time favorite made popular by the famous Miss Jessie Matthews several years back, *Dancing on the Ceiling.* This one surely deserves to be on every British Hit List." [*PB:*124]

Disc Jockey: "Well, rock 'n rollers, it's time for our mystery-guest contest. If you guess the name of our next artist, our sponsors will send you two tickets to the RKO theatre in your neighborhood. Now the clue to this singer, and this is the only clue I'm going to give you, is that she had two of the biggest hits in the country." [*SB:*86]

Or by word pronunciation producing homophonic ambiguity:

35. It has been suggested by Garnes and Bond (1975:222) that boundary assignment (addition, shifting, and especially deletion) is a principal source of hearing slips but a minor source of speaking slips.

"Final results of the FFA contest are: Apple picking won by Dick Jones, Tractor driving award to Jack Davis. One of our own girls, Miss Betty Smith, was chosen the best hoer." [*PB:*43]

Salacious rereadings are especially difficult to guard against in regard to a class of words and phrases which can be called "leaky." Even without benefit of phonological disturbance, word interchange or structural ambiguity, such terms are treacherous, unstabilizing single meanings. Examples: *balls, can, behind, gas, parts, come, lay, globes, big ones, fanny,* [36] *piece, erection, business, rubbers, make, drawers, nuts, sleep with.* (A feature of leaky words is that each usually has a widely employed innocent meaning, whilst the salacious meaning is part of widely accepted, non-"literal" vernacular.) And as with any other source of prurient rereading, the audience can feel that they have caught out the announcer in an inadvertent breach of the moral standards set for broadcasting, that his efforts to avoid this have come to naught comically, and that he is "one down":[37]

[BBC announcer at the launching of the Queen Mary]: "From where I am standing, I can see the Queen's bottom sticking out just over her water line." [*PB:*120]

Contestant: "How much time do I have to answer my question?" Quizmaster: "Lady, yours is a little behind, so we'd better try to squeeze it in within five seconds." [*SB:*118]

Cooking Program: "Good morning. Today we are going to bake a spice cake, with special emphasis on how to flour your nuts!" [*SB:*32]

[OPA spot announcement] "Ladies, take your fat cans down to the corner butcher." [*PB:*131]

"It's a laugh riot, it's a musical treat, it's the film version of the hit broadway show, *Gentlemen Prefer Blondes,* starring Jane Russell and Marilyn Monroe. Yes sir, the big ones come to R.K.O." [*PB:*111]

36. Does not leak in Britain.
37. In the collections of leaky utterances I have seen, my impression is that the referent-person leaked on is more likely to be a woman than a man, whereas, in the case of announcing, the perpetrator is usually a man—if only on occupational grounds. I assume the underlying reason is to be found in our traditional sex roles, not our humor.

"Starting next week at the Paramount Theater you will see that rollicking comedy smash hit, *Pale Face,* starring Bob Hope, America's favorite comedian, and lovely Jane Russell. Boy, what a pair!" [*PB:*103]

"Calling all parents, calling all kids! Here's your chance to buy a Davey Crockett bed—yes, friends, Hunt's Furniture Store has Davey Crockett beds—it's a twin size bed, just right for the kids —with scenes of Davey Crockett in action on the mattress!" [*PB:* 109]

Newscaster: "Plans were announced for the parade which will follow the Governors' Conference. At two P.M. the cars will leave their headquarters just as soon as the Governors are loaded!" [*Pr.:* 55]

Announcer: "At Moe's Esso Station, you can get gassed, charged up, and your parts lubricated in 30 minutes!" [*PB:*36]

So announcers can fall into saying something that not only allows for unintended reframing, but also a reading that is either all-too-true or risqué. Here again, note, one faces a problem connected with the social control model. Second readings, whether a result of word inversion, mispronunciation, homonymous forms, ambiguous pronominal or clausal reference, or whatever, confront the perpetrator with a dilemma. The more unfortunate the unplanned reading, the more extended and substantial will be the apology that is in order; but the more elaborate and pointed the apology, the more attention will be focused on the difficulty, and in consequence, the more embarrassing will be the misfortune and the more needful of apology.

Moreover, there is this. Whether or not an error is itself interpretable as risqué or ironically apt, the attention that is focused on a corrected replay carries its own special vulnerabilities, and these too reflect on the peculiarities of the social control process. For in the heat of the moment, the announcer will more than usually flub the correction, and thus be stuck with having drawn attention not only to an error already made, but now to the making of an error—an error sometimes more risqué or ironic than the original fault:

Newscaster: "It is beginning to look here, that the Canadian Prime Minister is going to have difficulty with his dame luck cabinet . . . I mean his lame dick cabinet!" [*SB:*124]

Disc Jockey: "And that was 'South Town' sung by the Blue Bellies . . . I mean, the Blue Balls . . . the Blue Belles!" [*Pr.:*30]

Weather Forecaster: "Well, many of you who awakened early saw the dreary-looking, foreboding black clouds which indicate that we are in for a long rainy bleakened . . . I mean a long blainey leakend!!!" [*Pr.:*75]

Once it is seen that audiences take an active interest (and often a delight) in uncovering imperfections in the announcer's word production, it should be evident that the social control response—in this case, snickers and laughs the announcer can't hear unless he has a studio audience—can become something of an end in itself—indeed, an official one—here again pointing to the limitation of the social control model. This is clear in contestant shows and variety talk shows where persons quite inexperienced in broadcast talk find themselves required to perform verbally before a microphone. It appears that the very considerable amount of technical influency they produce is allowed to pass without particular notice (much as it would in ordinary conversation), but the slips, boners, and gaffes they produce are another matter. A studio audience is likely to be available and will establish through its open laughter that laughing at "incompetence" is part of what the show is all about:

[Anna Moffo, on Carson's "Tonight Show"] discussing her role as Brunhilde, stated, "In order to sing Brunhilde, all you need to wear is a pair of comfortable shoes and nothing else (AUDIENCE LAUGHTER). You know what I mean." [*Pr.:*80]

Quizmaster: "All right now, for twenty-five silver dollars: Who were the Big Four? Contestant: "Er . . . let's see . . . Jane Russell, Jayne Mansfield . . ." (AUDIENCE LAUGHTER) [*Pr.:*63]

"Laughing at" as an end in itself can also be clearly seen in the "What's My Line?" format, where unintended *double entendre* are automatically generated by the structure of the show. Panelists are required to guess the occupation of persons brought before them. The audience is informed beforehand so that it will be able to appreciate what the panelists can't. And, of course, the presented persons are selected for the show with embarrassments in mind.

"Is your product used by one sex over the other?" (*PB:*111) becomes an inadvertent but facilitated fault when the respondent has been selected because of being a mattress stuffer.

Here, incidentally, is another complication in regard to social control. When a speaker addressing a live audience learns from the sound of sudden laughter that he has made an error, he may feel compelled to jump in quickly with a strident candidate correction. This remedial utterance will inhabit the focus of attention created by audience response to the defective utterance. When it turns out that the speaker has hit upon the wrong aspect of his faulty utterance to correct, he will inevitably provide his listeners with a second breach and second opportunity for laughter, but this time at the critical moment when they have already started to roll downhill:

> Announcer: "Here's your question. There was a famous French author, who wrote many, many famous stories. He is the man who wrote 'The Black Tulip' and 'The Three Musketeers.' What is the name of this famous French author?"
> Contestant: "Oh golly . . . I'm nervous . . . let me see . . . OH! Alexandre Dumb-ass! (LAUGHTER) OH! Henry Dumb-ass!"

> Here's a question from *Double or Nothing*, CBS, that rocked the studio audience with laughter: Question: Where is the Orange Free State? Answer: California! I mean Florida! [PB:66]

2. We have considered the treacherousness of broadcast audiences. Consider how that the fact that listeners are on the prowl for faultables is worsened by a technical feature of broadcasts, namely, that very often the text is formulated totally in advance, and, of course, very often by someone other than the individual who is to read it aloud. Although one might think that pre-scripting merely eases the announcer's burden in this connection (giving him an opportunity to check through his text before delivering it), there are considerations on the other side.

In everyday fresh talk, whatever impression of speech competency the speaker manages to give is a product of his having a choice of words and phrases with which to realize his thoughts. As suggested, words he can't pronounce "correctly" without special thought, or whose meaning is not quite clear to him, he tends to avoid, and in such a fashion that there is no indication that a lapse has been averted. A favorable impression of competence can thus be generalized from the words that do get spoken. (One might therefore argue that speakers in general appear to be more competent than they actually are.) These avoidance techniques cannot readily be applied when a pre-fixed text must be read, or even when paraphrasing is allowed but certain personal names and place names must be mentioned. (Practice runs help, but are not always possible.)

> "And stay tuned for the late movie, Alexander Dumas' immortal classic *The Count of Monte Crisco,* starring Robert Donut." [*PB:*133]

> Announcer: "And now to conclude our program of Christmas Carols, our guest star will sing 'Come All Ye Faithful,' by Adeste Fidelis." [*PB:*13]

> "Now here's an interesting looking record—it's got a classical label, sung by a trio, John, Charles and Thomas." [*PB:*71]

> "And now back to our all-request recorded program. We've had a request for a record by that popular Irish tenor, Mari O'Lanza." [*PB:*127]

Indeed, freedom to embed required names in extemporaneous (albeit formulaic) elaboration can make matters worse:

> Disc Jockey: Now we hear one of my favorite selections by George Gershwin, with lyrics by his lovely wife, Ira. [*PB:*41]

Also, fresh talkers—especially in face-to-face everyday talk —are in a position to take the local environment and the local hearership into consideration in preselecting words and phrases so that likely alternative readings are ruled out. (Of course, in face-to-face talk, the social and personal identity of the listeners will oblige the speaker to preselect on the basis of a whole range of fundamental factors—propriety being at issue, not merely disambiguation. He will have to consider their age, sex, ethnicity, and religion relative to his, their "personal feelings," the information it can be assumed they possess, and so forth.) However, when someone other than the animator prepares a text out of the context of the animation, then, apparently, alternative frames are hard to avoid, even apparently by writers who are acutely alive to the need of doing so. As though the premonitoring which serves as a check in fresh talk can't be employed away from occasions of delivery. Thus, for example, the frequency of "leaky" words in spite of editorial vigilance.

3. I have suggested that prewritten texts have less flexibility than fresh talk, less of what permits the speaker to avoid words he can't use or pronounce "correctly," and avoid phrasings that aren't the best suited to the audience at hand. Consider now another problem associated with scripted texts. Without any failing other than not checking the script, an announcer may find himself lodged cold in a text that is incomplete, jumbled, or in some other way nonsensical. The embarrassment can be deep, speaking to the way we assemble things to say. In actual fresh talk, the speaker's thought or theme seems to serve as a running guide, ensuring that his statements don't run too far off the mark, even though he may have to search for a word or retract one he has spoken. If the speaker does "lose the thought" of a statement in midstream, he can make this evident with a trailing intonation, a ritualized expression of his situation. Reading a prepared text is a considerably different matter. Instead of constantly appealing to the overall thought behind the text as a guide, an aloud reader can rely on upcoming bits of the text itself. Announcers use these upcoming passages to determine how to parse what is currently being read, and thence to provide through stress, juncture, "feeling," pitch, and other prosodic markers a speaking that displays a plausible interpretation of the text. When, however, an announcer loses his text, or, rather, is lost by it, his effort to provide a usable interpretation prosodically can carry him in a direction that cannot be sustained by what turns out to follow. The fresh-talk speaker can warn us of losing his thought while at the same time reducing his claim to meaningful speech, but the announcer has ordinarily foregone such measures, for he has read what he takes to be the line in a confident, committed, "full" voice. In consequence he not only can create the impression that he is not in mental touch with the thought he was to have been expressing, but also that he is intentionally faking fresh talk. Here, then, a fault is discrediting:

> Weather forecaster: "The Mid West is suffering from one of the worst cold-spells in years, with temperatures dropping as low as twenty degrees below zero. Tomorrow's forecast is for continued mild!" [*PB:*71]

Commercial: "So remember . . . National Airlines has ten flights daily to Miami and also Florida!" [*Pr.:*59]

[Newscaster reading unchecked item]: "In the head-on collision of the two passenger cars, five people were killed in the crash, two seriously." [*SB:*68]

4. Another source of trouble, this time not restricted to texts that the announcer has not written himself: track error. Here is a frame problem, pure and simple. An editor—or the announcer himself during a practice run-through—interlards a text with cue signs, reading instructions, and other stage directions; and the announcer, during the "live" reading, construes these comments as part of the text and reads them along with it[38] (of the three forms of production—memorization, aloud reading, and fresh talk—only aloud reading seems vulnerable to this particular kind of confusion):

> When Pat Adelman, program director of Station KNOW, Texas, finished preparing the day's schedule, he left it in the control room. Later he made a change—instead of Les Brown's orchestra, he substituted a religious program which was to originate from New York. He scratched out Les Brown's name and wrote over it, Yom Kippur. When the new announcer came on shift, he picked up the schedule and exhorted his listeners to "Stay tuned for the dance music of Yom Kippur's Orchestra." [*PB:*9]

> Bess Meyerson, former Miss America and co-MC on *The Big Payoff,* popular network TV program, was interviewing a contestant on the program. She was handed a note from one of the members of the production staff, which told her that the contestant was London-bound, so as to get this added color into her interview. Believing that this note was an added reminder of the contestant's name,

38. Goffman (1974:320). Some of these instructions, such as the Spanish inverted question mark at the beginning of interrogative sentences, provide help without introducing the possibility of misframing. But other devices, such as the use of parentheses to mark out-of-frame comments, can lead to misinterpretation, in this case reading the comments as if they were parenthetical statements *in* the text instead of *about* it.

A similar problem occurs in *lingua franca* talk ("two parties speaking different native languages communicate via a third language"), where "What happens in fact is that questions about language (metaquestions) get taken as questions about meaning (object questions)" (Jordan and Fuller 1975:11, 22), a confusion, in short, between "mention" and "use."

she introduced him thusly: "Ladies and gentlemen, I would like you to meet Mr. London Bound." [*PB:*62]

"It's 8 P.M. Bulova Watch Time. On Christmas say Merry Christmas, and on New Year's, say Happy New Year." [*SB:*36]

5. Consider the framing issue arising because announcers must frequently cite the title of songs, movies, and the like. Such titles, of course, are meant to be treated as "frozen" wholes, set off from the utterance in which they are embedded; the constituent words of the title are meant to have their standard meanings *within* the title, not outside it. In terms of the work titled, a title can cannote something, presumably touching off a general theme to be found in what is titled. In terms of the utterance in which the title in embedded, the title can only mean what any other title might, namely, the name of some work. In effect, in the embedding or "higher" sentence or clause, a title's words are being *mentioned,* not *used.* However, announcers find that the titles they mention may be interpreted "literally," as words or phrases having the same status as the others in the utterance and readable in a single syntactic sequence:

> Station Break: "Stay tuned for our regular Sunday Broadcast by Reverend R. J. Ryan, who will speak on In Spite of Everything." [*Pr.:*63]

> "And now, Nelson Eddy sings *While My Lady Sleeps* with the men's chorus." [*PB:*93]

> Station Break: "Be sure not to miss THE COMING OF CHRIST, Wednesday, 8:30 P.M., 7:30 Central Time." [*SB:*11]

> "There's excitement in store on our *Million Dollar Movie* tonight with Ann Sheridan—stay tuned as Philips Milk of Magnesia brings you *Woman on the Run.*" [*PB:*108]

And, indeed, titles may be read off against each other, as though both were part of a single, extendable sequence:

> Commercial: "Starting Thursday for four days only, see Betty Davis in *The Virgin Queen* and *Tonight's the Night . . .* Starting next Monday be sure to see *Breakthrough* and *Emergency Wedding!*" [*Pr.:*15]

> Announcer: "Your city station now brings you a program of piano music, played by Liberace, in a program titled 'MUSIC YOU

WANT', followed by 'MUSIC YOU'LL REALLY ENJOY' on Melody Theatre." [*SB:* 112]

Disc Jockey: "Our HAPPY DAYS musical show continues with a medley; we will now hear, 'I'm Walking Behind You,' 'Finger of Suspicion,' and 'The Call of the Wild Goose!' " [*Pr.:* 23]

6. Next is the problem of page transitions. Studio "copy" that is two or more pages long requires the aloud reader to finish the last line of one page and start the first line of the next page in a time that can be encompassed by production margins. And this is routinely achieved with opposing pages. When, however, a page must be *turned*, an overheld pause or an overheld syllable may be required, which can intrude on the impression of fresh talk that is otherwise being sustained.[39] Very occasionally at this moment an unintended risible meaning also becomes available to listeners:

Commercial: "So stop by our downtown store and visit our fashion center. You will see our lovely models in heat . . . (PAUSE, TURNS PAGE) . . . resistant fabrics which will keep you cooler this summer." [*SB:* 14]

"Tums will give you instant relief and assure you no indigestion or distress during the night . . . So try Tums and go to sleep with a broad . . ." (turns page) ". . . smile." [*PB:* 137]

7. There is the issue of "juncture readings," an issue structurally similar to the page transition problem already considered. Program management tends to focus on the content of particular segments of the day's broadcasting, and upon fluent

39. When an individual reads to a physically present audience, it seems that pauses at page transitions—including ones involving the turning of a page—are "read out" by listeners, indeed so effectively disattended as to not be heard at all. Radio reading systematically disallows this collaboration, although televised reading might not. Interestingly, in music performances for live audiences, page-turn delays apparently can't be managed by means of the collaborative disattendance of the hearers, presumably because timing is much more fixed in music than in talk—in music being in effect semantic in character. Furthermore, a musician who turns his own pages cannot use that hand for music-making, this not being a problem when the mouth, not the hands, are the source of animation. (Of course, in singing and horn-blowing the timing of breath intake becomes very much an issue, the mechanics of animation here having to be made somehow compatible with the sustaining of sound.)

temporal linkage of one segment to the preceding and following ones. But this very smoothness creates its own problems. Any review of copy that editors, writers, and announcers have time for tends to be limited to the internal content of particular segments, that being the substantive unit of production. In consequence, unanticipated (and thus almost certainly undesired) readings are possible across the ending of one segment and beginning of another. Apparently these possibilities are not sufficiently considered in advance to avoid all juncture readability. Given the tendency for the audience to look for risible readings no matter how obviously unintended, segment junctures can produce faultables.[40]

> On the Arthur Godfrey program, time was running short, therefore two commercials were thrown together back to back. This was the dialogue that resulted from the rushed commercials. "Lipton Soup is what you will want for dinner tonight." (NEXT COMMERCIAL) "Thank goodness I brought an Alka Seltzer!" [*Pr.:*8]

> [Announcer, in solemn voice] "So, remember friends, Parker's Funeral Home at 4th and Maple for the finest in funeral arrangements . . . and now the lucky winner of our deep freeze." [*PB:*135]

> ". . . And the United Nations will adjourn until next week. And now here's a local news item: A lot of villagers were very startled today when a pack of dogs broke loose from a dog catcher's wagon and raced crazily through the field of a well known tobacco plantation . . . Friends does your cigarette taste different lately?" [*PB:*70]

As they can in conjunction with titles:

> Announcer: "So folks, now is a good time to spend planning your Christmas holiday. . . . Take your youngsters to the Radio City Music Hall to see 'Snow White and the Seven Dwarfs'. . . . We now pause for a short sponsor's message!" [*SB:*95]

> "Before our next recorded selection, here's an item of interest—last night at the Municipal Hospital there were 42 babies born . . . and now . . . *Don't Blame Me.*" [*PB:*92]

40. What one has here, of course, is an example at a higher (utterance) level of the unexpected reading that is possible across morphemic boundaries.

Formulaic broadcaster phrases for satisfying program requirements such as continuity, timing, and identification, can themselves allow for unanticipated readings:

> Announcer: (After having mike trouble) "Now due to a mistake, The City Light Company presents your garden lady, Peggy Mahaffay." [*SB:*114]

> Newscast: "This is DIMENSION, Allen Jackson reporting on the CBS Radio Network from New York. Today's big news story is the national spreading of the flu epidemic . . . brought to you by the Mennen Company!" [*Pr.*:29]

> Announcer: "Due to circumstances beyond our control we bring you a recorded program featuring the Beatles!" [*Pr.:*11]

> Announcer: "Excuse me, Senator . . . I am sure that our listening audience would like to hear more about the fine work that your important Congressional committee is doing . . . but unfortunately, Margaret Truman is about to sing." [*Pr.:*22]

And indeed, the news format can call for a succinct review of vital facts, which in turn requires a disconnectedness, and "implication block," across adjacent utterances which hearers may not allow:

> Newscaster: "And word has just reached us of the passing of Mrs. Angela Cirrilio, who died at the age of eighty-seven. Mrs. Cirrilio was a noted amateur chef who specialized in Italian cooking. There are no survivors." [*Pr.:*58]

> Local News: "Mr. Baker, who applied for the job, seemed to be very well qualified. He is obviously a man of sound judgment and intelligence. Mr. Baker is not married." [*SB:*82]

> "And in the world of sports, Yogi Berra the great Yankee catcher was accidentally hit on the head by a pitched ball. Yogi was taken to Fordham Hospital for X-rays of the head. The X-ray showed nothing." [*PB:*127]

8. As already suggested, a radio station's broadcast output is planned as a continuous flow of sound production across all of the hours the station transmits. This requires that most segments will begin at a predetermined moment in chronological time and end at another, similarly predetermined. Only in this way can a

particular program be fitted to the one just preceding and the one to follow to produce a continuous ribbon of broadcasting—a functional equivalent of the conversational ideal of no-gap/no-overlap. Yet different announcers, different authors, different sponsors, and different support personnel will be involved—in fact, with "remotes," even different program sources.

It follows that because the content of a segment is usually itself predetermined, in order to maintain required continuity an announcer must not only begin any given segment at the right moment, but also pace his aloud reading to end his text exactly when his allotted time is up. This fitting of reading time to allotted time whilst not breaching production margins is an important part of the professional competence of announcers. But, of course, contingencies can arise, requiring more slowing down or speeding up of reading pace than will be overlooked by hearers.

9. The "ribbon effect" raises some other questions. Modern technology makes it possible to construct a smooth flow of words (and images, in the case of TV) out of small strips that are of greatly disparate origin. For example, a beginning-of-hour news program can involve a local announcer's introduction, a sound-jingle "logo" from a cassette, a cutting into a national hookup precisely in time for a time beep, then four minutes of national news. The news itself may be broken up into three sections to allow for interspersed commercials, each news portion in turn broken up by "remotes" involving taped on-the-scene comments introduced by an on-the-scene announcer, and leading into the excerpted comments of an official or other actual participant. Following the national hookup news, there may be a minute or two of local news and weather, finally closing with a recorded sound logo. Although heard as a continuous stream of sound, with no gaps or overlaps, a few such minutes can be made up of a great number of small segments, each of which has to be very nicely timed and patched in and out if coherence is to be maintained. Here in the extreme is the way in which technology and planning bring to a traditional mold—the expectation of no gap, no overlap—an artificial filling that is more variegated and compacted than could be expected to occur in nature. And, of course, the technology that allows disparately produced strips of talk to be orchestrated so that a unitary flow of words results, also opens

up the possibility that the "wrong" segment will be brought in at a juncture, or that an ongoing segment will be "cut into" by another accidentally. In consequence, the possibility of unplanned and undesired readings across properly unrelated strips:[41]

> Our lovely model, Susan Dalrymple, is wearing a lovely two-piece ensemble . . . *(Station Cut-In)* . . . with a rear engine in the back!" [*SB:*28]

> "It's time now, ladies and gentlemen, for our featured guest, the prominent lecturer and social leader, Mrs. Elma Dodge . . ." *(Superman cut in)* ". . . who is able to leap tall buildings in a single bound. SWISHHHH!" [*PB:*16]

> "The recipe this afternoon is for potato pancakes. I'm sure you will enjoy them. You take six medium sized potatoes, deep fat . . . and I am sure your guests will just love them." *(Cut in)* "Funeral services will be held promptly at two o'clock." [*PB:*79]

> "So remember, use Pepsodent toothpaste, and brush your teeth . . ." (CUT IN [to a cleansing product commercial]) ". . . right down the drain!" [*Pr.:*26]

> Emcee: "You are quite a large man . . . how much do you weigh?" Man: "About two hundred eighty-five pounds, and I . . ." (COMMERCIAL CUT IN) ". . . have trouble with hemorrhoids." [*Pr.:*32]

As might be expected, unanticipated boundary readings seem especially likely when an ongoing program must be interrupted for an unscheduled special news bulletin:

> A local TV station carrying a network telecast of a prize fight from Madison Square Garden in New York, interrupted its coverage to inform its audience of the death of a local politician. Upon cutting back to the fight, the announcer was heard to say, "That wasn't much of a blow folks!" [*Pr.:*48]

> On the Ed Sullivan program, movie actor Van Johnson was singing a spirited song about the pitfalls of show business, which highlighted such problems as mikes breaking down, poor lighting, the show must go on, etc., when a CBS news bulletin broke in, inter-

---

41. There is a children's game that efficiently accomplishes much the same effect. The adverbial phrase *between the sheets* is added by one player to the end of every sentential utterance of the other.

rupting his song. After Harry Reasoner finished his bulletin about the Greek-Turkish Cypriot crisis, the station cut back to Johnson, who was singing, "It's just one of those things!" [*Pr.:*105]

Wild Bill Hickok had his program interrupted by a newscaster just after four shots were fired by the program's sound effects man. "We interrupt this program to bring you a bulletin from the Mutual News Room. L.P. Beria has just been executed, according to an announcement from Moscow Radio. We now return you to *Wild Bill Hickok.*" At that moment, Guy Madison was reading this line: "Well, that should hold him for awhile." [*PB:*42]

10. Consider the contingencies of "modality integration." Much radio announcing involves only the spoken voice, but radio drama involves the simulation of the sound associated with various physical events and actions.[42] And, of course, sound effects can be introduced at the wrong time, or the wrong ones at the right time:

"Beyond the head waters of the Nile, Stanley continued his search for Livingston. Dense jungle growth and the ever-present danger of the Tse-Tse fly made the journey more hazardous. Supplies were

42. The technological vicissitudes of staging a radio drama can, of course, be much greater even than those of staging a multisource newscast. When in real life lovers sit in the park in season, they themselves don't have to secure the services of birds, brooks, and falling leaves to ensure a parklike effect; for what we mean by parklike is what occurs there without particular users' help. The problem of coordinating the various effects is no problem at all for the lovers: the prior effort of the park authorities in conjunction with mother nature does it all—parks being (like the real forests Turner painted) social constructions based on community resources expended over a certain period of time. But if you are to make a radio drama of all this, sound-alternatives to visual effects and sound-mimicry of actual sounds will have to come from different sound-makers. Production conventions allow the show's producer to severely limit the number of these streams of sound required to set the scene, and he will also be allowed to play them down once he has played them up, so that ongoing interference won't have to be tolerated. But when sound effects *are* scheduled to appear, they have to appear on time. It is just this coordination that can break down, so that the sound counterpart to action comes too late or too early or fails to come or is of the wrong kind. (I might add that in addition to communally constructed ongoing backgrounds for action, there are extensive scenes set up with one celebrative occasion or affair in mind: specially constructed reviewing stands for an inauguration are one example; tent facilities for a large garden party are another. Radio dramas can involve scenic resources that are also occasion-constructed, but, of course, here one deals with a simulation of a social occasion, not the real thing.)

264

getting low, the natives had almost reached the breaking point, when suddenly, in the distance, they heard the sounds of a village . . . (HORNS, TRAFFIC SOUNDS, CITY SOUNDS)." [*SB:* 56]

The issue is even more acute in television. TV commercials are likely to involve the close interweaving of scripted words and visual demonstration of the working of the sponsor's product. Should a hitch develop in the physical manipulation of the product, the product itself can lose credibility, and in addition all the cues for the scripted words can be thrown off, resulting in confusion. Here, incidentally, one can see in paradigmatic form the intimate bearing a nonlinguistic fault can have upon the speech stream:

> "There's no reason to be satisfied with old-styled refrigerators. This Westinghouse is completely automatic—a self-defrosting feature takes care of that. Let's look inside—just the slightest push on this snap-open door and uh! wait a minute—just push—wait a minute. Oh, this opens—I guess you'll just have to take my word for it." [*PB:* 76]

> "Well, now, you can have this model plane all for yourself, and it's a lot of fun. You just take the kit and it comes completely set up for you. All the parts are ready to put together. You take the part and you well—now you—well, this section here is—well it's—just a minute now. It must be a little stiff and you—this is a very educational toy . . . It teaches children how to cuss!" [*PB:* 108]

11. For technological reasons in broadcasting in general, and radio broadcasting in particular, single-point transmission prevails; quite small sounds occurring at this point and very little of what occurs away from this point are transmitted. If a single meaningful stream of sound does not issue from this point, then the interaction fails in a way that the informal face-to-face variety cannot, in that the latter is unlikely to be so pinpoint dependent. (For example, a fellow conversationalist in a somewhat different microecological position can easily take over should a speaker be struck dumb.) One manifestation of this issue is the dead air problem: if no transmission occurs—that is, if the announcer or other source of meaningful sound is for any reason silent for more than a few seconds—then audiences are left hanging. They may be inclined to think that the station has ceased to

function, and in consequence turn to another; and other listeners, searching their dials, won't know that they have passed through a station.[43] Another expression of the single point problem is the high cost of extended overlaps at turn changes, and, especially, the high cost of interruptions. (In everyday conversational interaction, of course, simultaneous sounds coming from sources even slightly separated in space can be sorted to a degree binaurally to avoid confusion; multiple sound sources in radio can't be separated in this fashion except under special stereo conditions.) On the same grounds, "creature releases," such as burps, hiccups, sneezes, and coughs can be magnified, becoming something the announcer is likely to recognize as disruptively noticeable. (Thus the remedial practice of using a power potentiometer [the "pot"] to cut out [by "back-cueing"] disruptive sounds, such as coughing, page-turning, the slow first revolution of a record, the clicking of the mike key, and so forth, the resulting moment of silence being more manageable than the sound alternative.) So, too, if the announcer draws back from the microphone or turns his head slightly, the consequence in sound will be very great, to avoid which the announcer must maintain a fixity of posture while "on" that is rarely required in ordinary face-to-face interaction.

12. Just as the microphone generates a small zone in which any sound present gets broadcast, the recipient then being unable to pick and choose among the sounds, so the microphone's power source introduces the condition that when the power is known to be off, it can be confidently assumed that nothing in the vicinity will be transmitted. And, of course, it will always be possible for an announcer to err in his belief as to which state the micro-

---

43. In ordinary, informal face-to-face talk, the sudden stopping of a speaker's words *can* cause the listener bewilderment and even alarm, but the local scene is likely to provide the listener with a million cues as to why a sudden pause should be taken in stride—merely a reflection of the fact that a multitude of legitimate claims will impinge upon the person speaking in addition to the one obliging him to complete whatever utterance he is in the middle of. Many of the "good reasons" the speaker has for suddenly stopping will be visible to the listeners; other reasons, part of what the speaker alone has in mind at the moment, can be "externalized," as when a speaker in midspeech stops, *then* slaps his forehead, *then* says, "My God, I forgot to bring the letter." These visual presentations being available to the speaker, he can afford to suddenly stop; these sources not being available to the radio announcer, he can't.

phone is in, alive or dead, open or shut. Thinking that he is merely talking aloud to himself or to nearby station personnel or into the off-air, broadcaster to control-room hookup, he can find that the mike is open and that his words are being "carried." Similarly, he can think he is out of range of the microphone when he isn't. Broadcasting live from the site of some action, he may inadvertently pick up utterances from nearby participants that violate FCC standards. Here, simply on technological grounds, is a frontstage, backstage problem of awesome proportions:

["Uncle Don," after closing his children's program and wrongly assuming the microphone was off]: "I guess that will hold the little bastards." [*PB:* 18]

After he [an announcer filling in on the "board" during a bad cold epidemic] cut off the mike switch and put on a musical recording, someone asked him how he felt. He said, "I feel like hell, and I'm full of Anacin." A few minutes later the phone rang, and a fan requested that he repeat that recording, "I Feel Like Hell, and I'm Full of Anacin." [*PB:* 23]

"It's nice to see we have such a nice crowd here tonight. It's a great turnout; we've got some wonderful matches for you. Now the main event of the evening is gonna be two falls out of three. Chief Bender is going to wrestle with Sando Kovacs—promises to be real exciting. First let's get a word in from our sponsor." (OFF MIKE) "Hey, Mac! Where's the can?" [*SB:* 63]

[Arlene Francis, doing a studio audience warmup on *What's My Line,* miscalculated her allotted warmup time and said]: "There are thirty seconds to go, if anyone has to." This advice was heard by millions of her listeners. [*PB:* 26]

Nor is the announcer alone in having to contend with this issue. Associated collaboratively with the radio announcer will be a circle of technical support figures who may be monitoring his words (directly or electronically) and watching his gestures, but who—so far as the audience is concerned—are ostensibly not present at all. Speaker's collusion with them is thus technically facilitated, if not required—as when a DJ announces records that are played by the studio engineer. And just as an announcer may find himself broadcasting when he least expects it, so may support personnel find that the words they thought were private, or

restricted to a nonbroadcast ("talk-back") channel, are heard by
all the station's listeners:

> "In Pall Malls, the smoke is traveled over and under, around and
> through the tobacco; thereby giving you a better tasting smoke
> . . ." (ENGINEER FLIPS WRONG SWITCH AND PICKS UP UN-
> SUSPECTING DISC JOCKEY) ". . . How the hell can smoke go
> through a cigarette, if it don't go over, under, around and through
> the tobacco?" [*Pr.:*98]

> [As Frank McGee, NBC-TV commentator, announced a switch of
> cameras from one city to another, his director was heard through
> what should have been only McGee's earphone]: "Oh, yeah, the
> line isn't ready yet and you're stuck with a five-minute ad-lib job."
> [*Pr.:*57]

> [Singer on local high school amateur hour]: "For my old Kentucky
> home far away." [She hits high, off-key note, and announcer,
> believing he was off-mike, says]: "Oh God, who goosed the so-
> prano?" [*SB:*60]

As suggested, when TV, not radio, is considered, the discrediting
event can be visual, not aural, but no less an embarrassment to
what has been said:

> Upon finishing a commercial for a nationally advertised beer, an
> announcer took a drink of this "wonderfully tasting beer," and a
> roving camera picked him up spitting his mouthful into a trash can.
> [*SB:*46]

13. Note, finally, the vulnerability of the announcer to technological faults that have nothing to do with a script or its sound
presentation per se, but only with the efficacy of its nonhuman
transmission. Power and equipment failures which entirely cut
off an announcer's words tend not to be attributed to his own
incompetency, whereas weakened or overlayed transmission can
be. So, too, music records that get stuck, crudely reminding listeners that it is a record they are listening to, and providing them
also with an accurate gauge as to how closely the announcer is
attending his duties—the measure being how long the repetitions
continue. (In fact, of course, it is often the studio engineer who
is responsible here and whose attentiveness is actually being
measured.) Cartridge ("carts") voice segments can also get stuck,

but here the embarrassment is less easily assigned to the mechanics of reproduction, for apparently we are more ready to keep in mind that radio music comes from records and tapes than that speech does.

One general point should be made in connection with the speech faults that have been reviewed here. Although the linguistically oriented literature devoted to what seems to be taken as "speech in general" is quite helpful, an analysis deriving from what are essentially ad hoc examples (or, even worse, traditional views of sentence grammar) cannot be expected to carry one very far. A significant amount of the speech trouble that announcers get into is to be traced to such matters as transmission technology, staff division of labor, format and editing practices, sponsorship, FCC regulations, and audience reach, and cannot be analyzed without reference to the ethnographic details of the announcer's work.

VII

Having considered some basic sources of speech faults in broadcasting, one could go on to consider the announcer's means of managing them. And this in a sense is what I propose to do. However, this task is very much complicated by the precarious nature of the concept of speech fault itself, regarding which some general strictures have already been reviewed. Before proceeding to the management of faults, then, I want to raise again the question of their nature, and document from radio talk the reasons already considered as to why the conventional view is too restrictive.

The mission of the professional announcer is to follow consistently a very narrow course. Whether engaged in fresh talk, memorization, or aloud reading he must be able to do so with very little stumbling or mumbling. Unexpected hitches, from whatever source, must be managed inaudibly. Unintended framings must be avoided. When there is a set text, the announcer must be able to stick to it quite fully and at the same time fit its delivery precisely into the time slot alloted to it. He is obliged to stay in role and not, through word or inflection, intentionally or inadvertently betray his tacit support for what he is saying in whoever's name he is saying it. Finally, he is obliged to provide meaningful sound no matter what happens, dead air and nonlexical eruptions being unacceptable. Observe, the maintenance of these standards does not require that no hitch in transmission occurs, only that such as do are not readily identifiable as his responsibility, and in the event of a hitch, that he provide a coherent account whilst sustaining his customary calm delivery.

When things are going well, that is, when performance obligations are being satisfied, the announcer is presumably projecting an image of himself as a competent professional, this being an image he can seemingly live with. A prearranged harmony will then exist among station, sponsor, audience, and the announcer's own self-image. And the work that the announcer is doing to carry off this "normal" competency will be hidden from us.

Now it appears that in lieu of a proper participation study of job socialization, one way to open up to view what the announcer is accomplishing when we think he is achieving nothing noteworthy is to examine the talk of radio performers whose ability is marginal. It is from them that one can most readily learn what it is that professional announcers have learned not to do and aren't doing. Incidentally, as will be seen, what one finds buried thus in the ontology of professional socialization will help us characterize ordinary informal talk.

And here again is a limitation of the social control model. Professional announcing, that is, network announcing that will strike the listener as unnoticeable as a thing in itself, allows announcers to commit themselves projectively to their profession. They can afford to project a self that would be embarrassed by a hitch in the proceedings because, indeed, they (and incidentally, the station's equipment and support staff) are unlikely to produce such a hitch. Given the prestige hierarchy of stations, it is apparent that an announcer who starts out on lesser stations by making mistakes or by being rambunctious will either leave this line of work or acquire "self-discipline," in this case the ways and habits necessary to produce professional broadcasting.

And yet whatever course a neophyte is destined to take, it will still be understandable that he currently holds the professional model at a distance and in emergencies try to save himself, not the program. For if a beginner's effort to maintain sober and faultless speech production is doomed to lead to a considerable number of failures, the effort in the first place may have to be undertaken self-defensively. Especially so in that even on its own, failure here is self-breeding. Once unnerved, the announcer is likely to err, which in turn may unnerve him more, which in turn leads to more error, this time as the center of attention. And once a remedy has been introduced, this remedy will be something that breaks the flow itself and may itself require remedy. Once started out in error, then, announcing can quickly unravel, and the announcer finds it costly—often apparently too costly—to present himself as taking the whole job seriously, or at least the part of it obliging him to speak faultlessly. On the other hand, once errors are consistently avoided, announcing quickly rolls itself up into tight production, for the announcer then can afford to play it straight. Thus, for the announcer, both failure and success have adaptive consequences as circular effects.

I admit now that not only unskilled or alienated announcers or those faced with transmission breakdowns provide us with material. There are also those announcers who are apparently concerned to "broaden" their role, bring "color" to their show, and come through as interesting, vital, unique persons—in brief, as "radio personalities." This they attempt to achieve by allowing more of what will be thought of as their integrity and individuality to show through, more, that is, than would show were they to adhere to the scripted forms. And, as already suggested, that announcers might be concerned to make their words compatible with their sense of who and what they are personally is to open up rather fully what it is that any one of them might consider a fault, that is, an utterance that allows for (if not warrants) some standing back from, some qualification, if not correction, on his part. In shows formatted to be "informal," such correction becomes a mainstay, for an announcer can take some sort of exception to almost any of his own statements if he is of a mind to do so. Indeed, a DJ who is shifting into becoming a stand-up comic and is guiding his show accordingly may define the standard information provided in spot announcements, recordings, weather reports, and time checks merely as an opportunity (and one he better seize) to elaborate and digress, to adumbrate in a manner approximating free association. His reputation and his market value will depend on his being able to qualify and extend required announcements—in effect, to correct them—with remarks that no one else would choose because no one else would have hit upon just these remarks as something whose corrective relevance could be shown.[44] Here something like a Freudian view begins to have appeal. If an announcer speaks a word or phrase that could easily have been misuttered, with consequent production of an embarrassing second reading, then he can assume that such an eventuality might be in his hearers' minds even in absence of the misuttering; and if not actually in their minds, then certainly recallable thereto. And so after successfully avoiding the slip, the announcer is in a position to make something out of what would have happened had he not. There being no real error to remedy, the announcer can address remarks to a latent one. In sum, having broadened analysis from faults to faultables and from faultables to the risibly interpretable, one must broaden analysis still a little more to include *remark-ables.*

It follows that no two announcers will be in total agreement as to what calls for correction and what doesn't. Thus, on the same station on successive airings of the same program, one announcer will say:

This is John Nisbet, filling in for the vacationing Bob Ross.

and a second, with somewhat different sensibilities, that is, with a somewhat different image to sustain, will say:

---

44. Public service station DJs of classical music programs, alas, provide a good example here. On first taking on the program (which sometimes means when the station is first beginning *and* the DJ is first acquiring basic competencies), he will tend to stick to music, often long selections, with brief comments in between identifying performers, title, composer, and record company. As the DJ acquires more ease with his duties and more musical lore, however, he seems doomed to begin to extend the spoken bridge—culling from liner notes, proferring personal opinions, remarking on past local performances, and so forth—until eventually the program becomes a showcase for the display of his frame space, and only brief pieces of music can be aired or single movements from larger works. Listeners in search of music must then turn to stations that are less public spirited and ostensibly provide less service. In a word, classical music programs seem to have a natural history; they begin with music bridged with words and end with words bridged with music.

This is Mike Gordon, filling in for the vacationing Bob Ross—as we say in radioland.

Or, faced with the final item in the hourly news, an item often selected to provide a light, if not comic, note to end on, the second announcer will say:

And finally, in what news people call the kicker . . .

in this way again giving the impression that it is not only discriminating members of the audience who feel uneasy with media jargon.

What a particular announcer "lets go by," then, is not merely something he did not perceive as an error but listeners might, or something he observed to be an error but hopes listeners might not notice, or something obviously noticeable but too embarrassing to try to correct; rather he may let something go by simply because according to his own standards and interests nothing has occurred upon which to hang a qualifying comment. Yet what he sees as something to pass over without further thought, another announcer can hang his career upon. Moreover, the individual announcer and his personality need not be the fundamental unit here. Certainly a sense of characteristic practice is generated, and certainly in the close study of any one announcer's verbal production over time personal and habitual locutions can be uncovered; but variability is also uncovered. What an announcer lets go by one day or week, he may elect to distantiate himself from the next. The basic unit, then, is not the person but the set of stances available during any given moment. And although it may appear that the tack taken by an announcer is an expression of his personality, in fact one finds that the choice was necessarily made from a handful of established possibilities, and that what should impress is not the idiosyncrasy of the choice, but the conventionality and paucity of the options.

Return to the argument, then, that very often one can learn that a fault has occurred only after the announcer has displayed an effort to draw attention through comment to it, and that in many cases nothing "objective" exists in what has occurred to account for its ultimate treatment as something to remedy.

The argument must be qualified. Just as some announcers

will find grounds (or rather opportunity) for correction and adumbration where no such reworking of the prior utterance could be anticipated, so it is plain that some words and phrases receiving remedial treatment were glaringly obvious candidates for it by virtue of broadly based cultural understandings. Some slips produce an alternative reading that is so widely evident in our society, and some assertions are so contrary to the way we know the world to be, that these acts provide reasonable grounds for saying that a "fault" is objectively present. Even had the speaker been unaware of the risible or erroneous implications of what he had said, large numbers of listeners could still be depended on to be more observant, and, being observant, to observe the same thing:

> Weather forecast: "Of the 29 days in February, 126 were clear."
> [*PB:*97]

> Newscaster: "Word has just reached us from London, that England's Queen Elizabeth has given birth to a baby boy. The infant son weighs seven pounds, fifteen inches!" [*Pr.:*5]

> Commercial: "So, dad, it's time for that new dinette set for your ever-growing family . . . and at Travers for only $99.00 you can now buy a seven-piece set consisting of six tables and a large-sized chair!!!" [*Pr.:*7]

> Newscaster: "The only way the man could be identified was by the fact that he was standing in the road alongside his stalled automobile with a cool tit in his hand." [*SB:*41]

> "This is a final warning! Failure to report to your alien officer may result in your deportation or prostitution!" [*PB:*68]

> "It's 9:00 P.M. B-U-L-O-V-A. Bulova Watch Time. This Christmas, buy the new Bulova President: curved to fit the foot!" [*PB:*93]

Indeed, in these cases were both the speaker and his hearers to have noticed nothing out of line, there would still be good grounds for saying that they had all "overlooked" a fault that was "really" present. After all, a great many other members of their speech community—both announcers and station listeners—would certainly feel that something had gone wrong. Further, speaker and hearers would themselves be subject to being told later what they had "missed," and could then be counted on to "realize" that they had missed something, and what it was they had missed. Even in the case of errors that whole populations within a language community would miss (as when most Britons and some Americans would fail to appreciate that "futility outfielder" is "obviously" an all-too-true version of "utility outfielder"), there would still be the possibility that they could readily be shown why other sectors of the community would hear an "obvious" slip.[45]

And so too with the question of not being able to tell always whether an announcer is genuinely unaware of the error he has committed or has merely given the appearance that this is the case in order to avoid drawing more attention to his unfortunate lapse. This is a genuine question, sometimes, answerable, incidentally, by listening in on what the announcer says to his support personnel as soon as he is off the air. But the question itself presupposes (and I think with warrant) that within a broadly based speech community *certain* verbal constructions would inevitably be judged to be faults.

Here the question of perspective must be addressed. I believe it is perfectly sound to distinguish between faults in speaking and faults in hearing, and that lots of "objective" faults can be found that are clearly one or the other, not either or both. And that like the student, speaker and hearer know these possibilities exist. When one focuses on only one of the two sources of trouble (in this case, on speaker faults), one can still attempt an inclusive approach that tacitly treats such faults from both speaker's and hearer's point of view. Doing so, however, one should be clear that the bearing of one point of view on the other—the "interaction" between the two—is a problem in its own right.

Thus one can say that in the face of an utterance that makes no sense or only improper sense, a hearer may correctly attribute the cause to his own mishearing or to speaker's misstating, or incorrectly do so, where "correctly" and "incorrectly" derive

45. Something of the same line of argument can be made about the "objective" character of some slips of the ear, and about the possibility, in principle, of distinguishing speech production faults from hearing produced faults, in spite of some obvious complications. Here, see Garnes and Bond (1975).

from the encompassing perspective of the analyst, not the hearer.

The hearer, of course, may sometimes find himself quite unable to decide whether it is he or the speaker who is at fault. Here an encompassing view can lead one to say that hearer may be deficient in this connection, for on various grounds it is sometimes possible to show that responsibility can be "correctly" attributed in such cases. But in other settings it can be shown that the hearer's doubt has better warrant, for some troubles, it appears, are objectively indivisible. Thus, if hearer turns away at the moment speaker drops his voice, a mishearing can be *jointly* accomplished. Whether speakers and hearers appreciate that in principle such joint responsibility is possible, is, however, another matter, and a social fact in its own right. As is the possibility that on particular occasions, the hearer may perceive himself or the speaker to be solely at fault, when in fact joint responsibility is at work.

Announcing provides useful illustrations of these perspectival issues. As already considered at length, listeners eagerly search for alternate readings they know weren't intended. The announcer knows this, attempts to guard against it, and treats such interpretive opportunities as he fails to block as faults on his part. And this is the interpretation (however labored) required for the unintended meaning. Presuming that he has tried to block such framings, listeners can jump on any that occur and snicker at his failure—a failure they see from his point of view—even though in fact he may never discover that they have caught him out on this occasion. But of course, the possibility of being put down in this way is built back into the announcer's general conduct, a stimulus to his routine precautions. So each of the two parties takes the other's point of view and each—in a way—takes it that this is taken.

A somewhat different possibility is presented in regard to full-fledged misunderstandings, that is, hearings that fail to grasp what the speaker had intended. Knowing that listeners are prone to err by deleting word boundaries, an announcer may make a special effort to check his copy for such junctures, and speak very carefully when he broadcasts these passages. He incorporates an anticipation of audience tendencies. Failing in this, their error becomes his fault. Again there is a collapsing of the two points of view, but here the speaker is doing the collapsing, not the listener.

All in all, then, the point of view of speaker and hearer must be kept separate, but each point of view involves close, although perhaps different, commitment to the other's point of view. Divided by an obvious barrier, announcer and listener are yet intimately joined, the announcer to the situation of the listener, and vice versa. All of which an encompassing view must find a place for. Incidentally, it is this interpenetration of points of view which provides one reason (but not the only reason) why a single individual (such as Kermit Schafer) can collect apparent troubles with some confidence that other hearers *and* announcers will agree that something had gone wrong.

A final point. When an announcer makes an all too obvious slip of the kind considered here, the chronicler and the student, like the members of the audience, apparently feel no need to explain in detail what feature of the world is violated by the slip, the assumption being that the matter is self-evident and can be taken for granted. And by and large it can be. Admittedly it would be worthwhile to try to formulate the underlying presuppositions that inform wide arrays of "evident" errors, especially insofar as these understandings are of a generalized character and not themselves made explicit by those who employ them. But that, surely, would be a separate study whose findings could in no way deny that certain errors were widely perceivable, and perceived as "obvious." (Which is not to deny that a cultural group will have its own beliefs about the workings of the world, and thus its own relativistic bases for "obvious, objective" error.)

The required reorientation is now evident. Although many faults stand out in a very obvious way—clearly a fault to nearly everyone in the speech community—other faults are very much a question of discretion, namely, what the announcer himself wants to disaffiliate himself from. Differently put, because it turns out that when an obvious fault is committed, one apparent consequence for, if not intent of, the announcer is to distance himself from the event—from the image of incompetence it might imply—one can take this disaffiliation as the key matter and go on to address anything the speaker attempts to dissociate himself from, including, but only incidentally, errors in the obvious sense. An utterance, like any other personal act, projects an image of the actor; and actors, act by act, endeavor to maintain a personally acceptable relation to what they may be taken to be exhibiting about themselves. And given the circumstances of the action, the personally acceptable can be extended upward to the personally desired, or downward to the personally least unacceptable.

As suggested, instances of this remedial behavior usually will not come from fully professional, network announcers of news and commercials (especially not from those who are happy with their role), but rather from those who have frequent cause for remedial action: incompetent announcers, alienated announcers, and announcers on special interest stations. Along with these there is reason to include those who have (or are trying to acquire) an M.C. role on an informal "personal" show. It is the conduct of these performers that will be our guide.

VIII

I turn now to an examination of the practices announcers employ to manage faults that have not been avoided and, not having been avoided, are treated by them as something to openly address. But on analytical grounds, this concern now resolves into a larger one: namely, what announcers do to project a self different from the one they have apparently just projected, whether projected through their own speech faults, their own official text, or the comments, prerecorded or live, of anyone else whose contribution to what gets broadcast they might be partly identified with. Differently put, I will now examine announcers' frame space, apart, that is, from the standard alignments allotted to them. What we will thus consider, incidentally, is what professional announcers in the main have learned never to need. "Role distance" is involved or, more accurately, "event distance."

1. AD HOC ELABORATION. While aloud-reading a text, the announcer may briefly assume the authorial function and extend his copy, drawing on what is to be taken as his own fund

of knowledge or personal experience, amplifying, specifying, and so forth. Transition into and out of this parenthetical elaboration (and the consequent switching between aloud reading and fresh talk) will commonly be marked by a change in voice and tempo. A similar license can be taken when the main text is itself in fresh talk, the asides departing from what would ordinarily be the routinely required development. Note, whether it is a fully scripted text or a planned fresh talk that he extends, the announcer need not openly betray the spirit of the anticipated presentation, that is, the line it was intended to develop. But however much his ad libs are in keeping with his official theme, they suggest, if only faintly and fleetingly, that he is not completely bound by his duties, and that his standard voice is not his only one.

Personal elaboration can occur through minor (and formulaic) parenthetical insertions within an utterance:

The time in our fair city is . . .

. . . directed by a man with the unlikely name of Victor Ewell . . .

. . . no less than Frederick the Great . . .

. . . now unfortunately out of the catalogue . . .

. . . that really wonderful music by . . .

. . . directed, of course, by Neville Mariner . . .

or as a tag at the end of a segment of the expected text:

. . . well, actually it opened last night.

[After reading the closing human interest note in the news]: Sort of does your heart good, doesn't it?

I might mention in passing something about the piano Glenn Gould uses.

. . . 5 percent chance of rain. [Dryly] So leave your umbrella in its stand. You do have an umbrella stand, don't you? No home should be without one.

Observe again that the significance of such elaborations will vary greatly depending on initial tacit assumptions concerning the rightful place in the talk of the personal resources of the speaker. In much everyday talk, of course, participants seem to be accorded the right to dip into their fund of knowledge and experience at will, providing only that canons of tact and relevance be sustained, and these sometimes minimally. An academic lecturer, speaking from notes, develops a text that can fully intermingle elaborative parenthetical comments with thematic development. In contrast, in court proceedings, counsel's questioning (especially "cross-questioning") can be held to a rule of strict relevance; what the judge chooses to consider irrelevant, he can openly characterize as such.

Broadcasts themselves display a wide range of definitions regarding extraneous, unscripted, "personal" elaboration. In those talk shows and interview programs in which the M.C. is concerned to develop an attractive "air personality" and is allowed to use a format that is not "tight," parenthetical extensions of any current thematic line may be perfectly standard, and well within both the rights and competence of the speaker. Popular DJs may feel that free association is the mainstay of their reputation, and are much motivated to dredge up incidental comments about almost everything they are obliged to talk about. (Probably they could not become "popular" without doing so.) In national hourly news broadcasts, a closely timed text is likely to be adhered to, and the reading rate tends to be high, with silences considerably compressed. Here the speaker, however professional, may be unable (and in a sense unwilling) to shift smoothly to fresh talk when necessary—say, to cover the failure of a remote commentary to come in. On such occasions the announcer can be expected to stumble a little, inadvertently change tone, slow up the tempo, and speak his ad-libbed filler with less than usual conviction.

2. METACOMMUNICATING. I refer to the ways in which the announcer may—whilst retaining the two-party character of direct announcing—change footing at points not scheduled for this, shifting from speaking in a collective "station editorial" voice to one in which he speaks more specifically for himself, and himself in his capacity as animator of the text he is delivering.

a. Central here is the shift in footing necessarily involved when a strident correction is employed, the stress projecting the image of a speaker struggling to get his words right. The image that was supposed to be projected, namely, a self that merges with the voice of the station, is undermined:

. . . at Temple Cit . . . Temple University Center City Cinema . . .

Station Break: "Stay tuned for WOODY'S PECKER SHOW . . . WOODY'S WOODPECKER SHOW!" [*Pr.:*33]

Apology tags employing "I" in their construction, which sometimes follow such corrections, make the change in footing explicit, for here the personal pronoun underscores the fact that the plea is being presented solely in the speaker's own name.

b. Consider now some variants of the "pronunciation frame." For example, the "phonetic trial" approach. Instead of treating a word (or phrase) in the usual way—as an unthinkingly available resource to say something with—the speaker seriously reframes the bit of text as something to try to pronounce, much as a child might for whom trying pronunciation was an appropriate developmental task. The speaker picks his way through the word's pronunciation, often with the help of some sort of letter-by-letter, syllable-by-syllable articulation, and often giving a sense of self-oriented, self-directed rehearsal or experimentation:

. . . played by (slowing up) Ań ať ólé Fisť oó lárié.

. . . and as pianist Lydia Pé trá skí yań . . .

Sometimes the rising intonation of a question is employed, as if the announcer were openly underscoring that the "correct" pronunciation is unknown, the one employed being offered merely as a possibility—a possibility that seems to await what can't be delivered, namely, confirmation or correction by the hearer. These gambits, note, shift the attention of hearers from the sense of what is being said to production contingencies involved in saying it, a metalinguistic shift from the semantic reference of an utterance to the mechanics of its animation.

Note, too, that the question of ritualization is involved—in a somewhat ethological sense. Although for any speaker the prosodic features of these utterances may originally have been simply a by-product of having to piece out the course of the pronunciation syllable by syllable, no doubt the sound pattern becomes a format in its own right, something a speaker can employ when for a whole range of reasons his intent is to reduce tacit claims to his knowing what he is doing.

c. In the same way that an announcer can direct attention to the requirements of pronunciation, he can change footing and display the pleasure he takes in the word's sound when he himself seems not to have a problem with pronunciation. Again, the pronunciation frame, and the implicating of the animating process as a subject matter in its own right:

> . . . playing the hurdy-gurdy. Delightful sound. Hurdy-gurdist, if that's what you call him.

> That was Benjamin Britten's Simple Symphony. Try saying that fast—Simple Sympathy . . .

> Similarly. Sim/a/l/ar/ly [as if savoring the sound of the correct pronunciation] . . .

And as suggested, in the face of foreign words, an articulation flourish may be employed, an overrounded, slightly unserious venturing of native pronunciation, sometimes followed by an accounting:

> Ber nar do pas qui na. I love to pronounce those Italian names.

As with "phonetic trials" a switch is here involved from use to mention.[46]

d. When an announcer reads a text other than one prepared by himself or his coworkers, he is likely to provide a clarifying and identifying "connective," tying what is being said to the party originally saying it, as in the phrase, "according to an AP release." In brief, a certain scrupulosity is observed in the matter

---

46. Mock uneducated hyper-Anglicization is another example of the pronunciation frame. But although its use is not uncommon in face-to-face talk (sometimes, of course, as a strategic cover for felt ignorance of both the native and standard Anglicization forms), no instance appears in my radio sample. There is one example of a translation played straight, but then followed up by a guyed apology that is probably more stereotyped in its unserious ironic form than in the literal: "Well, here's his *Waltzes Noble* and *Sentimental*—pardon my French."

of tacit claims to authorship. Sometimes a connective may have to be parenthetically introduced when the text is meant to be heard as a quoted one and contains anaphorical expressions which might not otherwise be properly interpreted. (For example, when the liner notes on a record jacket cite Mahler's wife's biographical comment on Strauss's behavior after the premier of the Sixth, and uses "we" to refer to the persons backstage at the time, the announcer must make sure that hearers won't take *him* to be saying that he was among those present.) During the reading of such a quoted text, or when a long, cited passage might possibly cause listeners to forget initial authorship disclaimers, a "reconnective" may be parenthetically injected, as in, ". . . caused the explosion, Chief Wilson goes on to say." The point here is that by injecting unscripted connectives and reconnectives, an announcer may show extra circumspection, taking added care not to be attributed with the knowledge and experience implied in what is about to be, or just has been, heard. As though the requirements of modesty forced the announcer to break the illusion of his discourse at an unexpected point—a Brechtian technique.

Interestingly, announcers are sometimes faced with a text whose reading might give the impression that they themselves have introduced stylistic license. In such cases they need an equivalent to *sic,* the sign a writer can use following a quoted word or phrase to indicate that the apparent imperfection belongs to the original text, not to its transcription. Here the announcer can discreetly employ an interjected connective:

> . . . while speaking at the podium Judge Sirica just keeled over, UP states, and was taken to the hospital suffering a massive heart attack.

Scrupulosity, and the slight change in footing its maintenance can require, may involve more than the insertion of a connective. The reading of excerpts from liner notes of a recording is a standard way in which DJs generate something relevant and informative to say. And presumably because such citations can easily pass as an expression of the announcer's own knowledgeability, some speakers are careful to introduce authorial disclaimers:

I have Paul Cleb, who wrote the liner note for this particular recording, to thank for that.

[Regarding Schubert's age when he wrote his posthumous trio]: It's very easy to sound erudite, but I learned this from the liner notes.

We are grateful to a Mr. Bent for a brief life of Chausson. In the liner notes he says . . .

D'Indy is said to have said . . .

This sort of nicety can be carried to the point where backstage secrets of the broadcast are revealed—all presumably in the interests of avoiding pretense. For example, in reporting the weather forecast, an announcer can gratuitously inform on how the station receives the forecast:

> . . . according to the National Weather Bureau [change in voice] and Ma Bell . . .

while incidentally employing an ironic tone throughout to convey his personal belief that there is reason to be a little skeptical of the reliability of the prediction.

In ordinary conversation the unqualified expression of an intention or belief can readily be interpreted in self-aggrandizing terms—an act that is immodest, intractable, demanding, presumptuous—and further, can restrict the maneuverability of listeners who might disagree, leaving them no easy way to present a contrary view. A very standard strategy, then, is the perfunctory hedge that hopefully mitigates some aspect of avowing, these forms being almost as common in broadcast talk as in the everyday kind. As already suggested, however retiring a maker of such comments is, he nevertheless must draw attention to the production format of his statement—that is, to himself in his personal capacity as animator, author, and principal—and this in its own right constitutes an intrusion of self. Thus, a broadcaster's hedges may question his own belief or competency (and thereby, of course, reduce the potential discrediting of a mistake):

> . . . piece played, if I'm not mistaken, by . . .

> . . . Burgemeister, if I pronounced that correctly.

> . . . that tune was a hit around 1965, 67—I think.

or the right to inject a personal opinion:

> If you ask me . . .

> If I may say . . .

> If I may express an opinion . . .

> And I must say, Bob Ross really outdid himself in that one.

or the implication that anyone other than himself might hold with the personal opinion he has interjected:

> . . . played the harpsichord with a very subtle touch, it seems to me.

> . . . what is for me my favorite Bruckner symphony, for what that's worth.

> [After saying you can learn a lot about a period from its history]: That's sort of an armchair musicologist's note. I don't know. At twenty-five after seven I guess . . .

But, of course, the cost of these modest disclaimers is the addition of yet another extraneous utterance, another utterance in which the announcer vents a personal view—even though this second departure can provide something of a bridge back to format duties.

There are other sources of broadcaster hedge. The announcer may feel that standard industry phrases for covering standard items may commit him to pretentions he is uneasy with, so he will ad lib some self-disclaiming, dis-identifying comment:

> . . . the probability of precipitation—or the chance of rain, as we say in the street . . .

> . . . and the glass, as they say, is rising . . .

> And the barometric pressure—for those of you who are fans of barometric pressure—is . . .

Even the title of a composition can provide warrant for an ironic remark:

> And we're going to continue now with a composition by Roger Sessions written in 1935 called Concerto for Violin—pretty basic simple title there—with Paul Zukofsky performing on violin.

A similar self-dissociation can occur when available materials, such as liner notes, lead the announcer to convey obscure, technical, or learned facts, recital of which might be taken to imply pedantry, traditionalism, pomposity, and so forth:

> . . . born in 1757—for those who care.

> . . . Brandenburg Concerto no. 1 in F, BVW 1046, if you're interested.

> I know you want to know John Stanley's dates. They are . . .

> . . . Wolfgang Amadeus Mozart [lightly], to give you his full name.

One has here what is sometimes called self-consciousness—an individual's readiness to turn on his own acts to question their propriety, originality, sincerity, modesty, and so forth. This self-consciousness, as already suggested, is also found on occasions when an announcer discovers that his own extemporaneous formulations have led him to employ what might be heard as a stereotyped phrase, these being the circumstances in which he may respond to his own words with an ironic phrase of self-dissociation:

> . . . without further ado, as they say . . .

> . . . who could ask for anything more—to coin a phrase . . .

> Time marches on, inexorably, if you will—if you can handle that kind of language this early in the morning.

A repertoire of ironic, self-dissociating phrases not only allows an announcer to counteract self-projections he feels might be questionable, but also frees him from finding unobjectionable phrasings in the first place. A remedy being available, the fault that calls it forth can be indulged without danger. And on occasion it appears that a self-alien word or phrase may be introduced just so colorful disclaimers can be brought into play. Indeed, mock, unserious immodesties can be employed, the assumption apparently being that because these acts are not seriously assayed, their doer must certainly know how to conduct himself modestly. So to cut a modest figure, modesty itself is hardly a qualification, being something that its possessor might not frequently be in a position to demonstrate the possession of; in any case, such demonstrations would remove him from the center of attention where evidence of character can be efficiently conveyed.

e. The parenthetical remarks that have been considered so far follow rather closely upon the faultable for which they are meant to provide a remedy. Disclaimers can, however, reach back further for their reference, providing the speaker with a special basis for intruding himself as animator into the discourse. To open up the matter, consider the question of "textual constraints."

Whether starting with a word, phrase, clause, or sentence, and whether the unit is written or spoken, one can move from there to some larger segment of discourse of which the instance unit is but one part. Attempts can be made to try to uncover the constraints and license that apply to the instance unit by virtue of its being part of a larger whole.

One issue, presumably, is that of topical coherence, namely, the requirement that a theme, once established, be adhered to throughout a segment of discourse; thus, "digression," and the obligation to curtail it. Another issue is repetition. For example, no matter how long a book is, the writer is obliged to be concerned about the repetition of ideas (except by way of summary), and about using the same expressive phrase "too often," the same descriptor in close sequence, and any particular illustration more than once. So, too, in the case of news columns, the initial mention of a subject tends to spell out his full name and place him socially, whereas each succeeding mention will employ more abbreviated forms, with some stylistic obligation to use different ones.

An interesting point about these textual constraints is, apparently, how readily repair of their breach can be attempted by means of some sort of remark; for example, the ubiquitous, "As already suggested" and "To repeat an earlier argument." So, too, digression excuses: "Not to change the subject, but. . . ." An explanation, I think, is that many of these constraints seem to be aimed at showing that the writer (or speaker) is alive to, and mindful of, the whole course of his communication. Consequently, his showing that he is aware of his lapses even as he commits them is to employ an alternative means of demonstrating that he is awake to his communication obligations. Repetition constraints also seem to be designed to sustain the notion that something fresh and unique is occurring with each word and phrase; here, however, excuses and apologies for too quickly repeating an expression can only provide a partial remedy.

Textual constraints have a special bearing on broadcast talk, for in the ordinary course of affairs there seems to be very little "segmental depth" to the announcer's obligations. It is almost as if he assumes his audience is constantly changing, and therefore that anything he says one moment need not constrain (or, contrariwise, provide much anaphoric background for) what is to follow. (Thus, new listeners are not likely to feel for very long that they are out of touch with what is going on; after no more than a sentence or two, they are likely to be able to follow fully what the announcer is talking about.) Nonetheless, some constraints do apply, especially on shows that run for an hour or more. When these constraints are breached, remedies require the announcer to step out of role momentarily and address his own text in his capacity as the formulator of it. Thus, coherence excuses:

> . . . what those three facts [culled from liner notes] have in common, I don't know, but there you are.

And, of course, repetition excuses:

> That was the ubiquitous J. P. Rampal—if we may use that expression twice in one morning.

> . . . that incredible—and I use that word again . . .

> . . . delightful, if I may be permitted to use that word again.

Interestingly enough, announcers may make a back-reaching reference that implies more listener continuity than might be considered conventional, and by this very breach, mark what they say as an unserious, self-referential break in frame, drawing attention to the discourse as discourse:

> We will continue with some . . . pre-nineteenth-century music—for want of a better name. [Then, after the recording in question]: We have been listening to "pre"-nineteenth-century music [this time the neologism being uttered unseriously, presupposing the prior accounting].

[After playing Milhaud's four-piano sonata, the announcer goes on to say with an ironic touch]: Now a piece for only two pianos.

And indeed, because announcers must routinely repeat some of the same information before and after a record, or periodically repeat the same advertisement or public service notice, they are in a position to "play" their own speech errors, repeating a difficulty, but this time in quotes, as it were—presupposing that the listener will appreciate that the announcer is not making a mistake but mimicking a mistake already made. And once again, the process of animation itself becomes an object of reference, not merely the vehicle for reference:[47]

> . . . an eight-minute walk from the Haverford station, not an eight-mile walk, as I believe I said yesterday [laugh].

f. Consider "counterdisplays." Immediately following an erroneous statement, doubtful pronunciation, or misconstructed word, an announcer may do more than merely respond with a flat correction (or even a strident one) and a perfunctory apology. At whatever cost to timing and prescribed text, he can break his pace and, in an openly self-admissive tone, unhurriedly introduce a rather extensive redoing of the faulted passage, the repair work requiring a clause or sentence. The new addition often includes a self-reference and, much to the point, is executed with fluency and control, a display of aplomb presumably supplying immediate evidence that the announcer is now (and characteristically) in control of himself and his situation, admittedly guilty but yet unabashed. The old animator is cast off, as it were, carried right into the talk by "I," leaving a new animator in full charge of matters—the one able to fluently intone the correction. In any case, the attention of listeners is turned for a moment from the text to a consideration of the individual animating the text.

Counterdisplays can be achieved merely by executing in a

47. This raises the issue of the "topical life" of a fault: when a speech fault occurs, and after appropriate notice is given it by the speaker, at what point in remove will he find it inappropriate to make a joking reference to his difficulty, and how many such references can the original contretemps bear? Note, this is a different life from the more significant one distinguished by Schegloff et al., where the issue is how many turns from the turn in trouble can speaker or hearer allow before remedy is referentially ambiguous and therefore inappropriate.

well-enunciated, well-rounded manner what might otherwise be a correction and a perfunctory apology:

> . . . a three-record set. I *beg* your pardon. A two-record set.

> Sportscaster: "The proceeds of the Annual All-Star Game goes to indignant players—I beg your pardon, that is indigent ballplayers." [*PB:* 82]

Formulaic phrases may also be involved as part of the controlling action:

> Did I say Tuesday? It's Wednesday I mean, of course.

> . . . at 31 . . . make that 3200 East Charleston . . .

> . . . low to mid-thirties. Did I say low to mid-thirties? I meant low to mid-fifties. Not in the low thirties, for heaven's sake . . . and at night . . . that's when it'll be in the low thirties.

> The time is sixteen minutes, make that fourteen minutes to twelve.

> Short-līved or short-lived, if you prefer.

> . . . not rubber workers but rather auto workers, I should say.

> Seventy-two degrees Celsius. I beg your pardon. Seventeen degrees Celsius. Seventy-two would be a little warm.

And, of course, a quip can be essayed, the aptness of the remark functioning to demonstrate how fully the speaker can bring his mind into gear in spite of his apparent confusion:

> . . . if I can get my tongue straightened out.

> Excuse me . . . get the frog out of my throat.

> . . . Gilbert . . . let me try that again. Wait till I get my false teeth in here again.

> My tongue is not cooperating this morning.

> One of the listeners said I said January instead of February. Oh, it's going to be one of those days.

Observe, irony can be injected into a counterdisplay by the pat metalinguistic device of referring to self in third person, this reflexive frame break presumably further distancing the current animator from the one under criticism:[48]

> . . . well deserves your enjoyable listening to, he says in a not very well-expressed way.

> . . . and now, he says as he catches his breath . . .

Counterdisplays—like other correction strategies—involve a special risk, namely, that having openly directed the full attention of the audience to the correction, a counterdisplay may itself contain a garbled version of what was meant to have been the correct version. But here there is the further embarrassment of projecting a pointed claim to self-control which discredits itself, and under concertedly audible conditions:

> "Place the sports and foons on the . . ." "I mean the sporks and sphoons . . . !" "Of course I mean the porks and soons." [*PB:* 50]

> Announcer: "And now, Van Cliburn playing Tchaikovsky's Piano Concerto Number One in Blee Fat Minor . . . I beg your pardon, that should be Fee Blat Minor!!!" [*Pr.:* 36]

g. Perfunctory apologies and excuses always seem to have a self-reference, explicit or elided, and can thus be taken as providing a brief report by the speaker on his state of mind and his feelings. So, too, the little flourishes contained in counterdisplay reports on the speaker's intentions, proper purpose, and actions. Now consider self-reporting as a practice in its own right.

One way an announcer can face a production hitch *and* comply with the norm that there should be no dead time, is to constitute his own situation—his actions, obligations, predicament, feelings, opinions—as the subject matter to describe, this being a source of copy always at hand. After all, as a source of emergency fill, the individual animating is in a special relationship to himself. If he is willing to change footing and introduce references to his own circumstances at the moment, then he need never be at a loss for something to say; for inevitably on occasion

---

48. The device can also be used by an announcer to deal with questionable comment insertions: ". . . he added, parenthetically."

of unexpected crisis, he will be experiencing something, if only shock. (Perhaps one exception should be made, namely, that although in face-to-face life we sometimes elect to report that we are bored or have nothing to talk about, such an admission might hardly serve as something to mention in broadcast talk.)

Some hitches responded to by self-reports can clearly be attributed to agencies beyond the announcer himself:

> This has taken me rather by surprise, but I want to say that the sound should certainly be soon restored.

> I don't like to make such announcements, but there you are.

Further, the announcer can report on his efforts to set matters right, even while he executes them:

> However, we don't seem to be getting through. Can you tell me the situation, Chuck? Will we get through? No? Well, then, let's turn instead to . . .

The price, of course, is that the speaker must thrust himself into the content of the program as part of its subject matter, adding to what may already be a deviation from expected text. It should be noted that biographical self-reports delivered in response to an emergency can themselves be delivered calmly and fluently, showing that the speaker is in command of at least one part of himself—whatever has happened to the rest of the world.

Self-reports can also be used in reference to a hitch that the announcer can only questionably treat as beyond his responsibility; indeed, the self-report can be a means of establishing reduced responsibility:

> For more information—no I don't have a number for that.

> It doesn't say exactly when these classes will start.

> I can't quite make it out, but I think the name of the pianist is . . .

> For more information about this festival . . . and there is no address; it doesn't even tell you where it takes place. But this is the festival . . .

Of special interest are those hitches in continuous broadcast flow that are apparently clearly traceable to the behavior of the announcer himself. Here, too, as in less blameworthy confusions, he may introduce a running report of his own remedial actions and his own predicament as someone trying to assemble a proper production, including references to the mechanics of show production, these being backstage matters ordinarily concealed from listeners. The minimal case here is the standard "filled pause," whereby the speaker, momentarily unable or unwilling to produce the required word or phrase, gives audible evidence that he is engaged in speech-productive labor.[49] Although the sound involved doesn't appear in itself to suggest much organization, it seems at least to convey that the speaker is still at the microphone addressing himself to the subject matter at hand, that transmission and reception are still in working order, and that words will soon return to the air.[50] But, of course, this minimal effort is not

49. In everyday conversation, filled pauses occur when the speaker needs time to think through an issue, or to find words to encode a thought already arrived at, or to choose from an array of encodings already brought to mind; and so also when his intent is to insure that listeners obtain the impression, warranted or not, that any of the above is the case (see James 1978). Thus a speaker can use a filled pause to convey that he himself is having no trouble with a thought or its direct encoding, but rather must give attention to finding a phrase that exactly matches his recipients socially—given their assumed knowledge of the subject at hand, their right to full disclosure, their relationship to him, and so forth. Filled pauses, of course, also function "to perceptually segment the speech stream for the listener and/or to allow the listener time for processing the speech at such points" (Beattie 1979:64), to mark a "turn transition relevant" place, and, contrariwise (as suggested), to hold the floor after finishing a point when wanting to continue on with a different one.

50. Although it might seem that announcers who have recourse to filled pauses as a means of holding the floor (or, rather, the air) are not overly conscious of what they are doing, the practice can, of course, be guyed. For example, there is a West Coast announcer, well loved by many of her station's subscribers, who uses a long string of nonsense syllables where an unobtrusive filled pause would otherwise be. She uses a similar string of sounds to exaggerate the mess created when a word is garbled:

> Yesterday, noted criminal lawyer ah F. Lee Bailey who had joined Miss Hearst, de Miss Hearst, defec defibbabab. Let me try it again. Take it from the top. Yesterday, noted criminal lawyer F. Lee Bailey . . .

> The crimes include a series of roba bab a booble—a series of bombings in San Francisco.

> An article in Pravda which is described by a-authorities in Moscow who work for Reuters as a comment from the very highest level of Soviet foreign . . . policy . . . or something like that . . . baoobaalaboodal . . . In Angola . . .

all that is found. Well-articulated verbal statements are not uncommon:

> I've lost my place, I'll have it for you in a moment.

> The U.S. government is urging American, British, and Canadian residents to leave Angola because the fighting is going to spread. The . . . very briefly . . . Oi boy it's after nine o'clock . . . in the Middle East there's been another message sent from Israel through the United States . . .

> PUBLIC SERVICE ANNOUNCEMENT: "So be sure to think of our less fortunate friends overseas. They will appreciate anything that you can give. A few cents a day will feed a Korean elephant, so send your money to Care, care of your local postoffice—Did I say elephant? I don't know where I got that. I mean orphan." [*SB:* 99]

> Now what else can I tell you . . . Oh yes. I will give you I will tell you that . . . lots of folks have subscribed today.

> I was going to say it was a nice name before I tripped over a syllable.

> . . . first since 19 . . . since 1757. I almost said 1957. Of the Masque by . . .

> Let me look at this for a moment.

> A ride is offered on October 2nd. Let's see when is that, it's oh, next week sometime, it's Thursday.

> This is by . . . let me see if I can get the right section here.

> I would like to refrain from announcing the name of the songs in that they are German and I can't pronounce German very well.

> . . . although Saudi Arabia opposes it. This according to the Iraqi oil minister after the opening session [sound of paper rattling] and rattling all this paper here [more rattling, this time as a demonstration of rattling].

> Stay tuned for Aeolia where they will be reading—if you wait a moment I'll be able to tell you . . . here it is . . .

> I just got lost in the liner notes.

Next. Someone is trying to tickle me here. We'll have the . . .

Well, let's see. Okay, that's about it.

. . . in . . . let me see here, in 1932 . . . the number is . . . here we are . . . it's . . .

Let me see who the performer was.

Disc Jockey: "Before I bring you the hurt record by trumpeter Al Hit, 'The Girl from Ipana' . . . here's a word about Ipanema toothpaste . . . wait a minute, I got that all fouled up . . . that should be Al Hirt and 'The Girl from Ipanema'!!!" [*Pr.:* 128]

Okay—we've seen all that before *(sotto voce)* ahh here is another news story which I should . . . around here in this great mess of papers here and I don't know what to . . . I know there's something here—I ought to remember to staple them next time. Well, would I be offending anyone if I said, well, that's the news for now.

It looks like—seem to have run out. I know there was something else I was going to read on. Pardon the shuffling of papers. Okay. The forty-nation Islamic conference . . .

Franklin P. Zimmerman, musical director . . . Oh yeah, here we go. On the final concert on the steps of the art museum . . .

Local News: "And the farmers of Boynton County have banded together to form a protective chicken-stealing association . . . (PAUSE) . . . that sounds like they are doing the stealing . . . of course, you know that is not what I mean!" [*Pr.:* 43]

Self-reporting can be tied to the pronunciation frame, both involving deviation from scripted projection:

In German that's Ver Clar ta Nacht. That's as far as I can get.

Niels W. Gade. I guess that's the way it's pronounced. It's spelled G-A-D-E.

Theatre de [slows up] well, I don't think I'll attempt that in French. It's the Theatre Orchestra of the Champs Elysees.

Here's that word again. I have to look at it for a moment to make sure I can pronounce it.

It should now be clear that self-reporting is not to be considered merely as a desperate measure to which resort is taken in a crisis. During informal face-to-face talk, its role is central, and no conversational mishap is necessary to warrant calling it into use. On some programs (and some stations) a similar impression is given; the speaker seems licensed to tap in at will into what would ordinarily be taken to be his silent backstage thoughts concerning his current situation:

> Gee, that was an awful joke. I shouldn't have told it on the air. Someone dared me.

and these may involve production matters about which he has cause to be pleased, not chagrined:

> [At the end of a show that runs till twelve]: Talk about timing. It's exactly twelve o'clock.

I have cited many examples of self-reporting because I believe that each of them has something to teach us about a fundamental feature of all speech, namely, the continuous decisions every individual must make regarding what to report of his passing thoughts, feelings, and concerns at any moment when he is talking or could talk. The self-reporting resorted to by marginal announcers when they get into a bind points not only to the kinds of trouble that major-station announcers are likely to avoid, but also—and more important—to remedies they might not employ were they to fail to avoid such predicaments. The obligation and right to restrict one's self-reporting, appears, then, to be a significant feature of formality. The self-reporting essayed by marginal announcers establishes informality, and links their style of talk to what is characteristic of everyday conversation. Which fact, in turn, leads to a critical question: What self-concerns, fleeting or otherwise, do conversationalists have in mind but forebear reporting, and this on the various grounds described as "self respect"? Which question, in turn, suggests a general conclusion: To do informal talk is to walk a very narrow line, often with no appreciation of how carefully one is walking; it is to blithely use self-reports up to a point, and silently foreswear such autobiography thereafter.

3. SUBVERSION. In various circumstances an announcer in effect betrays the different interests and entities in whose name

he ordinarily speaks. It is as if (on these occasions) he were under self-imposed pressure to stand up and be counted, that is, to express his "own" personal feelings and views about what it is he is obliged to utter, whether or not this expression comports with the stand he is supposed to take. And it seems that in maintaining a required line, a speaker finds himself admirably placed to infiltrate a contrary one simultaneously, modifying the original two-party, direct-announcing format to do so. Observe, in creating a clear contrast between official voice and "personal" voice, the announcer makes very evident that what we have been listening to until now is not a spontaneous expression of his full inner self. Note also that because an individual has more than one set of self-defining loyalties, he can feel obliged to convey reservations regarding what he has already established as a line that is opposed to the official one.

a. A common technique for subverting station commitment is to override a "personally" unacceptable strip of the text with phonological markers—tempo, voice articulation, intonation contour—which have the effect of "keying" the strip, giving it sarcastic or ironic implications. Standard, too, is the overt collusive aside, an unscripted, frame-breaking editorial comment conveyed *sotto voce* and rendered just before or after the derided strip. The two techniques—often combined—allow the announcer to align himself collusively with the audience against a third party: the station management, the source of the copy, individuals or groups mentioned in a news text, indeed, even society at large:

> [In progress is a commercial for a Florida hotel]: We're up to our armpits in people. [Aside to audience] One of the more elegant statements of our time.

> . . . what the weather forecast calls a dusting of snow . . .

> . . . snow flurries, or as it says here, slurries.

> . . . by, well, as the liner notes say anyway, the dean of the American musicians, Wallingford Riegger.

> A hostile Izvestia article said today [and then into singsong] twenty-six years after the victory of the people's revolution a great country has ended up in a economic and political wilderness. Okay.

> But his remarks according to the Associated Press indicate that
> he [Frank Church] has personally seen a copy of a letter on CIA
> file [and then with shock], that he had written to his mother. Hmm.
> [And then in *sotto voce* singsong] They got nothing better to do than
> . . . Okay. Senate Republican leader Hugh Scott said . . .

> He examined the crew of the Pueblo, the U.S. spy ship which was
> captured by North Korea. [And then sarcastically] So that's what's
> happening there . . .

May I add that we have here a nice example of the kind of
ritualization that speaking is full of (Goffman 1979:23–24, and
this volume, pp. 153–54): the speech markers announcers employ
to establish collusive communication with their invisible audience are an integral part of intimate face-to-face talk; their use
in broadcasting involves a transplantation.

    b. Consider the role of punning. Distinguish "self-punning"
(use of one's own utterance as the object of one's own pun) from
"other-punning" (use of another's utterance as the object of one's
own pun). Announcers when alone at the microphone are, of
course, restricted to self-punning. By dint of a pun, an announcer
can arbitrarily introduce an editorializing line where none might
otherwise be available to him. He can momentarily betray his text
and textual role, displaying a self that puts little weight on the
duties at hand. It is as though a "joke" were being used as a cover
for departure from the script:[51]

> . . . that was the music of Johann Wilhelm Hertel to open our
> program this morning as we go hurtling along.

Another connection in which self-punning occurs is worth
noting. The announcer makes a "serious" blunder, one which
introduces an unintended reading that is readily evident and
improper. Apparently he then wants to show that he has not been
completely thrown off balance by the mishap. So he continues in
the vein he has inadvertently established, adding what is in effect
an intentional pun (overloaded with a leering sound, presumably
so that the key—and his purpose—will not be mistaken). Here,

---

51. In face-to-face talk, other-puns, of course, are possible, and there
have characteristic functions, one of which is to allow the punster to be heard
from, without his having to get the floor (or take the floor) to accomplish this.

it seems to me, the announcer sacrifices the line he was meant to maintain in order to save himself. Having accidentally started his listeners down the wrong path, he gives them a further shove in the same direction. He demonstrates that he not only knows what it is they might find risible, but also that he has sufficient distance from his official task and sufficient wit to organize additional remarks in accordance with the unanticipated interpretation. One has, then, a sort of counterdisplay, but one that follows from an unintended second meaning, intentionally extending it:

> . . . rain and possibly peet . . . Pete who? . . . ah, ah . . . Rain and possibly sleet.

> Commercial: "So, men, be sure to visit Handleman's hardware store on the mall for the finest in tools for your tool kit. Our special for today only is precision wenches for only two dollars each . . . (GIGGLING) . . . Of course I don't mean that you can get a wench for two dollars . . . I mean that you can get a wrench for two dollars!!!" [*Pr.:*119]

> Disc Jockey: "We hear now a song from the new Columbia album featuring Very Jail . . . Oops, I ought to be in jail for that slip . . . of course, I mean JERRY VALE!!" [*Pr.:*120]

> Commercial: "So, friends, be sure to visit Frankie's restaurant for elephant food and dining . . . The portions may be elephant size . . . but I meant to say *elegant* food and dining!" [*Pr.:*11]

Elaboration of the unscheduled reading is sometimes managed with an off-mike aside, as though listeners were now being addressed in a different capacity—a different "participation status" —half-acknowledged overhearers of remarks that are to stand as partly self-directed:

> Political Program: "Everybody is watching the new incumbent with a great deal of interest. They are watching his every move, and are wondering where he will stand when he takes his seat! . . . That sounds like a nice trick if you can do it." [*SB:*85]

> Newscaster: "And the FBI is expecting to make an announcement shortly, linking their newly discovered cues to the Clue Kux Klan . . . that should be, kooks to the Koo Klux Klan . . . clues to the Ku Ku . . . I'm sorry . . . I never liked the organization anyway!" [*Pr.:*104]

[Bess Meyerson narrating TV fashion show]: "Our next model is shoed with the latest high hells . . . I mean, is wearing high hell . . . well, sometimes they may feel like hell . . . but what I meant to say is, high heels!!!"[*Pr.:* 76]

[Announcer doing Rem Cough Medicine commercial]: "So when you have a cough due to a cold, always keep some Rum on hand!" . . . "This may be good cough medicine, but I don't think it was what the sponsor had in mind." [*SB:* 20]

As a device for displaying control in a situation, extending one's own unintentional pun carries a price: to take this tack is to forego leaving open the possibility that one has not seen one's own *double entendre* (due, hopefully, to having a pure mind), as well as the possibility that at least some hearers have missed it, too. Thus, the following, an actual error and a hypothetical correction, has a chance of getting by some hearers:

Hillbilly Disc Jockey: "And now, Zeke Parker sings 'My Hole Has a Bucket In It.' . . . Sorry . . . 'My Bucket Has a Hole In It.'"

The actual correction played it less safely:

Hillbilly Disc Jockey: "And now, Zeke Parker sings 'My Hole Has a Bucket In It.' . . . Sorry . . . wrong number . . . that should be, 'My Bucket Has a Hole In It.'—That's quite a difference!" [*SB:* 13]

Note also that although second-reading extensions—like all other overt remedies—have the undesired effect of drawing attention to the fault, announcers seem almost always careful to leave something unstated. Something is usually left to the imagination. Therefore, no absolutely incontrovertible evidence is provided that they have "caught" the worst implications of the unsought interpretation or that they consider the audience able to do so. Leaving something unsaid here seems to ensure a tacit character to the communication, and it is just this tacitness in this context that produces a sense of collusion with the audience, a covert coalition against the official copy.

   c. It is thinkable, and it sometimes occurs, that an announcer openly turns against his sponsors and his text and presents reservations without employing mitigation, indirection, or cover of any kind. A collusive tone or register is not employed, the announcer showing unwillingness to credit the official line sufficiently to be sly or prudent in his rejection of it, incidentally disavailing himself of the opportunity to use expressions whose distancing implications he could deny were he to be directly questioned by station authorities.[52]

> Portugal's main rival parties today stepped up their pressure for radical solutions to the present political deadlock. Following anti-Communist rioting throughout the conservative north last night, the Communist Party leader Alvaro Cunhal said uncertainty about who rules the country, how, and with what backing was at the heart of the crisis. The Socialists meanwhile brought thousands of people out into the streets of the capital, the North and the South to demand the removal of Communist-backed prime minister Vasco Gonçalves. This Alvaro Cunhal statement, coming shortly after the appointment of three generals to rule the country and the formation of a . . . of a . . . excuse me, folks, this is what happens when you get in the middle of a paragraph that you don't want to finish, and I do not want to finish the paragraph and I will explain to you [ironically] that occasionally even Reuters' wire service tends to be biased. Reuters reports that . . .

> Gonçalves spoke to the five thousand laborers in Lisbon last night. One member of the Communist Party was shot dead and up to one hundred persons were wounded in an anti-Communist riot, or so-called by Reuters, in the northern town of Ponte de Lima.

There is an environment which seems to strongly incline the announcer to subvert his text: when he reads the text itself without prior check, that is, "cold," and finds, while doing so, that it contains an "impossible" statement—one that any listener could be expected to judge as senseless and contrary to the working of the world. At such times there is an appreciable possibility that the announcer will openly break frame and comment to his hearers candidly about the copy he was given, saving what he can of his own image at whatever cost to station programming:

> Sportscaster: "And in the world of baseball: The Los Angeles Dodgers lead the San Francisco Giants 3–3 after eleven innings!

52. The movie *Network,* a lamentable 1978 effort to provide something of an exposé of the broadcasting industry, featured a newscaster who, on the occasion of his last broadcast, decides to say what he "really" believes. Pandemonium and a high rating result.

. . . I've got two words for this report . . . im-possible!!!" [*Pr.:* 35]

Political Program: "The 67-year-old candidate for the Senate, now of Peoria, was born on a farm in Columbia County 58 years ago. That doesn't sound right but that's what it says in my script!" [*SB:* 84]

Commercial: "Try this wonderful new bra . . . you'll especially love the softly lined cups that are so comfortable to wear. You gals who need a little something extra should try model 718. It's lightly padded and I'm sure you'll love it. I do! . . . I mean I like the looks of it . . . Well . . . what I am trying to say is that I don't need one myself naturally, as a man . . . but if you do, I recommend it . . . How do I know? I really don't . . . I'm just reading the commercial for Mary Patterson who is ill at home with a cold!" [*Pr.:*92]

If you're confused by that [weather report] well so am I and I'm looking at it.

d. Consider next the possibility that an announcer may momentarily "flood out" into speech that seems to have broken free from the special circumstances of its production, namely, broadcasting. If the announcer's involvement is great enough, what we can hear is something like the "direct register" (Goffman 1974:361–62):

[Sportscaster during a Newark Bears' ball game when Ernie Koy hit a home run]: "Jesus Christ! It's over the wall!" [*SB:*114]

e. A related possibility is "exposed" collusion. Support personnel (never meant to speak on the air) are ordinarily available close at hand and/or through an off-air earphone channel. And, of course, a switch can totally cut the announcer off from the broadcast audience, while making staff auditors immediately available. Any urge the announcer might have to make undercutting, collusive comments about the audience is thus organizationally facilitated. Therefore, as already illustrated, there will be occasions when an announcer *thinks* that his staff-directed remarks are not being broadcast when indeed they are. At point here, however, is a further possibility: under no misapprehension that the microphone is closed, the announcer can blurt out a behind-the-scenes comment to technicians present, using a "rough," informal voice, as if momentarily blind to—or uncaring about—its wide reception:

> Stay tuned. At a quarter to nine there'll possibly be somebody in here who can read news better than I with a more updated and more ah understandable newscast. This is [to off-mike personnel] —did I do an ID? Well, I'll do another one anyway. This is KPFA in Berkeley at 94 . . .

> Newscaster: "And rumor has it that the North Dakota lawmaker has been ill for quite some time and this illness was caused by his death. We tried to reach him but we were told at the Executive Mansion that he is away at present on a little vacation. (FRUS-TRATED, OFF MIKE) Who typed this goddamn thing?" [*SB:* 88]

I might add that given the vulnerability of announcers to impossible texts, one might expect that on occasion copywriters and editors will purposely set up an announcer (or be thought by the announcer to have done so), a blurted remonstrance being a possible consequence:

> [Cardinal baseball network]: "Our sponsors today are Lucky Strike cigarettes, Camel cigarettes and Chesterfields . . . (CONFUSED AT THE COMPETITIVE PRODUCTS) . . . All right now, who's the wise guy?" [*Pr.:* 45]

All of these blurted communications, note, are to be distinguished from talk the announcer openly directs to support personnel by way of officially bringing them into the talk already in progress with the distal audience—albeit, like the latter, only as recipients.

    4. SELF-COMMUNICATION. One of the basic resources of the announcer (perhaps even more than of the ordinary speaker) is that of conveying something that listeners will be privy to but which cannot stand as something they openly have been given access to. The audience is, as it were, forced into the role of overhearers, but of messages the announcer is sending only to himself or not to anyone at all. Several varieties of this self-communication are to be found.

    a. Caught in the middle of reading something that doesn't quite make sense, or that makes all too much sense of a wrong kind, the announcer can allow his concern about what is happening to invade his words, much as if he were addressing a query to himself, this expression providing "notification" that a fault of some kind is occurring. Indeed, because the eye can take in an upcoming segment before the segment itself is encoded into speech (a sort of forward monitoring), the aloud reader can know that a mistake is imminent even though none has yet been transmitted; so self-directed concern and doubt can seep into his words well in advance of what will shortly show why such alarm is warranted. This seems to be an enactment—an "externalization"—of self-monitoring, the latter being a function that is ordinarily unobtrusively sustained. And with this ritualized expression, the work of animation becomes the subject of attention instead of the means for organizing it:

> Fashion Commentator: "And now for the latest from the fashion world. It is good news for men. Women are not going to wear their dresses any longer . . . [self-questioningly] this year." [*SB:* 51]

Interestingly, an announcer may extend this self-querying practice, casting his speech production deeper and deeper into the shadow of doubt and wonderment, until his speech peters out into silence. We are allowed first to catch only a glimmer of the speaker as animator, but gradually we see more and more, until finally a complete change of footing has occurred and the speaker is present before us solely as someone whose audible self-concern has been made available for our overhearing:

> Musician: "For my next selection, I would like to play a medley of Old Stephen Foster favorites; among them will be 'Jeannie with the Light Brown Hair,' 'My Old Kentucky Home,' and 'My Ass Is In the Cold . . . Cold . . . Ground.' " [With the last word, speaker's voice fades entirely away.] [*SB:* 56, and recording]

These dwindlings are sometimes followed by a hedge:

> That tune was a hit around 19–60–5?–6?–4? *I think* [this last said as if talking to himself].

These means of displaying self-doubt are not presented as subject much to conscious control, and yet, of course, they can serve an obvious function. Although they advertise the speaker's predicament, this exposure specifically saves him from "announcer's leap"—namely, throwing himself into a statement as though he were fully alive to what would end up as its meaning (and moreover was enormously convinced of its validity), only to find out too late that the utterance made no sense.

b. The self-communicative expressions so far considered involve "tone of voice," and are carried across word boundaries. They are to be considered along with segmented interjections, these blurtings constituting self-communication in a more obvious sense. Thus, consider "response cries" (Goffman 1978, and this volume, chap. 2)—imprecations and semiwords such as *Uh-oh!, Eek!, Yipe!*—which appear to be directed to no one, not even the self. Through these blurtings, the announcer ostensibly leaks evidence of his alignment to what is occurring, which expression has the form of something that is beyond self-control. In this way the announcer makes his audience privy to his own feelings (not the station's or sponsor's or any generalized "we"), shifting the audience's status to that of overhearers. Because response cries employ standard sounds, well-articulated and properly pronounced (even if not official lexical items), and do so right at the moment of crisis, they provide evidence that the speaker is fully alive to what has happened and, moreover, has not been completely disorganized by it. Paradoxically, then, these vocalizations are ritualized indicators of incapacity for verbal expression, whilst at the same time uttering them demonstrates (and apparently often intendedly so) that all control has not been lost:

> "Stay tuned now for a dramatization of Dickens' immortal *Sale of Two Titties.* Uh! I mean *Tale of Two Cities."* [*PB:77*]

Allied to response cries are interjective expletives of various strengths, which rather clearly display what is presumably the announcer's own personal "response" to a source of trouble, in these examples his own animating:

> Newscast: "We switch you now for a report from CBS's Dallas Texas . . . I mean Texas Townsend . . . Good Lord, I mean Dallas Townsend." [*Pr.:6*]

> Commercial: "So ladies, we urge you to shave at Cook's . . . I mean shake at Cook's. What I really mean is that you can shave at Cook's . . . Lordy, I mean save at Cook's!" [*SB:8*]

Commercial: "So remember, for the finest in profane gas . . . I mean propane gas . . . darn it . . . remember the Federal Profane Gas Company . . . Propane Gas Company!" [*Pr.:*30]

[Film Commentator]: "Hollywood stars as well as those here in London are usually faced with the problem of losing weight before starting a new picture. But not in the case of the talented Shelley Winters, who in her latest picture, *The Diarrhea of Anne* . . .oh! . . . *The Diary of Anne Frank,* found that she had to gain 53 pounds. When asked how this was done, she replied she had to go on a very strict high colonic diet . . . Oh, mercy. [*PB:*138, and recording]

Self-directed interjections, I might add, sometimes precede another, and fuller, change of voice, namely a shift into exposed comments to support personnel:

Sportscaster: "And in the Eastern Playoffs of the NBA tonight, it was Philadelphia 122, Cincinnati 114, with Cincinnati winning that one . . . (Off Mike) . . . I'll be goddamned . . . now how the hell is that possible! Hey, Charlie . . . who the hell typed this!" [*Pr.:*95]

c. Along with response cries, consider less formulaic, often more extended strips of communication that the audience is made privy to, but that aren't openly addressed to them. For an under-the-breath delivery is available to the announcer, a sort of non-theatrical aside through which he can momentarily take up a footing radically different from the one he has been otherwise maintaining. Here, then, self-talk—remarks of an interjective character the speaker apparently addresses to himself. Through this arrangement, the speaker can employ self-accusations, showing in his response to his own error that he is, for example, surprised, shocked, and chagrined at making the mistake, and, at the very least, is perfectly aware of what the audience may think he has done. And with the proper modulation of his wonderment, he can indicate that he is really well organized and self-possessed, in a word, bemused. Note, this kind of self-communication can also be employed by the announcer to cut himself off from responsibility for faultables attributable to the station's equipment, the sponsor's advertising agency, the presumably prepared copy, and so forth:

. . . overnight lows . . . what am I saying . . . the highs today will
be in the low 80s and the overnight lows [laugh] will be in the mid
60s.

No, that can't be right.

Now what have I done?

. . . for more information . . . no, I don't have a number for that.

. . . send a stamped . . . no, that doesn't apply.

. . . narrated by Leonard Bernstein and performed . . . is that the
right version, yeah . . . by the New York Philharmonic . . .

Announcer: "Our next selection to be sung by our great baritone
soloist is Rachmaninoff's 'Oh, Cease Thy Sinning, Maidenform.'
. . . That should be, 'Oh, Cease Thy Sinning, Maiden Fair' . . . Oh,
great, Maidenform is a bra!" [*SB:*112]

"Beat the egg yolk and then add the milk, then slowly blend in the
sifted flour. As you do you can see how the mixture is sickening.
I beg your pardon, I didn't mean sickening I meant thickening" *(Off
mike)* "Oh, I goofed there, I know." [*PB:*81]

Commercial: "This is KECK, Odessa, Texas. When you think of air
conditioning, think of Air-Temp at a price everyone can't afford
. . . so if you don't want to pinch tit . . . (FLUSTERED) . . . pitch
a tent on the front yawn . . . lawn—buy Frigi-King . . . er, Air-
Temp, for your home. (OFF MIKE) God damn, I'm glad that's
over!" [*Pr.:*91]

"And now, audience, here is our special TV Matinee guest that
we've all been waiting for—world famous author, lecturer, and
world traveler, a man about town. Mr. er—er, Mr. . . . Oh! What
the hell is his name?" [*PB:*111]

d. An announcer can use the verbal channel to address his
own faultables, as would a critical member of the audience. He
can use the perspective of the audience not merely as a guide in
formulating excuses and accounts, but also as the substance of
a self, a self that is, for example, amused at the mishap that
has occurred and is ready to mock the speaker who caused
it.

In the mild and most common form, the announcer allows
an override of laughter to creep into his voice, betraying that he

himself feels what he is saying is risible[53]—perhaps even beating the listener to the punch:

> We'll confine, we'll continue [laugh] . . .

Such self-amusement may be carried to the point where the announcer frankly "breaks up" into privately directed laughter over what the speaker (who happens to be himself) has said:

> Disc Jockey: "And now it's time for another record by that svelte, smooth singer of songs . . . slinky Pinky Lee . . . (BREAKS UP) . . . of course, I mean PEGGY LEE!!" [*Pr.:* 124]

> Announcer: "And as I stand here at my vantage point overlooking the Hudson River on this historical Fourth of July night, I can see the fireworks eliminating the entire Riverside Drive . . . (Laughing) . . . I mean illuminating!!!" [*Pr.:* 96]

Indeed, laughter may build upon itself until the announcer appears to give up all effort at self-containment, all effort to provide any text:

> "In the wonder of science, the Hayden Planetarium has heard from a Minnesota man who claims that the shape of the aurora borealis can be changed by flapping a bed sheet at it from the ground. The Planetarium doubts this but the man says he did successfully flap sheets in his backyard one midnight, although his wife kept hollering at him to cut out the foolishness and get back in the house!
> . . . [The announcer gives up trying to maintain a newscasting register, breaks up with laughter, and then, barely containing himself, attempts to continue.] This Sunday evening be sure to hear Drew Pearson on ABC. Pearson has received many awards for his work, and one of his treasures is the *Saturday* Revoo *of Literature* . . . [The last error is too much and he floods out again, a few moments later regains enough composure to continue on, and

---

53. There is an interesting transformation of this practice. After a "humorous" commercial skit taped by professional actors, the announcer coming in may allow the initial moments of his talk to carry a self-laughter override, half in collusion with the audience, as if thereby to add to the realism of the skit. The implication is that he, too, thinks it funny (presumably because this is the first time he has heard it) and is so close to his audience that he need not forebear allowing his appreciation to be sensed—which implication is quite beyond belief.

finishes with a mock slip.] . . . This is ABC, the American *Broad* Company." [*Pr.:*15, and recording]

It would be wrong here to present too simple a picture of the footings—the frame space—available to the announcer. Finding that he has committed a hopeless error—hopeless in the sense that the unanticipated reading is very obvious and all too meaningful—the announcer may present a corrected reading in a tone of voice to suggest that he tacitly admits to the audience the impropriety he has called to mind and indeed, is not so station-minded as to deny the relevance and humor of the reading he has inadvertently allowed. And yet by refraining from laughing outright, and by adhering to what would otherwise be a standard correction format, he can carefully manage his subversion so as to convey self-respect *and* station discipline.

It would also be wrong to assume that because a distinction can be drawn (and certainly heard) between collusive asides to the audience, and aloud asides to self, to no one, or to station personnel, any given formulaic remedy will be employed in only one of these participation frameworks. For example, upon making an "error," an announcer may repeat it in wonderment, as if holding it up so he himself can get a better look at what he somehow said, projecting thus a little dialogue of self-communication:

. . . mostly skunny.
Mostly skunny?
No, mostly sunny.

Good Wednesday morning.
Good Wednesday morning?
Good Tuesday morning.

However, self-quoted errors (like the pun extensions already considered), can be presented not as overhearable self-communications, but as collusive asides to the audience:

. . . vins of . . . winds, not vins—vindows . . . must be those new false teeth of mine.

. . . no, not an eight-mile walk, my goodness, just an eight-minute walk from the [laugh] just an eight-mile walk—no, no, just an eight-minute walk.

In the meantime I want to tell you about a very live [laugh] *live* . . . very good program of . . .

A second example. It was suggested that when an announcer discovers that he is lodged into the reading of an "impossible" text, he can allow his voice to dwindle as he gives increasingly candid (and increasingly self-directed) expression of his bewilderment over what is happening (see 4a, above). A somewhat similar sequence, but perhaps even more ritualized, is the "despairing give-up." An announcer utters a "wrongly" constructed word or phrase, attempts a standard correction (flat or strident), fails to get it right—indeed, may worsen the product—tries once again, fails once again (all the while with increasing stridency) until finally, as if in angered resignation, he changes footing, transforms his audience into overhearers, and utters his final words on the matter aloud and uncaring, half to himself.

> Newscaster: "This is your eleven o'clock newscaster bringing you an on the pot report . . . I mean on the spot retort . . . I mean on the tot resort . . . oh, well, let's just skip it!" [*SB:*6]

> Sportscaster: "That was a great game that Drysdale pitched last night. Now wait a minute, it wasn't last night, it was the night before, and it wasn't Drysdale it was Koufax. Or was it? Wait a minute. (OFF MIKE) Hey, Joe. Oh, yeah. No! Wait a minute, now I'm all fouled up over here. Now I don't remember if it was night before last . . . (EXASPERATED) . . . to hell with it!" [*SB:*51]

> Announcer: "Our music-appreciation hour continues as we hear an instrumental selection by a well-known flautist. We hear now a sloat flulu . . . a fluke solo . . . I mean a sloat flulu . . . Nuts—I'm back to where I started!!" [*SB:*33]

The ritualized, patterned character of this response is suggested by the fact that it is not merely announcers who employ it; others fall back on the device, too:

> [Contestant on CBS musical quiz program, asked to identify a recorded musical composition]: "It sounds like Smetana's Buttered Bride . . . er . . . Battered Bride, oh the hell with it." [*SB:*25]

And as might be expected, much the same ritualization can be employed in collusive asides to the audience:

Local News: And this station is glad to be the first to bring you news of our mayor's death . . . that is, we are glad to be the first station to bring you news of the mayor's death, not that we are glad of the mayor's death . . . You know what I mean." [*SB*: 98]

[Actress during interview asked for her reaction to the opportunity to appear in the TV series "77 Sunset Strip"]: "I'm delighted to appear in a SUNSET STRIP . . . I mean I'm delighted to strip . . . Oh, my goodness, you know what I mean!!!" [*Pr.*: 123]

All of which forces a further conclusion. What is heard, say, as self-communication must depend on more than the actual formulaic words the speaker employs; prosodic features (in the absence of visual cues) are critical. Thus, to repeat a previous example, "Oh! What the hell is his name?" is an utterance that clearly breaks frame, involving a change of footing in which the announcer comes to speak wholly in his capacity as an animator; but whether self-communication is presented, or an aside that is rather openly directed to the audience that isn't present or to the support personnel who are, depends entirely upon intonation, "phrasing," and sound cues of head orientation. (In consequence, the illustrations I have provided of collusive asides and of self-communication are not, as printed, self-sufficient, although the LP and tape transcriptions almost always are; the reader must take my word for the frame in which they are to be "heard.") Nor, in many cases, would currently available transcription techniques for limning in prosodic features be discriminating enough to establish how the utterance is to be framed; a gloss in the form of bracketed stage directions would have to be employed. Thus, although an announcer may orient off-mike interjections in four different directions—to no one, to himself, to the remote audience, to support personnel—and be clearly so heard, no convenient notation for such facts is available. I might add that these issues cannot be adequately considered unless one appreciates that participation framework will always be a structural presupposition of our hearing of an utterance.

So far in reviewing the frame space of announcers, I have limited the discussion to occasions when an announcer serves as the sole official speaker. Many of the remedial practices described, however, are also to be found when two announcers share the speaking duties, as in some newscasting and record-playing programs. In these formats, one finds that instead of one announcer splitting himself into two voices (an official one which utters a faultable, and an unofficial one which contributes a remedial comment), the job can be split between the two participants, sometimes one announcer carrying the remedial (and distancing) comments, sometimes the other:

> First announcer: "It's Thursday, October the twenty-first."
> Second announcer: "Hold it, Cameron, it's Tuesday."
> First announcer: "You're right, I'm wrong. It's Tuesday."

> First announcer: ". . . and it will be a nippy forty-two degrees tonight."
> Second announcer: [*Sotto voce*] "I could stand a nip."
> First announcer: "Get away from here."

Indeed, the two-person, speaker and kibitzer format may be the underlying structure in all of this communication, the one-announcer form being an adaptation.[54]

From the examples given, it is plain that when a dialogue is conducted before the microphone, a straightforward statement said in good faith by one speaker may be reframed by the other in an apparent spirit of raillery and fun:

> Bennett Cerf: "Is the product made in Hollywood?"
> Arlene Francis: "Isn't everybody?" [*SB:* 78]

> On *Name That Tune*, on NBC-TV, a contestant was asked to identify *Hail to the Chief*, which was played by the orchestra. MC Bill Cullen tried helping the girl by hinting, "What do they play whenever the President's around?" She answered, "Golf." [*PB:* 92]

54. Certainly a two-party model is required in the vast number of childhood jokes, riddles, and snappy comebacks that work by inducing a standard interpretation of an utterance and, once induced, provide the uncommon verbal environment that neatly establishes an unexpected but cogent interpretation.

The late Marilyn Monroe was asked if she had anything on when she posed for that famous calendar photo. She told her radio and TV interviewers, "I had the radio on!" [*Pr.:*49]

In a television interview several years ago, Senator Margaret Chase Smith of Maine was questioned about her Presidential aspirations. Asked what she would do if she woke up one morning and found herself in the White House, she replied, "I would go straight downstairs and apologize to Mrs. Eisenhower, and then I would go right home." [*Pr.:*52]

On the popular Art Linkletter program, a youngster was asked what he wanted to be when he grew up. He replied, "A space man." He was then asked what he would do if he ran into a Martian. The youngster snapped back with, "I would say, 'Excuse me.'" [*Pr.:*56]

In brief, "quipping" or "snapping back" is possible, the provision of a response that admittedly derives from a misframed interpretation of the other's remarks. All of which leaves open the question of how frequently an announcer covertly sets himself up for his own misframing of his own remarks, allowing one part of him to produce a dually interpretable utterance so that another part of him can get a quip off by humorously extending the initial error, serving then as his own straight man. (Again, what seems generic to two-person play can be managed by one person.) And from here it is only a step to seeing that an announcer may intentionally phrase a statement so that hearers can construe the phrasing in an officially unintended way, to the disparagement of the subject matter.[55] Or, learning that he has inadvertently al-

55. This possibility must itself be distinguished from two other keyings: the serious citation of faults and corrections in talks on speech behavior, and the unserious introduction of faults and corrections when these happen to be the topic under consideration:

> When I [Kermit Schafer] was interviewed by Maggie McNellis over NBC Radio in connection with the release of my new book, *Your Slip is Showing,* Maggie came out with the following: "It now gives me great pleasure to introduce to you the author of that hilariously funny book, *Your Show is Slipping*—radio-TV producer Kermit Schafer!!! . . . er, I'm sorry, Kermit . . . I got the name of your book wrong . . . please excuse the shlip-sod introduction." [*Pr.:*127]

On the next page, the last in his book, Schafer concludes with, "This conclues . . . this conclees . . . that is all!!!" [*Pr.:*128].

lowed a double meaning, the announcer may attempt after the fact to give the impression that he had slyly intended it. In consequence of which, hearers may be left uncertain as to whether the risible ambiguity was or wasn't intentional.

x

The notions of speech fault and self-correction imply a simple sequential, remedial model basic to the traditional notion of social control. Starting from a baseline of acceptable talk, a fault then occurs, a correction is made, and the speaker returns to the baseline of talk unnoteworthy for its blemishes. Or, schematically:

baseline → fault → remedy → baseline

To which the standard variation could be added, namely, a sequence in which the remedy appears immediately *preceding* the trouble, the better to deal with it:

baseline → remedy → fault → baseline

For announcers, the schema would read something like this: The text an announcer must read, recite, or extemporaneously formulate sets the task. Ordinarily his competence at delivery, along with technical support from the station's equipment and staff, ensures that a flow of words is sustained that is acceptable to the station, provides a single, clear line for the audience to follow, and implies an image of the particular announcer he is prepared to accept. This, then, is the baseline. Then a fault occurs in speech production that the announcer feels he can't handle simply by passing over, whether the fault is an influency, slip, boner, or gaffe, whether the responsibility is to be attributed to himself or to station programming. Presumably something has been evoked that he feels is incompatible with the station's requirements or with his own reputation as an announcer. A remedy is then attempted and, typically, the announcer is thereafter free to return to the base line he had been maintaining before the trouble occurred.

This paper has argued that such a framework is inadequate to handle error in radio talk. Several grounds were suggested for extending the basic social control sequence, the aim being to make the formula fit the facts.

First, when a speaker is obliged to adhere closely to a script, or at least a format, any self-correction will itself constitute a deviation from what is prescribed as the text, and will itself establish a need for remedial action, with consequent prolongment of the remedial sequence. The following is therefore found:

$$\text{baseline} \rightarrow \text{fault} \rightarrow \text{remedy} \rightarrow \text{remedy for remedy} \rightarrow \text{baseline}$$

the question being open as to how any remedy can be the last one.

Second, as argued repeatedly, the notion of fault must be broadened to include "remark-ables," namely, anything the announcer might treat as something to not let stand. He can editorially extend what has been under discussion, deride in various ways what he has been obliged to say, and provide a risible alternative reading—one that listeners themselves may not have thought of. And if neither an obvious error nor an opportunity for skittishness arises, nor even a latent error, then a determined announcer can allow himself to commit an error with malice aforethought, just in order to be able to make something out of it.[56] And the point is that —more than in the case of ordinary self-correction— *these* makings-something-out-of-it, these remedial actions that other announcers might not be venturing at all, themselves provide deviations from the base line. Thus they are themselves candidates for remedy, even as the individual who produced them is already someone who has demonstrated a taste for working deviations for what can be gotten from them. For the more an announcer must coerce a faultable from what has just occurred, the more the remedy is likely to display an attempt at wit; the less the remedy is likely to be merely remedial, the more it will itself be questionable. So the shift from fault to faultable, and from faultable to remark-able, increases the likelihood that

56. A possibility perhaps even more exploited in face-to-face talk. Thus, for example, it has been recommended that individuals who begin to use an untactful descriptor for someone present, then catch themselves and rush in with a more acceptable alternative, will sometimes be acting tactically, committing the error for what can be safely leaked in this manner (Jefferson 1974:-192–93).

the social control sequence will be extended by an extra step or two:

> . . . rain and possibly sleet. They're not treating us well in the weather department. That's all I can say. [Dropping voice] That's all I should say.

Third, the simple remedial sequence can be complicated by the question of framing. Some elaboration is required. When an "obvious" fault occurs in announcing, it tends to occur in a nicely self-bounded fashion, the words just before and after it providing discernible contrasts and hence brackets for the spoiled strip. The prospective or retrospective correction then presents no problem with respect to what it refers to. By and large, no corroboration from the audience is required in order to ensure that they have gotten the point and will have correctly referred the remedy to what was in need of it. It will be clear to them that the remedy is not part of the copy, but the speaker's out-of-frame correction, and clear, too, when the correcting is complete and the speaker has reverted to his prescribed text.[57] The unavailability of listener back-channel response—a response which helps stabilize frames in face-to-face talk—is here not damaging.

When, however, the speaker elects to provide an editorial-like comment about a remedy he has provided, or, even more so, chooses to betray his prescribed text in the absence of evident error, then framing problems can arise. Hearers may not know whether a strip of talk is an out-of-frame comment on the text or a part of the text itself; and if they do appreciate that the announcer is not delivering his copy but commenting on what he is required to deliver, they still may not know precisely where this side-remarking ends and the official text begins again. In turn, because back-channel cues from hearers are not available, the announcer will not know whether or not his listeners know how he wants them to take what he is saying, or, if they do sense how he wants his comments to be taken, whether or not they are ready to do so.

A general solution for this framing problem is for the speaker

---

57. A more refined treatment of correction placement position is to be found in Schegloff et al. (1977:366 and 377), and Schegloff (1979).

to assume the role of his hearers and provide an approximation of their response, were they present in the flesh to provide the feedback he needs. The dialogic character of remedial work is thus maintained, but the announcer performs both parts of it. Thus, the "bracket laugh," a standard frame cue announcers employ to show that what they had been saying is not part of the text proper but a comment on it, and that now this commentative aside is terminated and the official text is about to be resumed.[58] The bracket laugh is in fact not unlike the laugh that members of a live audience might give to show that they have gotten the point and find it funny, the announcer often inserting his version at just the juncture the live audience would have selected. The difference is that he runs the risk of appearing to laugh at his own jokes. (But he does get a chance to imply by tone that he admits his remark might have been a little uncalled for, and that he makes no claim to a sure right to carry on in this fashion.) Observe, the availability of framing cues itself allows the announcer to venture a remark about aspects of his copy that other broadcasters would find no need to make something of, and to offer such remedies playfully in a tone of voice that might otherwise be miskeyed as serious:

> . . . that's the longest sentence I've ever read from an AP release [laugh].

> [During a weather forecast, wind speed is announced in a hoarse voice]: I think my voice left with those winds this morning [laugh].

> . . . Mozart composed while playing skittles. It doesn't say whether he was drinking beer or not, be that as it may and all that [laugh].

> . . . an Argo record—to give the British their due [laugh].

> [Transmission noise]: No, a bee didn't get loose in your receiver [laugh].

> [From the liner notes]: Music to entertain a king. In this case, King Henry VIII, in fact, his whole entourage [laugh].

Announcers seem particularly concerned that a hearer might miskey the enactment of pretension, and here they seem particularly

---

58. See the comment on "joking openers" in Goffman (1971:182). A close treatment of the placement of laughter is provided in Jefferson (1979).

prone to employ a bracket laugh to ensure proper framing. For example, after a straight reading of liner notes (on Buxtehude) that could be considered overbearing, an announcer may display his view of such erudition by means of mock personal elaboration of the notes, and then use a laugh (apparently) to make sure he isn't misinterpreted:

> One doesn't hear much of Buxtehude's chamber music [laugh], does one now?

Just as bracket laughs are often found after questionable remedies, so they are found after a remedy (serious or not) has been itself remedied:

> . . . by Karl Maria von Weber. That was pretty lively music, not to say bumptious—and I don't know why anyone would, except me [heh heh].

> One of the slogans flying at the park read, "Be prepared against war, be prepared against natural disasters, and do everything for the people. Dig tunnels deep, store grain everywhere, and never seek heg, heg, hegomany"—I should learn to read these things beforehand. Hegemony [laugh].

Interestingly, if the speaker's laugh comes right at the juncture between out-of-frame remark and the resumed text, a break in fluency is chanced. To deal with this issue, announcers sometimes delay their bracket laugh, displacing it until just after the prescribed text has been resumed, the laugh taking the characteristic form of a slight swelling of the initial words of the reestablished text:

> . . . barometer stands at twenty-eight degrees and
> falling. Crash. We⌐turn . . .
>   └[laugh]

> That's soprano, comma, trumpet, not soprano trumpet
> on this record.
> [laugh]

> How do you like that? He [meaning himself] got through
> the weather forecast without making a mistake. The⌐next . . .
>   └[laugh]

> And now that you're awake,⌐this is . . .
>   └[laugh]

In sum, once an announcer undertakes a digression, or ad libs a remark, or takes exception to a phrasing that would otherwise have passed unnoticed, he has the problem of getting back to base; so, whether or not he provides a mitigating comment on his comment, he may add a bracket cue to ensure that his hearers find their way back to his text. A full expansion of the remedial cycle in the case of announcer's self-correction would then be:

$$\text{baseline} \rightarrow \text{remark-able} \rightarrow \text{remedial work} \underset{\searrow}{\overset{\nearrow}{}} \begin{array}{l} \text{bracket cue} \rightarrow \text{baseline} \\ \text{reworking} \rightarrow \text{bracket cue} \rightarrow \text{baseline} \end{array}$$

I want only to add that a frame bracket laugh can also appear at the *beginning* of an utterance that is not to be taken literally but keyed, for example, as irony, sarcasm, quotation, or mock pretension:

> If my [laugh] if my memory serves, yes, Thomas Weelkes [a very, very obscure composer] was born in 1575.

—which would require a slight reordering of the elements of the remedial cycle.

As already argued, the less an announcer is in control of his circumstances, the more, it seems, he must be poised for these remedial sequences, these little essays in compensation, recompensation, and reconnection. He must, indeed, be ready in relatively serious shows to engage in just those shticks that professional announcers engage in when emceeing an informal show. In any case, these little remedial sequences turn out to be extremely well patterned, extremely stereotyped. The path of words along which the announcer retreats is likely to be one that is well worn. That is, the verbal and expressive rituals he employs to get himself back into countenance are relatively standardized and common to the trade. Indeed, many are common to talk in general. The individual who uses these devices in announcing is likely to have used them in off-mike hours. And when an individual does use these moves while announcing, he or she is not using them *qua* announcer but as a person who is stuck with a particular job and therefore stuck with the particular ways in which this work can go wrong. Social (indeed formulaic) this behavior is, and certainly it is displayed *during* the performance of an occupational role; but in the last analysis it speaks to the job of being a person, not an announcer. Which is not to say, of course, that just such a display of personhood may not become the mainstay of a radio or TV show.

CONCLUSIONS

1. Take it that a standard in much broadcasting is that the speaker will render his prepared text with faultless articulation, pronunciation, tempo, and stress, and restrict himself entirely to the copy. He is to appear to us only in the guise that his prepared material has planned for him, almost as though he were to hold himself to the character allotted to him in a play. And whether aloud reading or fresh talk is required of him, he is obliged to compress or stretch his talk so that it lasts exactly as long as the time allotted, just filling up the space between his "on" and "off" cues. Given this ideal, any noticed faultable may not only introduce irrelevant associations (if not misinforming us), but also divert the obligatory stream, presenting a view of someone stumbling—indeed a view of a stumbler—instead of a view of the person who has been programmed for the occasion. Further, remedies themselves necessarily add further diversion, further introducing a difference between what was to have occurred and what is occurring. More to the point, corrective actions can intrude the speaker upon us in a way we hadn't bargained for: his plight as a speaker of words. Substantive repairs, self-reports, and apologies—remedial acts of all kinds—thrust the person making them upon us in a more rounded and intimate way than the role that was meant to emerge for him might recommend. He becomes fleshier than he was to have been. After all, the very efficacy of an apology is due to its capacity to convince us that the person making it is a somewhat different person from the one who committed the offense in the first place, and how can this evidence be presented without deflecting attention from the original text to the announcer in his capacity as animator?

It was argued that announcers on small and on special-interest stations, and announcers employing a comic format, do not merely make errors and employ remedies for them, betraying their own role obligations to do so, but also make unscripted comments about strips of their performed text that otherwise would have passed by with no special attention. So, too, they may choose to treat error correction itself as requiring remedial comments. It was suggested that here repair work might be seen as merely one example of maintaining a dual voice, of commenting on one's own production even while producing it. And that at the heart of it is the characterizing, self-projective implication of any stream of activity and the capacity and license to introduce contrary images during its flow. Here role is a rough gloss, for it is really multiple voices and changes of footing that are at work. With marginal announcers, then, the shift is from errors in talk and their correction to definitions of the self that talk projects and the means of escaping these definitions—and then escaping the escape. And the study of speech faults and what is done about them proves to be an integral part of a larger matter: the study of how a speaker can construe a strip of his own speech to provide himself with something upon which to base a remark. How, in effect, a speaker can transform a linear text into a mono-dialogue. What starts with a consideration of error correction should end with an analysis of sequential movements within frame space.

2. Now finally I want to review the argument that an examination of radio talk, especially the differences between the formal and informal kind, can direct our attention to critical features of everyday face-to-face talk that might otherwise remain invisible to us.

As suggested, there are obvious differences between ordinary talk and radio talk of any kind, all a consequence of the presence in radio talk of absent addressees. Correction in radio talk is almost all of the self-administered variety; correction in everyday talk is considerably other-noticed, if not other-administered (Schegloff et al. 1977). (A member of an audience can write or phone in a correction, but the remedy will ordinarily have to be transmitted considerably after the error has occurred, by which time the announcer's subject matter and audience will have changed somewhat; if he is to make a public acknowledgment, he will have to replay the original context of the error to be sure his comments will be understood.) Radio listeners are free to laugh derisively and openly when a faultable occurs, not being bound by the tact that leads face-to-face listeners to pass over some of the faults to which a speaker seems oblivious.[59] Also as suggested, nonbroadcast talk would seem to allow for subtler changes in footing than does radio talk, in part because a speaker in everyday talk can obtain ongoing, back-channel evidence that his intention—his frame and its keying—is understood.

But there are deeper issues. The fresh talk to be found in informal conversation, and the simulated fresh talk to be found in network announcing, are similar on the surface but different underneath. Both tend to be heard as faultless and spontaneous, the first because the sort of technical faults that routinely occur are routinely disattended or flatly corrected (in any case, lots of warrant is available for them), the second because special skill has been applied to eliminate such faults in spite of very treacherous conditions.

In everyday informal talk, the conception of individual-as-animator that seems to prevail allows speakers a considerable margin of error and imperfection. They have the right to break down in minor ways; they can cough, sneeze, yawn, pause to wipe their glasses, glance at passing objects of interest, and so forth. Speakers can disattend these interruptions and assume that their listeners have done likewise. Further, conversational talk allows not only the disattendance of many minor faultables but also the introduction of candid corrections—restarts, filled pauses, redirections—as well as perfunctory excuses and apologies. In addition, stressed corrections abound. Corrections in general, then, whether flat or strident, themselves don't much require excuse and remedy. And many priorities are accepted as taking precedence over smooth speech production by virtue of the fact that many claims in addition to that of coparticipant in talk are recognized as legitimately bearing on the individual, even if he happens to be in the role of speaker at the time.

Informal talk allows still other liberties. Often a participant can forego speaking in favor of mere back-channel evidence of

59. Studio audiences are in a similar position. On various grounds they can behave like an absent audience, tittering and laughing in the face of the person who is the target of this response; indeed, they may be encouraged by a show's M.C. to do so (see Goffman 1974:372–73).

participation that passes the right and obligation of speaking back to prior speaker. If more than two participants are involved, there are circumstances in which one of them may move in and out of effective participation. A participant also has the right to generate discourse by referring to his own situation, including his situation as animator, telling us, for example, of the difficulty he is having remembering what he knows he knows, or finding the right words for what he has in mind—a form of self-involvement that need not be heard as a particularly eventful change in footing; after all, the speaker in any case is likely to have been uttering his own formulations in his own name. (It is as if the biography and officially irrelevant concerns of a talker are always accorded the right to some attention from listeners; that claim is presumably a feature of the way we are in informal, natural talk.) Also, he may be able to pun at will, responding with alternative interpretations, playfully reframing what he or another has said.

All of these deviations from a fixed role can themselves be of small moment because informal talk is defined as presenting the individual participant in this fuller way. No particular voice or footing is fixed for the speaker, so shifting from one to another voice needs no apology or excuse. Insofar as the speaker can claim the right to report on his own fugitive feelings, his own responses and passing concerns, then shifting from a wonted concern to a "personal" one requires no excuse; and what would be perceived as an abrupt change of footing in formal circumstances is here hardly perceived at all. And because no fixed, continuous script is involved, unexpected pauses and introjections are not disorganizing.

I am suggesting that the very license to employ these stratagems freely, very appreciably defines what informal talk is. To repeat: The right to disattend a multitude of minor faultables, to apologize easily in passing for ones that one elects not to disattend, to report self-concerns widely, indeed, to turn upon one's own words or the words of another in order to discover something to remark on—all these flexibilities are not generic to communication as such, but particular to the multiple selves we are allowed to project during informal talk. The right to shift topic either with a crude bridge for coherence or a perfunctory excuse for its total absence, to inject "side sequences" of long duration, to take physical leave of the conversational circle temporarily or permanently on any of a wide range of grounds—all these possibilities speak to the same looseness of demand. So, too, does the right to split voice and employ sarcasm, irony, innuendo in a rather open play of multiple address and behind this, multiple selves. A fixed footing is not required. In short, a wide frame space is legitimately available, albeit a formal stance is disallowed. It need only be added that this license in conversational talk is so much taken for granted by us that it is only by looking at such things as delicts in broadcast talk that the liberty we conversationalists have been enjoying becomes obvious. And it is through a microanalysis of these varieties of talk and the frame space they employ that we can begin to learn just what informality and formality specifically consist of.

Contrasting broadcast talk with the ordinary kind thus allows a glimpse of the distinguishing structural features of everyday discourse. However, at least one similarity between the two genres of talk is worth considering, too. Clearly, professional aloud reading of fully worded copy tends to produce a mere illusion of fresh talk. But then how fresh is everyday face-to-face talk?

Competent announcers with the permission of their stations editorially elaborate on their copy extemporaneously in the course of reading it, thus appreciably strengthening the impression of fresh talk overall. A lay speaker (or even a neophyte announcer), thrust before a microphone, likely would not have the ability to do this. Yet when one examines how this editorial elaboration is accomplished, it appears that a relatively small number of formulaic sentences and tag phrases are all that is needed. Providing that any one use of a particular remark does not immediately follow another use of the same remark, the illusion of spontaneous, creative, novel flow is engendered.[60] When one shifts from copy that is merely elaborated somewhat by extemporaneous remarks, to shows that are fully unscripted,

60. A structurally similar effect is found in gesticulation. Professional pop singers ordinarily employ a small repertoire of hand-arm gestures—perhaps six or eight—but so long as the same gesture is not repeated before others have been interspersed, the illusion is created that a uniquely developing flow of feeling is occurring.

fresh talk would seem to be a reality, not an illusion. But here again it appears that each performer has a limited resource of formulaic remarks out of which to build a line of patter. A DJ's talk may be heard as unscripted, but it tends to be built up out of a relatively small number of set comments, much as it is said epic oral poetry was recomposed during each delivery.[61] A lay speaker suddenly given the task of providing patter between records would no doubt be struck dumb—but this for a want of tag lines, not for a want of words.

Surely, the ability to engage in face-to-face "small talk" in natural settings depends on a similar resource, merely one that is widely distributed. No doubt grammar generates a near infinite set of sentences, but that does not mean that talk is novel in the same way. It would seem that a reason we can bring a phrase or sentence to mind before encoding it in speech (so that once we start encoding, the task can be finished without much thought) is that we draw on a limited compendium of pat utterances in doing so. The mind of the lay speaker is a repertoire of sayings —large when compared to the gesticulatory stereotypes of pop singers, but small and manageable in other respects.

However, even as a model this approach to the mind of the speaker is simplistic. The mind may contain files of formulaic expressions, but speakers are not engaged merely in culling from the roster. The underlying framework of talk production is less a matter of phrase repertoire than frame space. A speaker's budget of standard utterances can be divided into function classes, each class providing expressions through which he can exhibit an alignment he takes to the events at hand, a footing, a combination of production format and participation status. What the speaker is engaged in doing, then, moment to moment through the course of the discourse in which he finds himself, is to meet whatever occurs by sustaining or changing footing. And by and large, it seems he selects that footing which provides him the least self-threatening position in the circumstances, or, differently phrased, the most defensible alignment he can muster.

During his stint before the microphone, a professional's footing may be considerably set in advance; changes may not be

61. As considered by Parry (1971) and Lord (1960).

frequent and may occur at preestablished junctures—for example, station breaks. But for the announcers in some program formats and some announcers in most of their programs, local responsiveness will be considerable, the performer not knowing in advance what alignment he will find it desirable to take to what is happening currently. And certainly during ordinary informal talk, the speaker must be ready moment to moment to change footing in a way he hadn't planned for, else he will not be able to continuously sustain such viability as his position offers him. And error correction and apology introduces one such locally responsive change in footing, as does the remedial work sometimes then performed upon the first remedy. But this local responsiveness must not be misperceived. The predicaments a speaker is likely to find himself facing during the course of his talk cannot be established in advance. However, given the predicaments that do arise, his response to them plays itself out within the limited frame space available to him, and this space of alignment possibilities is itself not generated moment to moment, nor are the phrases and gestures through which he will represent the alignment he has selected. From moment to moment, unanticipated junctures at which interaction moves must be made will occur; but each move is selected from a limited and predetermined framework. (Even when an announcer follows the novel course of remarking on a latent error, an error that wasn't made but could have been, he must choose an utterance that could indeed stir the audience to some concern in this regard, and either has, or will, be seen as a likely candidate in this respect when he remarks on what he escaped doing. Perhaps even more than is ordinarily the case, the announcer here depends on standard understandings.) If what thereby occurs is something like a game, it is less like chess than like tic-tac-toe. But no less than tic-tac-toe, this game can hold attention; for the illusion is allowed that at every moment new responses are revealed.

Learning about the little maneuvers that announcers employ to keep themselves in countenance, and learning about the participation framework and production format in which these moves are grounded, is what gives warrant for something so trivial as the close analysis of radio talk. Catching in this way at what broadcasters do, and do not do, before a microphone catches at what we do, and do not do, before our friends. These little momentary changes in footing bespeak a trivial game, but our conversational life is spent in playing it.

REFERENCES

Baker, Charlotte. 1975. "This is just a first approximation, but . . ." In *Papers from the Eleventh Regional Meeting of the Chicago Linguistic Society*, pp. 37–47.

Beattie, Geoffrey W. 1979. "Planning units in spontaneous speech: Some evidence from hesitation in speech and speaker gaze direction in conversation." *Linguistics* 17:61–78.

Bell, Allan. 1977. "The language of radio news in Auckland." Ph.D. dissertation, University of Auckland, New Zealand.

Boomer, Donald S. 1965. "Hesitation and grammatical encoding." *Language and Speech* 8:148–58.

Boomer, Donald S., and Laver, John D. M. 1968. "Slips of the tongue." *British Journal of Disorders of Communication* 3:2–11.

Bourdieu, Pierre. 1975. "Le fétichisme de la langue." *Actes de la recherche en sciences sociales* 4 (Juillet): 2–32.

Clancy, Patricia. 1972. "Analysis of a conversation." *Anthropological Linguistics* 14(3):78–86.

Corum, Claudia. 1975. "A pragmatic analysis of parenthetic adjuncts." In *Papers from the Eleventh Regional Meeting of the Chicago Linguistic Society*, pp. 133–41.

Dittmann, Allen T., and Llewellyn, Lynn G. 1967. "The phonemic clause as a unit of speech decoding." *Journal of Personality and Social Psychology* 6:341–49.

Fay, David, and Cutler, Anne. 1977. "Malapropisms and the structure of the mental lexicon." *Linguistic Inquiry* 8: 505–20.

Finegan, Edward. 1980. *Attitudes toward English usage.* New York: Teachers College Press.

Finnegan, Ruth. 1977. *Oral poetry.* Cambridge: Cambridge University Press.

Fraser, Bruce. 1975. "Hedged performatives." In *Syntax and semantics: Speech acts,* vol. 3, edited by Peter Cole and Jerry L. Morgan, pp. 187–210. New York: Academic Press.

Friedman, Marc. 1970. Personal communication.

Fromkin, Victoria A. 1971. "The non-anomalous nature of anomalous utterances." *Language* 47:27–52.

Garnes, Sara, and Bond, Zinny S. 1975. "Slips of the ear: Errors in perception of casual speech." In *Papers from the Eleventh Regional Meeting of the Chicago Linguistic Society,* pp. 214–225.

Goffman, Erving. 1959. *Presentation of self in everyday life.* New York: Anchor Books.

————. 1967. *Interaction ritual.* New York: Anchor Books.

————. 1971. *Relations in public.* New York: Harper and Row.

————. 1974. *Frame analysis.* New York: Harper and Row.

————. 1978. "Response cries." *Language* 54(4):787–815.

————. 1979. "Footing." *Semiotica* 25(1/2):1–29.

Goldman-Eisler, Frieda. 1968. *Psycholinguistics: Experiments in spontaneous speech.* London: Academic Press.

Halliday, M. A. K. 1967. "Notes on transitivity and theme in English (Part 2)." *Journal of Linguistics* 3:177–274.

Hirsh-Pasek, Kathy; Gleitman, Lila R.; and Gleitman, Henry. 1978. "What did the brain say to the mind? A study of the detection and report of ambiguity by young children." In *The child's conception of language,* edited by A. Sinclair, R. J. Jarvella, and W. J. M. Levelt, pp. 97–132. Berlin: Springer-Verlag.

Hoffer, Jay. 1974. *Radio production techniques.* Blue Ridge Summit, Pa.: Tab Books.

Humphrey, Frank. 1978. *"Shh::!"* Unpublished paper presented at the Seventh Annual Colloquium on New Ways of Analyzing Variation, Georgetown University, Washington, D.C.

Hyde, Stuart W. 1959. *Television and radio announcing.* Boston: Houghton Mifflin Co.

James, Deborah. 1978. "The use of oh, ah, say and well in relation to a number of grammatical phenomena." *Papers in Linguistics* 11:517–535.

Jefferson, Gail. 1974. "Error correction as an interactional resource." *Language in Society* 3:181–200.

————. 1979. "A technique for inviting laughter and its subsequent acceptance declination." In *Everyday language: Studies in ethnomethodology,* edited by George Psthas, pp. 74–96. New York: Irvington Publishers.

Jordan, Brigitte, and Fuller, Nancy. 1975. "On the non-fatal nature of trouble: Sense-making and trouble-managing in *lingua franca* talk." *Semiotica* 13:11–31.

Kasl, Stanislav V., and Mahl, George F. 1965. "The relationship of disturbances and hesitations in spontaneous speech to anxiety." *Journal of Personality and Social Psychology* 1(5):425–33.

Keenan, Elinor. 1977. "Why look at unplanned and planned discourse." in *Discourse across Time and Space,* edited by Elinor Keenan and Tina Bennett, pp. 1–41, Los Angeles: Southern California Occasional Papers in Linguistics, no. 5.

Labov, William. 1972. "Hypercorrection by the lower middle class as a factor in linguistic change. In William Labov, *Sociolinguistic Patterns,* pp. 122–42. Philadelphia: University of Pennsylvania Press.

Lakoff, Robin. 1973. "The logic of politeness; or minding your P's and Q's." In *Papers from the Ninth Regional Meeting, Chicago Linguistic Society,* edited by Claudia Corum et al., pp. 292–305. Chicago: Department of Linguistics, University of Chicago.

Laver, John D. M. 1970. "The production of speech." In *New horizons in linguistics,* edited by John Lyons. Middlesex: Penguin Books.

Lord, Albert, B. 1960. *The singer of tales.* New York: Atheneum.

Maclay, Howard, and Osgood, Charles E. 1959. "Hesitation phenomena in spontaneous English speech." *Word* 15:19–44.

Morgan, J. L. 1973. "Sentence fragments and the notion 'sentence.' " In *Issues in linguistics,* edited by Braj B. Kachru et al., pp. 719–51. Urbana: University of Illinois Press.

Parry, Adam, ed. 1971. *The making of Homeric verse: The collected papers of Milman Parry.* Oxford: The Clarendon Press.

Pomerantz, Anita. 1977. "Agreeing and disagreeing with assessments: Some features of preferred/dispreferred turn shapes." Unpublished paper (reported in part at the American Anthropological Association Meetings, San Francisco, November 1978).

Schafer, Kermit. 1959. *Pardon my blooper.* Greenwich, Conn.: Fawcett Crest Books.

————. 1963. *Super bloopers.* Greenwich, Conn.: Fawcett Gold Medal Books.

————. 1965. *Prize bloopers.* Greenwich, Conn.: Fawcett Gold Medal Books.

Schegloff, Emanuel. 1979. "The relevance of repair to syntax-for-conversation." In *Syntax and semantics: Discourse and syntax,* vol. 12, edited by T. Givon and C. Li, pp. 261–86. New York: Academic Press.

Schegloff, Emanuel; Jefferson, Gail; and Sacks, Harvey. 1977. "The preference for self-correction in the organization of repair in conversation." *Language* 53(2):361–82.

Sherzer, Joel. 1978. " 'Oh! That's a pun and I didn't mean it.' " *Semiotica* 22(3/4): 335–50.

Shultz, Thomas R., and Horibe, Frances. 1974. "Development of the appreciation of verbal jokes." *Developmental Psychology* 10:13–20.

Shultz, Thomas R., and Pilon, Robert. 1973. "Development of the ability to detect linguistic ambiguity." *Child Development* 44:728–33.

Simonini, R.C., Jr. 1956. "Phonemic and analogic lapses in radio and television speech." *American Speech* 31:252–63.

Trager, George, and Smith, Henry L. 1951. *An outline of English structure.* Studies in Linguistics: Occasional Papers, no. 3. Norman, Okla.: Battenberg Press. (Republished, New York: American Council of Learned Societies, 1965.)

Urmson, J. O. 1952. "Parenthetical verbs." *Mind* 61:480–96.

Wilson, Thomas P. 1970. "Normative and interpretive paradigms in sociology." In *Understanding everyday life,* edited by Jack D. Douglas, pp. 57–79. Chicago: Aldine.

Yngve, Victor H. 1973. "I forgot what I was going to say." *Papers from the Ninth Regional Meeting, Chicago Linguistic Society,* edited by Claudia Corum et al., pp. 688–99. Chicago: Department of Linguistics, University of Chicago.

Zwicky, Arnold M. 1977. "Classical malapropisms." *Language Sciences* 1 (2): 339–48.

INDEX

331

University of Pennsylvania Publications in
Conduct and Communication

Erving Goffman and Dell Hymes, General Editors

Erving Goffman, *Strategic Interaction*

Ray L. Birdwhistell, *Kinesics and Context: Essays on Body Motion Communication*

William Labov, *Language in the Inner City: Studies in the Black English Vernacular*

William Labov, *Sociolinguistic Patterns*

Dell Hymes, *Foundations in Sociolinguistics: An Ethnographic Approach*

Barbara Kirshenblatt-Gimblett, editor, *Speech Play: Research and Resources for the Study of Linguistic Creativity*

Gillian Sankoff, *The Social Life of Language*

Erving Goffman, *Forms of Talk*

Sol Worth, *Studying Visual Communication,* edited by Larry Gross